GENERAL JACK'S DIARY 1914-18

GENERAL JACK'S JACK'S DIARY 1914-18

THE TRENCH DIARY OF BRIGADIER-GENERAL J. L. JACK, D.S.O.

EDITED AND INTRODUCED BY JOHN TERRAINE

CASSELL

Cassell Military Paperbacks

Cassell
Wellington House, 125 Strand
London WC2R 0BB

First published in Great Britain by Eyre & Spottiswode 1964
This edition published 2000
Reprinted 2001 and 2003

A CIP catalogue record for this book is available from the British Library

ISBN 0-304-35320-5

Printed and bound in Great Britain by
Cox & Wyman Ltd, Reading, Berkshire

Introduction

Brigadier-General James Lochhead Jack, D.S.O., was born in 1880, and died on December 22nd 1962. He fought in the South African War with the Argyll and Sutherland Highlanders and with the Scottish Horse, and was mentioned in Despatches. In the First World War he served in the Scottish Rifles (Cameronians), the West Yorkshire Regiment, and finally as commander of the 28th Infantry Brigade. During that time he won the Distinguished Service Order and Bar, and was twice mentioned in Despatches. He retired from the Regular Army in 1921, but continued to take an active part in the work of the Territorial Army. From 1931 to 1941 he held the appointment of Aide-de-Camp to the King. He was a Justice of the Peace for Leicestershire from 1928 until 1955, and a Deputy Lieutenant of that county from 1935.

This summary does not explain the special quality of the war diary which he kept from 1914 to 1918. Almost every day, while in France and Flanders, Jack made a cryptic jotting in a tiny pocket book, intelligible only to himself. Once out of the line, in reserve, or on leave, or in hospital, he worked up these minimal notes from immediate memory; and after the War it became one of his deepest interests to expand the resulting narrative with subsequent observations (readily identifiable), maps, illustrations and carefully preserved contemporary documents, until they filled four thick foolscap volumes. It was Sidney Rogerson, who served with Jack in the West Yorkshire, who first showed me one of these volumes, a presentation copy which General Jack had made for him. Later, the General himself showed me the rest, and the idea of this book was born. It is, in fact, an extract of about one-third of his original manuscript. Unfortunately, General Jack died before work on the book had even begun; the idea that what he had quite privately written would have general interest at first surprised him; at least, before he died, he had the encouragement of learning that this was so.

Many valuable – and some brilliant – books have been written describing the life of the infantry in the trenches, and in the great battles of the First World War. Almost all of them, and certainly the most famous (Siegfried Sassoon's *Memoirs of an Infantry Officer*, Edmund Blunden's *Undertones of War*, R. H. Mottram's *Spanish Farm*, Robert Graves's *Goodbye to All That*, or, in a different key, Charles Edmonds's *A Subaltern's War* and Sidney Rogerson's *Twelve Days*), take their place in literature because of their style, the quality of their writing, their deeply felt and superbly-expressed emotion. These are the testimonies of Britain's Citizen Army, the soldiers of the War who were only soldiers because of the War.

It is much more difficult to discover, at the regimental level (the trench level), the record of the Regular soldier. Generals and Field-Marshals committed millions of words to paper, and very interesting many of them are. But they do not show how the men who were trained for war, brought up to expect war, and soldiered on, with or without war, faced those same circumstances and situations that Graves, Sassoon and the rest have so graphically described. Did their training make them different men? If so, in what did the difference lie? Was General Sir Tom Bridges's famous statement – 'Our motto was, "We'll do it. What is it?" ' – correct? If so, what kind of men did it turn them into? Were they dull fellows? Were they less sensitive to death and suffering than their Citizen comrades? Did they ever give way? Did they have doubts and regrets? What was it that sustained them?

These are the questions which General Jack's diary helps to answer. His narrative fills in (deliberately) much of the detail of a soldier's life at war which alone can provide true answers to the great inquest into 1914–1918. This is not literature, as such; the language is the language of the mess, the orderly room, Standing Orders, 'reports in writing'. Men do not 'go', they 'proceed'; things do not 'begin', they 'commence'; one does not 'help', one 'assists'. So much the better; this creates a stiff strait-jacket for emotion and passion. If they can break through it, they must be powerful indeed. And, in my submis-

6

sion, they do break through it. With them go certain other qualities, not to be overlooked: a stern conception of duty; the keen attention to details at all times; the 'eye for country', sharpened by training – and by hunting; a sense of history, instilled by the Regiment. In short, this is a true chronicle of the British professional soldier, at a time when he was worth his weight in gold.

JOHN TERRAINE

EDITOR'S NOTE

As he left them, General Jack's diaries consisted of some 200,000 words, including introductory material, day-by-day entries, and voluminous appendices. My object has been to reduce this large bulk to about 60,000 words, for convenient publishing and reading. I have tried to follow two threads throughout the course of my editing: the preservation of as much narrative continuity as possible without interpolation, and the illumination of the character of the man. Mostly, what I have cut out is pure detail, in which his meticulous mind delighted, much of it topographical (map references for positions held or attacked, for example); there was also much pure repetition of daily routines which had to go, as long as sufficient remained to give the flavour of that 'nine-tenths boredom' which war is. A number of personal passages, referring to friends, and anecdotes from his past, have been cut; I hope without offence. I have tried to exclude all hearsay, except where it has a real significance in the development of Jack's ideas. All war fronts abounded in rumours, many of them worthless; nor did the 'bright' communiqués of the period greatly contribute to understanding. Beyond that, I have allowed myself to follow certain subsidiary threads in particular chapters, i.e. in Chapter I, the sense of the strangeness of it all; in Chapter IV, the feeling of the newcomer, taking over a proud but shaken unit (and here I had to cut many references to his own regiment, still his neighbours, which he visited frequently, and from which he continued to draw inspiration); in Chapter V, the disturbing task

7

of having to try to rehabilitate 1/Cameronians, passing through a bad patch; in Chapter VI, the novelty of his new command, and the new type of warfare in which it was engaged.

At all points, I have clung firmly to Jack's own style and usage, apart from correcting evident mistakes, and abandoning his military habit of putting every surname or place-name in capital letters. I have tried to confine my own additional material (*which throughout always appears in italics*) to explanation, either of the general situation as we now know it to have been, or of curiosities of military (or simply period) behaviour.

Contents

Illustrations

The photographs are all reproduced and described between pages 160 and 161. Grateful acknowledgement for their use is due to Major-General R. C. Money (Nos. 2–9, 11–16) and to the Imperial War Museum (Nos. 19–29, 31, 32). The other subjects are taken direct from General Jack's Diary.

MAPS
drawings by W. Bromage

Foreword

by SIDNEY ROGERSON

It was my privilege and pleasure to serve under James Jack while he commanded the 2nd Battalion, West Yorkshire Regiment, from September 1916 until wounded on July 31st 1917 in the opening assault of the Third Battle of Ypres, and to enjoy his close personal friendship right up to his death in December 1962. I was a subaltern when he walked over from our neighbours, the 2/Scottish Rifles, to take command. Later, as his diary records, I commanded a company, and ultimately became his Adjutant. In these positions I naturally saw much of my Colonel, earning his censure frequently, and his commendation less often. I saw him at close quarters, too, notably in the cramped confines of a dug-out which, sensitive to the cold as he was, he kept at furnace heat, and which was therefore purgatory to me with a more vigorous, youthful circulation.

It is true to say that during those months I never really knew him, however much I grew to love and admire him. For one thing, his sense of duty was far too strict for most of us young men to understand. For another, he had an almost exasperating punctiliousness in what often appeared to us to be unimportant details of military etiquette as well as discipline.

It was only in later years that I came to realise what his diary reveals so clearly, how these and other facets of his character enabled him, a stranger, to take hold of a battalion not a little sick and shaken after the terrible experience of July 1st; to nurse it back to health amongst the mines and minenwerfers of the Loos salient; and to harden and train it in the muck and misery around Les Boeufs until, when it went over the top on

July 31st 1917 at Ypres, it was recognised by High Command as one of the picked battalions of the B.E.F.

It was also, surely, one of the happiest battalions, and a spirit of gaiety, the result of increased confidence in their own efficiency, characterised the duties and recreations of officers and men alike. In a peculiar way the Colonel was able to set an example both of relaxation in play and of concentration in battle. It was a great accomplishment, described here with a modesty, almost a naïveté, which is most impressive. The diary is a record of achievement, but the emphasis is all on the regiment, and not on its commanding officer. It is painstaking pleading that the individual is subordinate to his task, all the more effective because it is so obviously unconscious.

General Jack was not easy for a young man to know. He was peculiarly averse from showing his feelings, or from admitting any but a few well-tried friends behind the veil which reticence hung before him. Yet without our really getting at the inner man, he managed not only to overcome our suspicions of a stranger in a short time, but also to endear himself to all of us. I could not then explain how he did it. He had none of the tricks of popularity, and it was the last thing he would ever have set out to attain. Again, the diary makes clear what in those distant days we were only able to discern as in a glass darkly. It is the revelation of a personality. It is something more. It is – and I as a temporary soldier of those years can say this – a testimony to the qualities and traditions of the best type of old Regular officer, a type whose weaknesses have unfortunately been all too often seized upon and laughed at, but whose merits are far too little appreciated by any but those who have served under him.

In this sense his diary is, I feel, very valuable. It not only reveals the sympathetic nature which lay behind the martinet exterior, but it is impressive evidence of the load of responsibility which rests on the shoulders of those who command men in battle, and of how the conscientious officer reacts to it. A great deal has been said and written about an officer's duty towards the men under him. Seldom can it have been said more effectively than in this diary. It should be read, marked and inwardly digested by those who aspire to command, and it

14

might well benefit those who are commanded without realising what is passing in the minds of those who command them.

For all the years of labour which Jack lavished on his Diaries – which between the two German wars became a major personal preoccupation – his ideas about their publication were modest, rising, indeed, no higher than his own regimental magazine, or at best the Journal of the Royal United Service Institution. I took a different view, which I pressed on him in season and out of season, without any clear idea of how the Diaries were to be made fit for presentation to the wider public I had in mind. Happily, I persuaded him to leave the matter in my hands, and at last, but not without manifest misgivings, he entrusted to me his four precious volumes of typescript. These I loaned to John Terraine, and eventually brought about a meeting between the two men. This book is the result. It presents the experiences of the veteran (already in 1914 a veteran of the South African War), annotated by a contemporary military historian who has staked out his claim to recognition as an interpreter of the war of 1914–18, the fiftieth anniversary of which we commemorate this year.

My great grief is that Jack did not live quite long enough to see his diaries in the form in which they will reach the public.

Portrait of Brig.-General James Jack

by

MAJOR-GENERAL R. C. MONEY, c.b., m.c.

late The Cameronians (Scottish Rifles)

I first met James Jack when, with about a year's service at home, I joined the 1 Cameronians in 1910 in South Africa.

Although he had a S.A. Medal he was still a Subaltern, and was our Adjutant. I got a place in the Subalterns' Polo team and saw a good bit of him for the next four years. Then again I was his second-in-command at the Depot 1920-21. His background was not military, laird or country squire or parson and so was rather different from the rest.

He was intensely reserved, inhibited perhaps by shyness. Never once did I hear him mention home, father, mother or relatives. His private world he protected by enacting the parts of his two heroes, the Duke of Wellington and Brigadier Gérard; on these he modelled all he said and did.

Thus one never came to grips with the man himself nor did he have any close friends. He had great nervous energy and driving power and drove himself (even in those days) too hard for his staying power, which I believe he undermined by deliberate starvation in order to keep down his weight for riding, since he could not afford 'weight carriers'!

He was a 'character' widely known in the Service, admired, trusted and liked because of his integrity, iron will and self-mastery, his immense courage both moral and physical, his sense of justice, his sound sense and puckish humour. He never allowed himself to fall below his own very high standard of behaviour and was in fact what a Regular Officer should be.

General Jack's Dedication

To the Glorious Memory of All Ranks of both Regular battalions of my Regiment, the Cameronians (Scottish Rifles), and also to that of my other comrades of the Old British Regular Army, who carried out to the end, with ability and unsurpassed courage, all their duties to their Country in the Great War.

James Jack 22 Aug. 1934

The Cameronians (Scottish Rifles)

I

Mons – Le Cateau – Marne
Aisne – First Ypres

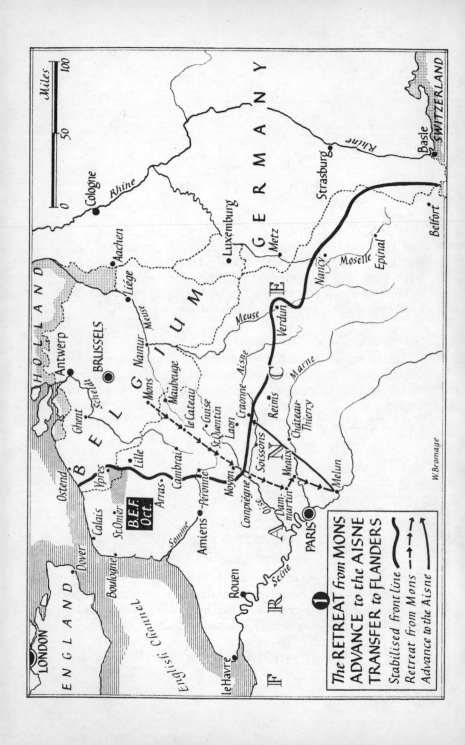

Miles
100
50
0

HOLLAND

GERMANY

Cologne · Rhine

Aachen

Luxemburg

Metz

Strasburg · Rhine

Basle

SWITZERLAND

Belfort

Moselle

Epinal

Nancy

BELGIUM

Antwerp

BRUSSELS

Ghent

Liège

Namur · Meuse

Mons

Maubeuge

le Cateau

Guise

St.Quentin

Laon

Craonne · Aisne

Reims

Verdun

Meuse

Marne

Ostend

Ypres

Lille

Arras

Cambrai

Péronne

Noyon

Compiègne

Soissons

Château-Thierry

Melun

Meaux

Dan-martin

FRANCE

Oise

Calais

Dover

St.Omer

B.E.F.
Oct.

Amiens

Somme

PARIS

Boulogne

Seine

Rouen

ENGLAND

LONDON

English Channel

le Havre

W. Bromage

The RETREAT from MONS
ADVANCE to the AISNE
TRANSFER to FLANDERS

Stabilised front line
Retreat from Mons
Advance to the Aisne

❶

At the end of July 1914 the 1/Cameronians were at an exercise camp in the Grampian Mountains, carrying out strenuous tactical training with other units of Scottish Command.

JULY 28TH

The Cameronians have not been in North Perthshire since 1689 when, under Colonel Cleland, who was killed, they defeated a large body of Highlanders at Dunkeld . . .

The past month's tension in Europe has been greatly increased by the news that Austria has declared war on Serbia.

JULY 29TH

In the afternoon, at a tennis party at Blair Castle, a bicycle orderly arrives with an urgent telegram for my battalion. Being the senior Cameronian officer present I open it and read that we are to return to Glasgow forthwith in accordance with the 'Precautionary Period' measures of the Defence Plan prior to Mobilisation.

Tennis ends abruptly; we return to camp; the brigade spends all night packing up beside the patches of pine woods and the splashing waters of the Garry.

The newspapers are full of the acute situation in Europe.

AT PRECAUTIONARY PERIOD STATIONS

AUGUST 4TH: FORT ARDHALLOW

Early in the morning of the 31st July the detachment under my command (2/Lieut Ferry and 60 other ranks) departed from Maryhill station, Glasgow, and two hours later took over Fort Ardhallow on the Clyde near Dunoon from its single custodian . . .

Except for a short parade before breakfast and cleaning up,

the men work for three hours in the morning besides three in the afternoon, digging trenches round the fort and erecting barbed wire entanglements as part of the defences. . .

On Sunday Germany declared war on Russia and invaded Luxemburg.

Yesterday she declared war against France, and her army, despite the protests of King Albert, has crossed the Belgian frontier. All Europe is in ferment.

AUGUST 5TH

About 2 a.m. I receive a telegram stating that Britain declared war on Germany at midnight . . .

One can scarcely believe that five Great Powers – also styled 'civilised' – are at war, and that the original spark causing the conflagration arose from the murder of one man and his wife . . . It is quite mad, as well as being dreadful . . .

MOBILISING AND TRAINING

AUGUST 8TH: MARYHILL BARRACKS, GLASGOW

Mobilisation has been proceeding at top speed and is now completed in the four days allowed for it. There has not been a hitch in the plans, nor an article deficient or out of condition.

Only one (? two) of our some 600 reservists has failed to report, and he may be abroad. But the presence in the ranks of such a large number of reservists to make our strength up to its War Establishment of 1,022 is most unsatisfactory for possible immediate battle. Although they require tuning up as soldiers in addition to conditioning for marching they are splendid fellows.

All ranks are in high fettle at the prospect of active service. But hating bloodshed as I do, and having had a hard if not dangerous fifteen months in the South African War (1901–02), together with many racing, hunting and polo accidents, I personally loathe the outlook. A queer soldier! . . .

The public are almost unanimous in considering that we must back up our Treaty to maintain . . . the independence of Belgium. The German Chancellor is said to have referred to the

Treaty as a 'scrap of paper' and is dismayed at Britain's dissenting from this view. Apart from sentiments of honour, what would be our position eventually if the Prussian war-lords held the ports just across the English Channel, and we were friendless as well as despised for abandoning our present obligations? We should invite trouble for ourselves later.

Luckily, a Liberal Government is in power and, in a National crisis, we can count on the aid of the whole Conservative Opposition Party. Were these roles reversed, unity would be less certain; as it is, two of the Liberal Cabinet have resigned rather than endorse our promises regarding Belgium – so it seems.

AUGUST 12TH

. . . The prospects are, of course, widely discussed in the mess.

Regarding our Allies: We hope that the French are again those of Marengo, Ulm, Austerlitz and Jena, with another Napoleon at their head; but the Prussians hammered them in their last big campaign (1870). We think that the immense Russian numbers will tell, and trust that their form has improved since the Japanese beat them decisively ten years ago.

Of our Adversaries: The Austrians are gentlemen rather than soldiers. Germany, however, is very highly organised for a European war. Her armies have a tremendous reputation, and have smashed all enemies quite easily during the past fifty years.

A Staff College friend . . . told me recently that the German infantry must be considered equal to ours notwithstanding their short service with no war experience compared with our long-service men, many of whom have seen a campaign. [He] added, 'Perhaps we are a little better at musketry.' Our cavalry and artillery, however, which take longer to train than infantry, should prove superior to their two-year men . . .

Since I am the junior captain in the battalion . . . I have sunk to the leadership of a platoon (55 men).

A note from the Remount Department tells me that my two remaining private hunter horses, Ardskull Boy and Home Park, have been taken for the army – the first war wrench . . .

During the past few days many friends have come to bid us God-speed. We have been packing up and now the barracks are bare. Everything not required for active service has been sent away; officers' and sergeants' mess silver to the bank; pictures, furniture and trophies to store; private property to our homes; unfit men, those under age for foreign service, and full dress uniforms to the depot at Hamilton.

The quartermaster has weighed our kits to the regulation allowance; mounted officers 50 pounds, dismounted officers 35 pounds.

Our quarters, lately so cosy if simple, are dismantled. The corpse-like roll of kit covered with a dust-sheet, which lay on a shelf in Sam Darling's room next to mine, has been packed away. I used to remark to him in jest how real his 'corpse' looked; he replied with his penetrating glance, 'Well, if ever we get into a European war few of us will see the end of it.'

AUGUST 13TH

Secret orders arrive for our departure tonight, but the battalion carries out its usual programme to avoid advertising the move to the public, among whom there are certain to be foreign spies. After the day's exercises are finished the pipes and drums play us back to barracks through thronged streets; but there is no fuss, just the friendly wave of hands. The four companies, each 220 strong and wearing full equipment, look splendid as they swing in at the barrack gate for the last time, at 'attention', to the regimental march 'Kenmure's On and Awa' . . .

Between 11 p.m. and 1 a.m. (14th) the battalion departs unobtrusively, with one absentee, in four special trains from Maryhill station. . . a few loiterers give us a cheer and wish us good luck.

AUGUST 14TH

. . . The battalion embarks at Southampton in the afternoon; the ship weighs anchor after dark and proceeds under Naval escort to France – so we suppose. The men are in great spirits.

Britain has declared war on Austria, and newspapers say that the French are attacking successfully in Alsace-Lorraine.

IN FRANCE

At 8 a.m. the ship enters the port in dull weather. We are almost the first British troops to arrive and get a tremendous reception. French sentries on the jetty, temporarily relaxing professional stiffness, cheer and throw their caps in the air. The sea-front is packed with people who join in the enthusiasm, which is redoubled when the 'Tommies' . . . strike up the 'Marseillaise' with great fervour, although imperfectly as music. This good impression soars still higher as our men cast their cash on the quay to be scrambled for by urchins.

At 6 p.m. the battalion marches, pipes or bugles playing and the men singing, four miles through cheering crowds in a downpour of rain to Harfleur Camp on the top of a very steep slippery hill. The transport does not arrive till 10 o'c, having had difficulty with the ascent. Then rations and stores are issued; the ground becomes a quagmire. We spend a miserable night.

AUGUST 16TH: HARFLEUR CAMP

. . . It rained all last night but the day breaks fine . . . and soon all is well.

The French public are very anxious to examine how 'les anglais' wash, shave, eat and sleep; we can scarcely keep them out of camp by courteous means . . .

The Germans are pressing through Belgium carrying all before them. Liége has fallen to the 16-inch Austrian howitzers after a gallant, useful defence of eleven days – we had hoped for longer.

At 9.30 p.m. the battalion marches to Havre and entrains at midnight for a Line-of-Communication station which, to the annoyance of our fire-eaters, is our present destination.

Many of the men's cap-badges and some tunic buttons are deficient, having been given to quickly-made French friends as souvenirs. Steps have been taken to stop this munificence otherwise we shall soon be naked.

AUGUST 17TH: BUSIGNY

. . . we detrain at Busigny, six miles south-west of Le Cateau, at 9.30 a.m. . . .

My half-company is detailed for station duties here . . . We accordingly 'fall in' and, preceded by one piper, set out as ordered for billets in the village a few hundred yards off. But our small procession unwittingly nearly ruins a kindly civic reception, as it is mistaken for the head of the battalion and I for the Colonel.

Besides being greeted with a hurricane of cheers, bouquets of flowers are thrust into my arms; these I hand to my sergeant to pass to the real Colonel (Robertson), who soon appears in front of his companies behind the pipes and drums in full blast to receive the garlands, and many more, along with a vociferous welcome reciprocated by our smart riflemen.

AUGUST 21ST

. . . Colonel Robertson is commandant of this sector of the Lines of Communication; I am station staff officer with a tiny hut in the station yard for an office.

Since we arrived on the 17th a constant stream of trains has passed through Busigny day and night (often at intervals of only fifteen minutes) conveying cavalry, artillery, infantry, as well as other troops, to the Point of Concentration of the British Expeditionary Force, near Le Cateau. Many of the trains stop here, and we see large numbers of friends pass by to the grief of our men at being left behind 'out of the show'.

Our duties are to prevent hostile agents from interfering with the railway lines and bridges, to keep men off the troop trains from leaving the station, to provide water for men and animals, besides tidying up.

Oakley with the other half of 'C' Company returned here on the 19th. He was horrified at the absence of comfort in the officers' quarters, a state which he described as 'pigging it'. So now, among other luxuries, café au lait and a buttered roll appear when we are called in the morning, and thick mattresses for beds on the floor at night, on his sound principle 'Be as comfortable as you can; you never know how long it will last.'

26

THE CAMERONIANS MOVE
TO THE FRONT

On August 22nd the British Expeditionary Force arrived at Mons. Early that morning the first encounter between British and Germans took place when 'C' Squadron, 4th Dragoon Guards, routed a patrol of the 4th Cuirassiers, belonging to the German 9th Cavalry Division. This was the leading element of General von Kluck's First Army, over 300,000 strong, and now attempting to complete the encirclement of the whole Allied right wing prescribed in the famous Schlieffen Plan.

French strategy, to which the B.E.F. under Field-Marshal Sir John French had to conform, had completely broken down by this date.

Already defeated in Lorraine and in the Ardennes, the French Commander-in-Chief, General Joffre, now pinned his hopes on a counter-attack by his left wing, the Fifth Army under General Lanrezac, supported by the British. But the Fifth Army had already sustained a partial defeat at Charleroi, and was actually in retreat as the British completed their advance to Mons. Despite information which fully revealed the threat to his left flank, Sir John French agreed to remain in position at Mons for a day, covering the French retirement; some officers at British G.H.Q. even clung to the hope of advancing further.

Meanwhile the British II Corps under General Sir Horace Smith-Dorrien (3rd and 5th Divisions) lined up along the Mons-Condé Canal, facing northward, while I Corps under Lieutenant-General Sir Douglas Haig drew up almost at right angles to this deployment, facing east. Smith-Dorrien's two divisions were thinly spread along some 21 miles of canal bank, and to strengthen them the newly-formed 19th Infantry Brigade was brought up on the left, near Condé. This brigade, under Major-General J. G. Drummond, was composed of units drawn from the Lines of Communication: 2/Royal Welch Fusiliers, 1/Middlesex, 2/Argyll and Sutherland Highlanders and 1/Cameronians.

AUGUST 22ND

. . . A telegram orders the battalion to Valenciennes forthwith as part of an independent brigade being formed there. We shall be in the 'cock-pit of Europe' sooner than we expected, to the delight of many.

We reach our destination by train in the evening, and are

billeted in a large school where some of my comrades object to the straw provided for bedding on the grounds that it harbours fleas, if not lice. I wonder how long we shall remain so fastidious? . . .

The cavalry have been engaged, and Uhlan (German Lancers) patrols have been seen only eight miles from here. How horribly close: I have kept thinking till now that the whole thing must be a dream. A huge European war about so little.

At night I am appointed staff-captain of the brigade and go to the station to meet the brigadier's train. When waiting for its arrival a group of Uhlan prisoners is escorted along, the French crowd round them shouting 'cochons' and other unfriendly names whilst drawing their hands suggestively across their own throats; the French officer in charge, however, prevents any bloodshed . . .

A group of renowned battlefields lies just ahead of us, Ramillies and Malplaquet won by Marlborough's men, Steenkirk where, in 1692, the Cameronians formed one of '12 heroic battalions whose onslaught was with difficulty repulsed by 53 French Battalions and 7 regiments of horse' (Fortescue). Our cavalry have been nearly in sight of the field of Waterloo . . .

SUNDAY, AUGUST 23RD: VALENCIENNES

. . . My day is spent in Valenciennes trying to collect the equipment of an infantry brigade over and above that held by battalions. The basis of British organisation is the Division, and as we are an Independent Brigade and not part of any division we are short of a full Supply Train, Ammunition Column and Field Ambulance, besides clerks, stationery and other requisites. A long hunt ensues for these with indifferent success . . . (Most of the deficiencies were made good that night.) . . .

Fragmentary reports are to hand of a hot engagement at Mons. The right of the brigade has been in action for the past hour or two and has defeated minor attacks on the lock bridges, but the pressure is increasing and extending westwards to the other battalions . . .

The Battle of Mons began about 10 a.m. with the arrival of the German IX Corps opposite Mons itself. The feature of the battle was the

28

*piecemeal arrival and engagement of the German Army Corps, IX Corps
on their left, then III Corps, then IV Corps (in the area of the 19th
Infantry Brigade). As each German unit arrived, it attacked the bridges
and locks of the Canal in front of it. The British infantry, entrenched
and well hidden, shot these attacks flat one by one in the first of the
many remarkable musketry displays provided by the Old Regular Army.
By the evening the Germans had had enough, but the sheer weight of their
forces (3 corps against one) added to information of yet another corps
(II) marching against the open British flank, and of French retirements,
made it impossible for the British to continue to hold their ground.*

About 11.30 p.m. when, following a frugal supper, we have just
lain down for a little rest, a motor cyclist brings orders for the
brigade to retire at once to a low crest near Elouges. We do not
know the reason for this move; nothing untoward has happened in our vicinity . . .

Johnson,[1] Churchill and I write the orders dictated by the
brigadier on our small Field Service notebooks (6 by 4 inches),
each making three carbon copies. These orders are shortly sent
to battalions by their orderlies on pedal bicycles.

Between one and 2 a.m. (24th) the advance troops of the
brigade quietly vacate their positions on the canal under some
fire from the enemy on the north bank . . . Owing to the sudden
move many stores have to be abandoned, among them being
some bottles of Oakley's precious port wine . . .

Before daylight, against the advice of Johnson who says I risk
being captured, I ride pistol in hand a few hundred yards down
the street to Quiévrain railway station to see that the Belgian
operators there burn the files of telegrams – surely a necessary
precaution. The flames take an age to envelop the last bundle
as I stand in the doorway half expecting to hear Prussian foot-
falls at any moment. Thankful to get safely away I retrace my
steps, slowly to minimise the chance of being shot at by our
men, with villagers peering anxiously at me from the darkened
windows. At Quiévrain cross-roads I am challenged, and find
a battalion lying with fixed bayonets ready for the enemy;
near them some cavalry and artillery are standing to their
horses . . .

[1] *Captain H. C. Johnson, King's Royal Rifle Corps, the Brigade Major.*

The hazy dawn of a fine summer morning ends an entirely sleepless night, and finds the brigade near Elouges commencing to entrench a defensive position. The country in front is open, with low whale-backed ridges providing an excellent field of fire . . .

We have been placed under command of the Cavalry Division, and I am sent to Audregnies for orders. Riding along I meet General Allenby whose tall handsome figure sits a beautiful dark charger. One of his staff tells me that the 19th Brigade is to assist the cavalry in securing the left flank of the B.E.F. . . . .

All this time we hear a very severe action raging a few miles north-east and east in the nests of slag-heaps, furnaces and industrial villages lying between us and Mons; the front is clearly marked by the smoke of bursting shells.

About 7.30 a.m. the 2nd Cavalry Brigade with Horse Artillery batteries trot past us to take up covering positions near the Mons–Valenciennes road. My word! they look superb, business-like and resolute.

The brigade is now on its way, but ready to deploy for action . . . The sun is baking hot, and the roads are crammed with fleeing inhabitants, their cattle, and waggons piled high with belongings. They keep asking us where to go and should have been evacuated before now for their sakes as well as ours as they greatly hamper the column. Besides, there may be German spies among them. A pitiful sight!

Sir Horace Smith-Dorrien, the lean, wiry II Corps commander, a fine soldier, overtakes me on his way back from the front in a car. He inquires how the men are getting along. I reply that they are in grand heart but overloaded in this heat, especially the reservists who are not yet fit for hard marching, and that the incessant blocks on the roads due to refugees are a great bother. He nods and is driven on . . .

Our destination is changed from Presieu to Jenlain, so thither I ride in the afternoon to arrange quarters, and to collect farm picks and spades for entrenching at night as the men's small tools are useless for serious digging. The villagers are, however, very chary about lending their gear.

The brigade arrives towards 6 p.m., having covered fully

eighteen miles since leaving the canal this morning, and with only one proper meal from the field kitchens during a halt. The men are tired, foot-sore from the cobbled roads, and irritated at a retreat for which they can see no necessity. They consider themselves quite a match for the 'Bosches' . . .

THE RETREAT FROM MONS

AUGUST 25TH: JENLAIN

After a hurried supper last evening duties occupied me till midnight. This morning I rise at 3.30 insufficiently rested, and proceed round the brigade area to find the ammunition motor lorries still with us; they should have been gone – and soon are . . .

About 4 a.m. the brigade receives orders to continue the retreat forthwith . . . towards Le Cateau. Hurriedly packing up it sets off in half an hour, the men now guessing that something is wrong elsewhere. Before we leave the enemy commences to shell the outposts which are forced to abandon some damaged transport and stores. Thanks, however, to German respect for our fire no infantry attacks follow till our trenches have been well bombarded for long after our departure.

Battalions halt in column of route near Vendegies about 8 o'c for breakfasts from their 'cookers' (field kitchens). During the meal an inquisitive German 'Albatros' aeroplane keeps circling overhead observing; one can easily distinguish the black Maltese cross on each underwing. When hostile aircraft come within effective range the nearest companies deliver rapid rifle fire to drive them up; otherwise troops remain as concealed as possible, or motionless at the sides of the road if no cover is at hand, in order to minimise the risk of detection . . .

The march is resumed about 9 a.m. The men are becoming tired and footsore. The incessant blocks on the congested roads make straggling difficult to prevent . . .

I am now told to ride to General Headquarters in Le Cateau for orders, and to arrange billets if we are to stop there.

Solesmes is crammed with the transport of our cavalry moving east . . . with French cavalry going west, with units of our 3rd

Division and a stream of refugees and waggons clearing off southwards. An awful mix-up! . . .

Rain is falling heavily as I trot up the attractive valley of the Selle. On the slopes just south of Neuvilly and Montay (near Le Cateau) the 4th Division, fresh from England, is digging trenches; it gives one a feeling of security to pass back through infantry in position. I devoutly hope that other 'fresh' divisions from the same source are at hand!

Le Cateau is full of troops, transport and civilians, all strangely imperturbed considering that the enemy is almost at the gate. At G.H.Q. (Sir John French's Headquarters), to whom I report on arrival in the late afternoon, the staff, clerks and typewriters are all in 'full swing', apparently free from any anxiety whatsoever. Tea cups and the remains of cakes lie on the tables. A charming, well-dressed, easy-mannered young staff officer hears the little I know of the day's operations, says that the 19th Brigade will billet here tonight, and that orders will be sent to it. Finally, he remarks sympathetically 'You must be famished; go and have a good feed in an estaminet and come back in an hour.'

Having consumed a large delicious omelette, coffee, and as many rolls and butter as I can hold, I return to G.H.Q. at the appointed time. My word! There is not a soul in the building, not a pen, all have 'flown' with every stitch they possess.

Meanwhile the inhabitants, also scenting danger, are making off . . . I now proceed to search for accommodation for the brigade, and select buildings on the southern edge of the town instead of in Le Cateau itself. This will entail the wearied men marching nearly another mile, but for safety's sake they must be lodged, however uncomfortable, on the reverse side of the place to the enemy. They will then be on their direct route south-west should we retreat again tomorrow as seems probable.

Between 7 and 11 p.m. the soaked and hungry battalions stagger into the square where they are met by their quartermasters and me as usual. It is heartrending to witness the exhaustion of all ranks after their march of almost 23 miles in steam-heat and heavily loaded, besides going into action about Romeries and Haussy in support of the cavalry. The men have scarcely been off their feet for three days besides having had no more than snatches of sleep or scraps of food because of transport delays through road-blocks.

The last battalion to report, the Welch Fusiliers, drop down on the cobbled square saying they can go no further . . .

The remainder of II Corps (3rd and 5th Divisions) were in a similarly exhausted condition; General Allenby told Smith-Dorrien that the men and horses of the Cavalry Division were 'pretty well played out'; the newly-arrived 4th Division was actually in contact with the enemy; and I Corps was eight miles away, on the other side of the Forest of Mormal, retreating southwards after a night of alarums. This was the situation which faced General Smith-Dorrien on the morning of August 26th, and which dictated his decision to stand and fight at Le Cateau, despite orders from G.H.Q. to continue his retreat. The battle which followed was one of the most remarkable British feats of arms of the whole War.

THE BATTLE OF LE CATEAU

AUGUST 26TH (THE ANNIVERSARY OF CRECY, 1346)

At 3.30 a.m. after a bare three hours' rest, I rose, swallowed a cup of coffee, an egg, some bread and butter; put on tunic and equipment, and proceeded round our scattered battalions to see that the ammunition and supply columns (my special responsibility) were getting ready to continue the retreat as ordered . . .

On reaching the town square I found it full of horse and motor transport, ambulances, and groups of soldiers who, losing their regiments on the previous day, had unofficially attached themselves to the nearest units in the hope of getting something to eat . . .

By about 6 o'c the last of the impedimenta had disappeared out of the town along the Cambrai road; the Fusiliers were falling in beside their piled arms; the other three battalions were entering the square.

All at once we were startled by shouts 'The Uhlans are in the town', and the outbreak of musketry fire in the eastern outskirts a few hundred yards away. Anxious moments ensued in expectation of the Germans bursting into the confined space full of troops.

At the first shots bayonets were whipped out of their scabbards and rattled on to the rifle standards. A few seconds later pickets of the 1/Cameronians (the nearest battalion) doubled down the streets leading to the square to block them to the enemy while the two machine guns, under Robin Money, were bundled off the limbers ready for action in an instant; the other battalions conformed as expedient. All this took place with considerable inward excitement although rapidly and without flurry . . .

The Battle of Le Cateau began with random clashes of outposts at about 4 a.m. The German artillery came into action about 6 a.m., marking another piecemeal deployment of the First Army. The main line of Smith-Dorrien's Corps ran for some ten miles parallel to the Le Cateau – Cambrai road, 5th Division on the right, 3rd in the centre, 4th on the left. The weakness of the position was its right flank, which made a right-angle bend at Le Cateau, running back down the valley of the River Selle. Smith-Dorrien hoped that Haig's I Corps would arrive to cover this vulnerable sector, but in the total absence of information or appropriate orders, that formation continued its retreat southwards. Thus, instead of British support, Smith-Dorrien quickly found German troops (III Corps) occupying this vital ground and taking his 5th Division (Major-General Sir C. Fergusson) in enfilade.

Protected by its pickets the brigade – the last troops to vacate Le Cateau – marched up the Cambrai road in column of route almost 'under the nose' of a forthcoming German attack just west of the town. Half a mile on we wheeled to the left along the straight Roman way to St Quentin, and now, for the first time, learned that the II Corps was standing to fight immediately . . .

As we passed through the infantry of the 5th Division, arranged in the usual firing line, supports and reserves, they were entrenching as well as they could with their wretched little tools, augmented by some village picks and spades; the field batteries were trotting to their stations, many of these only 200 to 400 yards behind the foremost infantry and practically in the open as there had not been time to 'dig in' . . .

The weather cleared after heavy rain and a hot sun tinted

the large fields of cut corn to a golden hue. The remainder of the open rolling landscape was mostly covered with ripened grass, but patches of vegetable crops showed about the redbrick villages, and greener grass beside the several small streams. Numerous roads and tracks intersected the countryside . . . No fences interfered with movement except immediately around the villages; the main roads were lined with trees and one or two small copses stood here and there . . .

It was beside one of these copses that the 19th Brigade, the only infantry reserve of II Corps, took up its position.

By the time we had reached our position at the wood the bombardment seemed to be general all along the front; we could see shells bursting across the Selle where the Cornwalls, East Surrey and the 3rd Cavalry Brigade were withdrawing . . .

Brief items of news regarding the 5th Division reached us occasionally; word about the 3rd and 4th Divisions less frequently . . .

Up till 1 p.m. the positions of the II Corps were nearly all intact in spite of the highest trials. In the early afternoon, however, the situation on the right of the 5th Division became critical. Not only had the infantry and gunners there suffered fearful casualties which undeniably shook some units in their shallow trenches, but the German 7th Division was working up the Selle to turn that flank.

The trickle of wounded who, carried on stretchers or sustained by damaged comrades, had since early morning hobbled southwest along the Roman way now amounted to a stream . . .

One by one the units of the 19th Brigade were drawn into the fight: first the 2/Argyll and Sutherland Highlanders, to support the 2/Suffolks (14th Brigade) who were putting up a magnificent fight, although severely punished by fire from front and flank; then the 1/Middlesex, to support the Highlanders; later the 2/Royal Welch Fusiliers and 1/Cameronians marched off to help the 3rd Division which had been driven out of the village of Caudry.

Meanwhile brigade headquarters had not been idle. Johnson, Turner and I at first carried out short reconnaissances to acquaint ourselves with the lie of the ground and with the general position of the troops whom the brigade might be required to help. Then there were orders to convey on horseback, besides messages and reports needing attention. Churchill had his hands full with his signal lines and message books . . .

On my occasional rides with orders and reports, and at our headquarters among the corn sheaves on the crest north-east of Reumont, the shell fire was insignificant; the front infantry and gunners bore all the blast. But one shell burst so close to Turner (A.D.C.) sitting on his horse, that I momentarily thought both of them must be blown to bits. Neither was touched, and the only notice taken of the explosion by the Brigadier was an indignant glance; perhaps it had wakened him from a 'nap'.

Less fortunate was a gunner officer nearby; he and his charger were 'blotted out' in an instant by another shell.

When not busy we slept, except one on watch; the corn sheaves were so comfortable, the day so warm, and we were *so tired* . . .

In the early afternoon I saw through binoculars a long enemy column . . . advancing across the railway near Le Cateau station some two miles distant. At once informing the Brigadier, he sent me riding to the 108th Heavy Battery, a quarter of a mile north of Reumont, to tell them. On the way I spied the drums of the Argyll and Sutherland lying beside a track while the drummers were collecting casualties, and made a note to have them retrieved when things should become quieter. But a moment later all to do with music was put abruptly out of my mind, for as I cantered close to the teams and limbers of an artillery brigade, massed in a slight hollow a little to the east of the heavy battery, tremendous salvos of shrapnel were bursting over them; for a few seconds the bullets were passing my horse and me in gusts . . .

. . . on return from delivering a message, I found the Brigadier leaving a conference at H.Q. 5th Division . . . General Drummond informed me that the II Corps was on the point of withdrawing; that I must try to get some infantry on our particular front to hold their ground for a little longer and cover it; that he must leave the matter to me as he had no reserves left, the

Fusiliers and Cameronians not having been returned to him; and that the situation on the front of the 5th Division had become so uncertain that he could give no detailed orders.

Even then (between 2.30 and 3.30 p.m.), as a result of the terrible shell and machine gun fire from the front and flanks, the advanced trenches of the right and centre brigades besides the close support batteries of this division were being overrun by the waves of the enemy assisted at 1,000 yards range, or under, by field guns. Our artillery with superb courage attempted to save their pieces, the teams galloping straight forward through the corn sheaves under annihilating rifle fire. Many teams were shot down but others succeeded in getting guns away, some of them no further than two to three hundred yards from the enemy . . .

Unknown to me my groom had been wounded and the horses were missing; I therefore proceeded on foot to carry out the Brigadier's instructions. Collecting one or two men, we hurried along a lane in Reumont where a shell decanted portions of a roof on to our heads.

Less than a mile towards Le Cateau we met part of a battalion leisurely retiring in extended order. General Drummond's request, which I delivered to the senior officer, was received with an incredulous stare, as if it were a demand for a money subscription. I was told that orders to withdraw had been received, and that our leading troops had all been obliterated leaving none between this battalion and the Germans. So it passed on without stopping, I feeling rather daunted.

Cautiously scouting around, we presently came on two companies of the Argyll and Sutherland marching quietly back in open order with tall, handsome Colonel Moulton-Barrett at their head. He answered the invitation to oppose the enemy a little longer by at once calling out '93rd (their old regimental number), about turn', the movement being executed on the spot with almost parade exactitude; his Highlanders were then again led forward to a suitable crest nearby. I told the colonel the situation as far as I knew it; he confirmed my information as to the front, from which we could now hear little firing. Posts of our cavalry were visible across the railway towards Escaufort.

37

The only other units whom I could discover, a company of the 1/Norfolk, some 1/Scots Fusiliers and several sections of the 59th Company, Royal Engineers, also willingly stood fast – the last-named seemingly delighted at the idea of fighting as infantry. These detachments being short of officers, I quickly helped them to select positions before myself returning to Reumont . . .

Towards 4.15 o'c I reached Reumont again to report and get orders but could find no trace of my headquarters nor of any soldiers. Churchill soon arrived on the same quest and said that poor Johnson had been killed.[1] A further search produced only one young staff officer and his orderly; the former thought that everyone else had gone back. The village was under shell-fire at this time; some houses were burning, and the church, full of wounded, had been badly damaged.

Being now most anxious for the safety of the troops recently placed by me, particularly as we could see groups of men approaching from the ridges nearer Le Cateau without being able to distinguish their nationality, I ran forward along the outskirts of the village to warn our friends to retire.

Presently a tremendous crash of musketry fire broke out in front.

Following a hedge which obstructed the view I came on the Argylls just below me, manning the bank of a road at the south-eastern corner of Reumont. They were firing hard at the Germans whose advancing infantry lines were flooding all over the ground from the direction of St Benin, the closest being some four to six hundred yards distant.

A fusillade of bullets was skimming the road bank and a wire fence stood between me and the Highlanders. Expecting to be hit at any moment, I called to the men to tell their colonel to retire at once; then, to their kindly warnings 'Be careful, Sir', climbed the fence, slid down the track, and hastened crouching along to Moulton-Barrett. He said he believed that all the other units had already retired – none of them was to be seen or heard. We quickly divided those present into two parts, he taking the one and I the other, and doubling back alternately to a hollow out of the enemy's view, re-formed between 5.30 and 6 p.m.

[1] *Major-General Drummond was wounded, possibly somewhat later.*

In spite of the heavy rifle fire and some shells to which we were exposed on our run across the open ground I do not think that a man was lost. Perhaps, moving diagonally, as we purposely did, made us a difficult mark. We were soon safe near Honnechy, where I left my companions and went to look for headquarters.

On October 11th 1914 Captain Jack was awarded the Legion of Honour 'for gallantry during the operations between August 21st and 30th, 1914'. 'Only at Le Cateau on 26th August was I very closely engaged with the enemy,' he remarks, and consequently attributes the award to his work on that day, and to the recommendation of Colonel Moulton-Barrett of the Argyll and Sutherlands. Major A. H. Maclean of that regiment was also nominated for the honour at the same time – 'But he died and I lived . . . and I always consider that I wear the medal as much for him as for myself.'

Jack had deep affection for the Argyll and Sutherland Highlanders, with whom he served for fourteen years of his Army life: in South Africa with their 1st Battalion (91st Foot) as a volunteer from 1898– 1900; with their Militia Battalion in 1903; and with their Territorials between 1925 and 1933. Old soldiers have long memories; in May 1960 Jack received a letter from an ex-rifleman of the Cameronians who told him: 'When on holiday last year in Jersey, I met an old Argyll and Sutherland Highlander, an Old Contemptible, and in chatting about the first World War he said he had warm memories of the Cameronians in the 19th Brigade and particularly of a Capt. Jack, who he said got them out of a nasty position at Le Cateau. You no doubt will remember the occasion.' It was, of course, the episode referred to above, and this remembrance was probably more satisfying to General Jack than the award of even so distinguished a French decoration as the Legion of Honour.

The Battle of Le Cateau cost the B.E.F. 7,812 officers and men and 38 guns. It won for General Smith-Dorrien this tribute in Field-Marshal Sir John French's Despatch (his subsequent remarks in his book '1914' deserve rather to be forgotten): 'I say without hesitation that the saving of the left wing of the army under my command on the morning of the 26th August could never have been accomplished unless a commander of rare and unusual coolness, intrepidity, and determination had been present to personally conduct the operation.'

The battle contributed mightily to the 'fog of war' – with, on the whole, beneficial results for the Allies. General von Kluck, so far from preventing the withdrawal of Smith-Dorrien's smaller and shaken force in broad daylight, as he should have done in theory, not only allowed it to get away, but then 'lost' it completely. 'After Le Cateau', wrote Smith-Dorrien, 'we (II Corps) were no more seriously troubled during the ten days' retreat, except by mounted troops and mobile detachments who kept at a respectful distance.' This was because von Kluck, never appreciating the direction of the B.E.F.'s retreat to the south, now marched off south-westward towards Amiens, thus creating a gap between his army and that of his neighbour von Bulow which made possible the French counterstroke at Guise on August 29th – which, in turn, helped to procure the conditions for the Battle of the Marne.

Misunderstanding, however, also flourished on the Allied side of the line. At the British G.H.Q. the impression gained ground that II Corps had sustained irretrievable damage; the Cavalry Division was thought to have been wiped out (it had scarcely been engaged);the 5th Division was believed to have lost all its guns. Sir Henry Wilson (Deputy Chief of Staff) told General Snow (commanding 4th Division): 'From Henry to Snowball: Throw overboard all ammunition and impedimenta not absolutely required, and load up your lame ducks on all transport, horse and mechanical, and hustle along.' Impressed by these gloomy forebodings, the French Liaison Officer at G.H.Q., Colonel Huguet (not a robust optimist himself), told Joffre: 'For the moment the British Army is beaten and is incapable of any serious effort . . . the 3rd and 5th Divisions . . . are now nothing more than disorganised bands, incapable of offering the smallest resistance. Conditions are such that for the moment the British Army no longer exists.' This was sickening news for Joffre, at the crisis of the campaign; how far it was from the truth, only the men who had actually fought at Le Cateau really knew.

THE RETREAT FROM LE CATEAU

After leaving the Argylls at Honnechy in order to seek brigade headquarters I was too exhausted to remember details clearly till the 28th . . .

At a cross-roads a field battery and the Cameronians were composedly halted as rearguard ready for the Germans, the latter with fixed 'swords', as bayonets are called by Rifle Regiments. Colonel Robertson said he thought Brigade Headquarters were ahead. His battalion had been lightly engaged that day but had had a very wearing time moving about to threatened sectors.

Rain was now falling. I soon joined groups of various regiments and some horse transport stumbling along, the men half-dazed from fatigue, being only kept together, and moving, by the exertions of their few remaining officers . . .

Some time in the night[1] a motor lorry gave me a short lift before stopping to park with others. During this brief pause a little food purchased and devoured at an estaminet made me very sick; I lay down under the lorry to rest till it was ready to proceed with its neighbours. Soon somebody pulled me out saying they were going on; so I rose, numbed by the cold and rain, scarcely caring what happened . . .

About dawn I met, and reported for duty to, Lieut-Colonel C. J. Hickie (? H.Q. II Corps). He was accompanied by one or two mounted orderlies and had also lost his headquarters. Both of us were now 'off our maps'. We had, I believe, strayed west of St Quentin. Scarcely any troops were to be seen, but I managed to borrow a spare horse from a single battery and went with the Colonel on a small tour to try and discover our whereabouts. Of soldiery we saw none, but heard heavy gun-fire to the north-west (British and French cavalry rear-guards).

Then we stopped in a village, loosened girths, watered and fed the horses, and bought for ourselves as well as the orderlies beer, raw eggs, rolls and butter. This delicious breakfast was cut short by the approach of mounted men from the north; so thinking they might be Prussians and that we might have wandered behind our rear-guards we girthed up and trotted away. The rain had now ceased, giving way to warm, bright weather.

Directing our way south by the sun we came upon the main St Quentin – Ham road, straight, white, tree-lined, and running through open cultivated country. On it an endless irregular procession of infantry, batteries, transport and refugees tramped slowly towards Ham . . .

[1] *26th/27th.*

A large number of valises and entrenching tools were absent, having been lost in action or thrown away by order or otherwise; all troops, however, had their arms, besides the residue of their ammunition. The officers were afoot, many of them carrying one or two of their men's rifles. The chargers bore equipment or exhausted soldiers, and towed a man hanging on to the stirrup on either flank. Transport vehicles gave similar assistance.

Frequently someone would fall or sit down for a rest, the first to be picked up by comrades and put on a waggon, and the second urged to his feet again. Here and there in this ghastly queue marched a fairly solid company, platoon or section.

Abandoned equipment littered the roadsides; at intervals waggons had been left for lack of teams . . .

During the morning things began to improve. Staff officers at road intersections disentangled the medley: '3rd Division on the right of the road, 5th Division on the left, 4th beyond the 3rd.' There the different regiments were sorted out and formed into companies. Ammunition and rations, previously dumped by the transport, were issued.

I heard of one young staff officer being amused – until quelled – at the difference between this Retreat and the Real Professional Retreat performed at Aldershot in perfect order.

In the twinkling of an eye organisation and food produced a happier air; so when the improvised companies had devoured a meal from the 'cookers' collected at these rendezvous, followed by an hour's sleep or a smoke and chat, they set out again like new men, soldierly and singing although dead-beat . . .

As to the French peasantry: deeply concerned as they were about their own security, and bitterly disappointed at being left to the enemy's hands, their kindness by deed as well as word all the way from Mons can never be exceeded. At no time did I see on their faces, or hear in their remarks, anything but pity for our men. They stood at their doors with pails of water, sometimes wine, long rolls of bread and butter, fruit, just what they had. We must never forget them.

Late in the afternoon I crossed the Somme at Ham on foot, having relinquished my mount earlier – I could *not ride* with that wearied throng *walking* – and was directed to Ollezy, four miles eastwards, where nearly all the brigade was already assembled in bivouacs and barns.

The distance marched from Le Cateau was about 44 miles, the weather hot, and the men had had practically no proper meal or rest for thirty-six hours or more. Colonel Robertson estimated that the Cameronians covered fifty-seven miles in that time . . .

In the evening, when visiting the bivouac of my battalion, I fainted – twice I was told . . .

AUGUST 30TH: COULOISY

At Ollezy at 4 a.m. on the 28th the stir of packing up awoke me from a deep sleep; I rose, washed, shaved, breakfasted and resumed duty.

Lieut-Colonel E. E. Ward, 1/Middlesex, the senior battalion commander, has assumed command of the brigade . . .

At 6 a.m. the brigade, covered by cavalry in contact with the enemy, commenced its march of 19 miles . . . to take up a defensive position at Pontoise about 5 p.m.. The country was latterly rather hilly, the weather hot, and the hour's halt on the way for dinners very welcome.

That night I almost collapsed from fatigue and although it was unnecessary charming Duval insisted on helping me to remove my accoutrements.[1]

Yesterday we stayed at Pontoise till the evening. The men urgently required rest, proper meals, and a wash. Their feet are terribly raw from seven days' marching and fighting, with no chance to remove their boots. The most exhausted have been carried on army waggons or on farm carts requisitioned locally.

There was, however, no repose at Pontoise for the battalion quartermasters nor for my office as the tale of deficiencies in stories and equipment is staggering, necessitating the making up of long indents in triplicate for replacements.

After this precious day's rest, which restored the men 'no end', the brigade marched at 8 p.m. to Couloisy . . . down the steep winding road to Attichy, across the Aisne, and up the

---

[1] *Captain Raoul Duval, French Dragoons, Liaison and Interpreter.*

43

heights to billet here about noon today . . . the dust very trying and the checks incessant throughout the fifteen-mile march. . . . The Germans have taken Péronne and are before Amiens. Their unbroken successes everywhere are very depressing for us. What is to be the end of it all?

Our rear-guards had a little respite after Le Cateau, but the enemy are again pressing on and there is an attractive sense of security in having these large rivers between us and them at night.

AUGUST 31ST

. . . On my way back [*from Corps H.Q.*] . . . I see a group of British soldiers escorting a Frenchman – none other than Duval – whose face is livid with anger. He has been arrested, stupidly, by a young British departmental officer as a German spy, many of whom are said to be in the Allied lines, and is being marched to Headquarters for identification. At a word from me his freedom is restored and I bid him enter our car; but, still incensed, he demands to know the name of his captor for the purpose of challenging the villain to a duel at the end of the War. My attempt to pass the matter off draws the fierce threat that if I do not get the name he will shoot me instead. Seeing that my friend must have some name, I go over to the now frightened subaltern and return with the bogus information that he is Lieutenant Smith of Stepney. This ends the unfortunate incident.

Poor Duval, a very fine Frenchman, arrested as a German spy, in his own country, by aliens! (His death at Verdun cancelled the risk of this duel.) . . .

THE ACTION AT NERY

SEPTEMBER 1ST: SAINTINES, IN OUTPOSTS
AND BILLETS

We are awakened before dawn by a few rifle shots in the village, and shouts that the Germans have entered the place. These are followed by the clatter of one or two mounted Uhlans down the street, and there is some local excitement which soon subsides.

The brigade marches at 6 a.m. Soon afterwards . . . a cavalry warrant-officer gallops up rather breathless and reports to Colonel Ward leading the column, 'General Briggs's compliments, sir. The 1st Cavalry Brigade at Néry (a mile to our right rear) is being attacked by the Germans, is in "rather a mess", and urgently requires help.'

The Middlesex and the Cameronians are diverted forthwith to Néry and I am ordered to ride there, find out the situation, and tell General Briggs that assistance is coming at once.

. . . I soon reach Néry. There is indeed a 'mess'. Close beside an orchard rows of cavalry horses lie dead in their lines; a little further on are the bodies of Colonel Ansell (5th Dragoon Guards), de Crespigny (Bays), together with many other casualties. Near the eastern houses General Briggs, to whom I report, is assisting to man a Vickers gun. On a crest some 800 yards away twelve German field guns, now mute, face us. Except for a few enemy bullets and the bursts from our cavalry machine guns all is quiet.

On the way back to my brigade I pass the Middlesex in extended lines working up a hollow on the flank of the German batteries which they take with little opposition along with 78 prisoners.

A sharp skirmish about the Néry–Bethisy road is now in progress between the German troopers clearing off northwards and part of our brigade, together with units of the 4th Division . . .

This was the famous action in which 'L' Battery, Royal Horse Artillery, so distinguished itself. When five guns out of six had been put out of action, Captain Bradbury (mortally wounded), Battery Sergeant-Major Dorrell and Sergeant Nelson kept the remaining gun in action against the twelve guns of the German 4th Cavalry Division. All three were awarded the V.C.

Jack was concerned at a British Cavalry brigade allowing itself to be surprised as General Briggs's command had been when the morning mist cleared, and the enemy opened fire at a range of less than half a mile. 'The mistake lay in taking too much for granted,' he comments. 'Unless units are certain that they are adequately covered by other troops they must send out pickets of their own.' This seems to be the truth of the matter: the 1st Cavalry Brigade had some idea that there were French cavalry or British infantry between it and the enemy. Patrols were sent out early that morning, one of them under Lieutenant Tailby of the 11th Hussars (later Jack's neighbour in Leicestershire). Tailby took nothing for granted; coming unexpectedly on the enemy, he had the presence of mind to snatch up a German trooper's cloak to take back as clear evidence of their presence, to convince sceptics. But the mist cleared suddenly, and the German guns opened fire simultaneously with the return of Tailby's patrol – a perfect surprise. Such, however, was the quality of the B.E.F. that the 1st Cavalry Brigade rallied at once, and, with the help of supporting units, drove off the Germans. Their 4th Cavalry Division withdrew, damaged, considerably demoralised, and with the ultimate loss of all its artillery.

SEPTEMBER 4TH: CHANTELOUP

This sickening retreat still drags on.

On the 2nd the brigade stayed at Fresnoy till the evening. Then in a night and day march of over 30 miles southwards, in stifling heat and frequently interrupted by checks, it crossed the prettily-wooded Marne at Lagny and lodged here early yesterday afternoon . . .

Near Dammartin French troops and civilians were feverishly felling trees, erecting barbed wire entanglements, digging trenches and building redoubts. From there our way led inside the new hastily constructed outer defences of Paris . . .

. . . the French liaison officer and I rode on to Chanteloup to arrange accommodation, the battalion billeting parties following on foot . . .

In warm weather we prefer bivouacking in the open – with a few cottages or barns added for messes and offices – to billeting in villages. Men in billets take longer to collect in an emergency; moreover, buildings quickly become unpleasant under shell fire. Another reason why the infantry bivouac is that every other corps comes before them in the matter of comfort.

The men are recovering their 'spring' after the intense strain of August.

Today the brigade is not to move. We are getting a chance to attack arrears of office work, which is a difficulty during constant marching. The number of 'returns', reports, and indents to replace lost or damaged equipment is pestilential besides being complicated by our being only 'attached' to a division or headquarters and the division, etc., changed frequently. The 19th is nobody's child . . .

Toil as I can, the piles of papers on my office table are still high; a fresh post seems to turn up as soon as one has got rid of the last.

SEPTEMBER 5TH

Reveille is at 1 a.m. Two hours later the brigade . . . continues the retreat 14 miles south . . . and bivouacs at Grisy, 15 miles south-east of Paris.

Brigadier-General the Hon. F. Gordon, D.S.O. (Gordon Highlanders), arrives to command the brigade, with Captain C. Heywood (Coldstream Guards) as Brigade-Major . . .

The recent halts and the reduced length of marches have enabled us to get at our maps. All officers of the B.E.F. left the United Kingdom with a large supply (about 16) of excellent maps of Belgium and Northern France; but at first we travelled so far and so fast, and without access to our valises, that we were often 'off the map". I have, in fact, at times owed my direction to a very small-scale French cycling map.

The regulation marching intervals – six yards between companies, ten between battalions, and thirty in rear of a brigade – may be suitable in peace-time; they are too little here. Traffic obstructions on the roads cause checks all down the column, adding greatly to the fatigue of the troops. Rules as to intervals have therefore been somewhat relaxed to fit the circumstances.

A few drafts of men, some new equipment and clothing have just reached us. The Glengarry bonnets and regulation caps are especially welcome since many men, losing their proper head-dress, had adopted comfortable but unsoldierly straw hats as worn by the peasantry. Besides appearance, those wearing them are liable to be shot as 'franc-tireurs' if caught by the enemy.

In the afternoon I proceed uncomfortably on the luggage-carrier of a despatch-rider's motor bicycle to Headquarters 5th Division at Brie-Comte-Robert, five miles away, for orders. Sir Charles Fergusson and his staff give me tea and seem to be in uncommonly good spirits for no reason that I can discover.

Perhaps the current rumours are correct, that the B.E.F. is being taken out of the line to refit. I wonder if the French and Germans are doing likewise? I am sure all three of us could do with a long holiday!

The B.E.F. has marched nearly 200 miles in the first thirteen days of the campaign – fair exercise considering all the circumstances.

The vigour and accuracy of camp rumours in all armies have often been a matter for wonder. It was a fact that Sir John French, in the doldrums after Le Cateau, had expressed the determination to retire across the Seine, south-west of Paris, to rest and refit his army. He told the Government: 'This means marching for some eight days without fatiguing the troops at a considerable distance from the enemy . . .' This remarkable proposition was overruled by the personal intervention of Lord Kitchener. French was now in a more amenable mood, and had agreed to conform to General Joffre's plans. Sir Charles Fergusson's cheerfulness thus had a quite different cause . . .

THE ADVANCE TO THE MARNE
ACROSS THE GRAND MORIN

SEPTEMBER 7TH: LA HAUTE MAISON

A marvellous change has come over the situation. We have been chasing the Germans back for the past two days.

Yesterday at Grisy when the brigade was formed up in column of route at 5 a.m. ready to march south as usual, an order arrived to say that on the 5th a new French Sixth Army,[1] north of Paris, had commenced an advance eastwards against the right flank of the German First Army, and that the B.E.F., French Fifth Army and Cavalry Corps were to move forward at once and attack the enemy on the Grand Morin.

This totally unexpected news almost passed belief after the long depressing retreat; all faces were bright as we marched 16 miles north-east . . . to bivouac at Villeneuve-St Denis.

Our brigade, in rear, had a quiet day. Even the cavalry and infantry advanced guards were not seriously opposed and picked up a few prisoners – a heartening sight . . .

[1] *General Maunoury.*

48

At dawn this morning the brigade moves, as part of the left column of the 4th Division,[1] 13 miles north-eastwards through wooded country.

As I ride along the column with a message a British sergeant comes to inform me that a French patrol has just told his post that a German 'army corps' is within 800 yards of it. (40,000 Prussians only a mile from our line of march!) Doubting the sergeant's knowledge of French and the size of the enemy's host I wish him 'good luck' against such long odds, but report the tale to Heywood lest there by any chance of our being surprised, even by bodies not so formidable. Nothing eventuates.

The leading troops having brushed back the German rear-guards, the brigade crosses the Grand Morin at Crécy without delay or difficulty, and reaches La Haute-Maison in the afternoon. Our corps advanced guard (4th Division) has met with considerable opposition near Pierre-Levée, and we bivouac in touch with the enemy . . .

I agree with Heywood that our marches are too short for a pursuing force. He considers that we should push on with more vigour, and forget about the retreat. This brigade is certainly in good form once more.

THE BATTLE OF THE MARNE

SEPTEMBER 8TH

Reveille is at 3 a.m. Two hours later the brigade, as the leading left column of the 4th Division, advances to drive the enemy out of Pierre-Levée, but they have already gone . . .

The Middlesex (advanced guard), on appearing over the open crests beyond Signy, comes under heavy shrapnel fire from hostile batteries on the north bank of the Marne and suffers some loss . . .

The shelling is most disagreeable but relatively harmless; it lasts for perhaps half an hour. Although there is not the least sign of unsteadiness in the ranks, General Gordon and Heywood persist in standing about (I cannot well do otherwise) with the salvos constantly bursting almost in our faces . . .

[1] *From August 30th, 4th Division and 19th Brigade formed III Corps under Major-General W. P. Pulteney, C.B., D.S.O.*

49

Crowds of Germans are seen scaling the heights across the river, and the guns are quickly firing on fine targets . . .

Further operations, however, are held up as the Marne bridges here have all been blown up, no boats can be found, and the north bank is lined with hostile machine guns and riflemen . . .

The B.E.F. has advanced generally from eight to ten miles today (our brigade nearly seven), making large hauls of prisoners, machine guns and artillery. In spite of the very fine resistance of the German rear-guards, the difficult wooded country along the Petit Morin and its steep banks, our cavalry, I and II Corps advanced guards have forced the passages of that river (which lay east of and almost outside the III Corps front) after hard fighting . . .

SEPTEMBER 9TH: SIGNY-SIGNETS

The brigade had 41 casualties yesterday, mostly Middlesex. Battalions spent a cold wet night.

At 4.45 this morning the 4th Division takes the high ground at Tartarel, but has no means of crossing the Marne whose approaches are under heavy fire.

After we have breakfasted well on bacon, eggs, coffee, rolls and butter before settling down to office work, the enemy shells our farm. A couple of explosions in the yard 'shift' us into the open, despatch boxes, maps and accoutrements in our arms, papers stuffed into pockets, horses, carts and other gear in charge of those concerned. In a few minutes our late residence is in flames from bursting shells and the General, much annoyed at the interruption to his work, will have nothing to do with houses for the time being . . .

Scores of the enemy are visible hurrying away up the slopes north of the Marne with our shrapnel bursting among them. A gratifying sight!

In the afternoon a heavy bombardment by our guns drives the Germans back from their bank, and the Engineers immediately commence to build a pontoon bridge.

At night six battalions of the 4th Division, led with great enterprise and covered by machine guns, cross the Marne under hot fire, two of them by boat near La Ferté and four by the canal barrage and damaged girders of the railway bridge near Chamigny.

Meanwhile the brigade assembles and marches four miles to La Ferté where we sit by the water's edge while the indefatigable sappers complete their work. During this tiresome delay word arrives that one of our motor despatch riders has been arrested as a spy on the grounds that he was asking too many question and 'does not look like a British soldier'. Excusable enough, poor devil, if he is dirty, unshaved and oily from his constant rides with messages, along crowded roads, and often in the dark without lights. The arrest is also excusable as the risk of spies is so great . . .

Tonight's news is . . . The I Corps has crossed at Nogent and Charly, and the II Corps at Nanteuil and Mery . . . They have made very large captures of prisoners and matériel. The bridges being nearly ready, the III Corps is on the point of crossing at Chamigny and La Ferté.

The left of the French Fifth Army has reached the Marne about Château-Thierry . . .

SEPTEMBER 10TH

The pontoon bridge having been completed the brigade marches in miserable weather through La Ferté, passing a few dead men and horses along with wounded in the streets. Then, in its turn, with irregular intervals and broken step to save the strain on the bridge, it files across the Marne at 3.30 a.m. . . .

A French cavalry brigade comes next, Dragoons and Chasseurs -à-Cheval, still in their uniforms of a hundred years ago . . .

A little way on civilians say that the enemy has mined the road; I am therefore much relieved at our diversion to another route as left flank guard to the 4th Division. We proceed northwards . . . the latter part of the 15-mile march (from Signy) in pouring rain.

The Germans made themselves very comfortable – perhaps even drunk – at the villages occupied by them. The ground in their neighbourhood is often literally covered with empty wine bottles, besides equipment, abandoned waggons, carts and exhausted horses. The inhabitants are furious at the wanton

damage done to property by their late 'guests', described
heatedly as 'Huns', 'bosches', 'barbarians', 'pigs' . . .

Owing to the breakdown of the weather as many troops as
possible are billeted . . .

The woods on the routes of the B.E.F. are full of German
stragglers. Our captures of prisoners and transport are, as
yesterday, very large. We have also taken many machine guns
and some artillery.

Our airmen – splendid fellows – report the roads to the north
crammed with long hostile columns in full retreat . . .

SEPTEMBER 11TH

The pursuit continues on a very wet day . . .

Since the 6th instant the B.E.F. has taken a very large amount
of material, besides thousands of prisoners who say that their
orders were to check us as long as possible and then surrender.
Many of them capitulated to the bottle first. On the whole,
however, their rear-guards have put up a fine defence – in
many cases a superb defence . . .

THE BATTLE OF THE AISNE

SEPTEMBER 12TH: MARIZY-STE GENEVIEVE

. . . At 6 a.m. the brigade marches behind the 4th Division in
pouring rain and on roads deep in mud . . . to Buzancy, where
we are in poor billets and very wet after covering 15 miles . . .

The Germans are destroying the Aisne bridges, evacuating
[Soissons] and withdrawing northwards under our shells together with those of the French . . .

Our landlady complains that some of her poultry – all 'laying'
of course – have been stolen by our men; General Gordon, who
is most particular about looting, therefore tells me to collect
the price from the units concerned and pay for the fowls. This
prompt settlement pleases the old dame . . .

The south bank of the Aisne has been cleared of the enemy,
but our 80-mile advance is meeting with hardening resistance.

*This was the last day of 'pursuit'; by a forced march of 40 miles in
24 hours from Maubeuge (nearly 25 per cent of the infantry dropping*

*out on the way) the German VII Reserve Corps arrived next day on the
Chemin des Dames Ridge, north of the Sisne, just in time to block the
advance of the British I Corps. In the ding-dong fighting which followed
the beginnings of trench warfare were seen, and the first stalemate
experienced.*

SEPTEMBER 13TH: BUZANCY

... I am up most of the night meeting and directing the horse-
transport with ammunition, rations and other stores. The steep
road gradients and turns give great trouble and cause much
delay.

Today the B.E.F. attempted to carry the German positions
north of the Aisne ...

The day's fighting has been very severe. All the crossings,
save that at Bourg, were strenuously opposed. The Engineers,
working like navvies, have repaired some of the bridges and
constructed others of pontoons to enable part of the field
artillery to pass to the north bank.

SEPTEMBER 14TH: BILLY-SUR-AISNE. IN RESERVE

... Today the B.E.F. again attempts to storm the heights north
of the Aisne. We, in reserve, are on too low ground dotted with
copses to get any view of the action which we hear raging along
the valley ...

It rains ceaselessly; our headquarters huddle miserably beneath waterproof sheets tied to trees to form shelters. The
brigade finds large working parties to assist the sappers in
repairing bridges and roads, as well as to dig trenches ...

*This is an early mention of what was to become the bane of the British
infantryman's life: fatigues, in the never-ending form of working
parties, carrying parties, wiring parties – everything except cheerful
parties – and usually undertaken during periods officially known as 'rest'
or 'training'. The French, fighting in their own country, were able to
provide over-age Territorials or civilian labour for much of this; the
Germans had no compunction about using the population of the occupied
territories. By 1918 the B.E.F. had over 300,000 men in Labour Units;
it was still nothing like enough, and until then the brunt of this duty
had fallen on the unfortunate infantry (in addition to the brunt of*

53

battle); throughout the War, sheer physical exhaustion was a major horror of trench warfare.

The 4th Division – whose headquarters are adventurously situated in a prominent café in Venizel – was to have attacked the Vregny plateau, provided that the 5th Division on its right and the French at Soissons on its left made sufficient progress. Since they did not, the 4th stood fast, except for a successful minor attack by the 2/Dublin Fusiliers . . .

German counter-attacks on many parts of the British front have all, latterly, been repulsed with severe casualties; but their bombardments continue to be severe . . .

. . . our Allies cannot, any more than we, make further headway.

SEPTEMBER 21ST: SEPTMONTS

After a foul eight days on the Aisne, in continuous rain and the ground a quagmire, the brigade was withdrawn from the Venizel area last night to these quarters, four miles from the river, behind the heights on its south bank, and clear of shelling.

It is heavenly to be under a roof again; to enjoy a bath, clean clothes, proper meals, regular rest and an office out of the wet. Meeting the supply transport delayed by bad roads till late each night, besides many duties throughout the day, robbed me too much of sleep.

One's feelings all this time out of attacks have been rather mixed; thankfulness for our safer rôle compared with those in the cockpit of the battle, yet regret at not sharing their dangers more equally . . .

The B.E.F. ceased attacking after the 15th as being too wasteful of life under present conditions. The French have done likewise.

German assaults, however, on the front of all our three corps (principally on the I Corps) have taken place daily without making more than very local impressions on our lines in return for heavy casualties. The Queen's, Northamptonshire, and other battalions have counter-attacked with the bayonet, settling many of the enemy . . .

We have heard of several unfortunate – and I think very

stupid – incidents due to our troops leaving their trenches to 'accept the surrender' of Germans approaching under a white flag. Others of the enemy, having no intention of giving in, thereupon opened fire on friend and foe with dire results to both.

The enemy's shell fire has continued to be very harassing; the other day I saw some of our batteries having a hellish time from it.[1]

At Venizel we heard the 'drum fire' of the French artillery at Soissons every night . . .

The ordinary field trenches give sufficient protection from field gun shells, but not against the enemy's howitzer fire on our present fixed positions. Moreover, the Germans have brought up 8- and 11-inch howitzers which, outranging our lighter pieces, can fire without interruption. Villages have therefore been scoured for strong farm tools with which properly to entrench.

I recently had a disagreeable ride to Bucy in pitch darkness on a pedal bicycle, without lights since none are allowed to show at the front . . .

On the return journey towards dawn I passed the wearied, depressed fragments of a battalion filing to the south bank of the Aisne following many days in action. After it an ambulance convoy lurched along the rough track, together with a stream of walking wounded – 'the Glory of war'!

The public at Home can never realise the repeated high trials sustained by regimental officers and men, nor the terrible conditions under which they carry out most of their duties here . . .

BEHIND THE AISNE IN CORPS RESERVE
(Sept. 21– Oct. 4)

OCTOBER 4TH: SEPTMONTS

We have been quietly and comfortably billeted here in corps

---

[1] *Their serious shortage of heavy artillery now began to affect the Allied armies. General Haig wrote in his diary on September 16th: '. . . the enemy's big guns possess a real moral superiority for some of our gunners. In fact, our gunners cannot "take on" the enemy's heavy batteries.'*

reserve since 21st September. Some drafts have joined to fill up the ranks. The brigade has been digging and wiring reserve lines of trenches on the heights south of the Aisne.

The Battle of the Aisne, which has cost us pretty dearly', has been dying down for the past fortnight. The foremost infantry of both armies are now too securely entrenched, 200 to 400 yards apart, for attacks to have much chance of success save at prohibitive price . . .The Germans have been slower than we in appreciating the power of the defence . . .

It is rumoured that the enemy's spies in this area use undiscovered telephones to communicate with their own army, and that they signal information to the German aeroplanes which are frequently overhead observing. Every effort is being made to stop these practices.

One afternoon when I was riding near the Fère-en-Tardenois to Soissons road a large open car came flashing along it from the south, the occupants all muffled up in spite of the sunshine. Their appearance and procedure were so like those of an enemy's agents that I would have tried to stop the car had that been possible. On my return I reported the incident; the number of barricades on the roads has consequently been increased while the guards on them have been instructed to exercise the greatest vigilance.

Important court-martial sentences are read from time to time on parade of all troops as a warning to them. Two recent examples were sentences of death for cowardice and desertion in the presence of the enemy, a sickeningly terrible end to these poor fellows. But if discipline is not strictly upheld on active service an army may become a rabble. I know that presidents and members of courts-martial impose this penalty with extreme reluctance, and only on irrefutable evidence which is minutely examined by the Judge Advocate-General at Army Headquarters before the sentence is carried out by a firing party.

Our Headquarters are in the château, a quaint and beautiful old building with five towers joined by a high wall round the courtyard.

[1] *About 20,000 casualties.*

The château was formerly a palace of the bishops of Soissons, and is now tenanted by a polished, aged Spanish noble who is most kind . . .

Before our arrival the grooms of another British unit billeted on him greatly displeased our host by tethering their horses in his rose garden and damaging his plants. In fact, he said he preferred the presence of the Germans. However, General Gordon's innate consideration and our good behaviour soon mollified the old gentleman so greatly that he has presented some bottles of wine to the mess although remaining unyielding to requests for permission to shoot a few of the multitude of pigeons that dwell in one of the towers . . .

The Daily Routine is:

At 4.30 a.m. (one hour before dawn) all troops parade fully equipped and 'stand to arms' till daylight. This is a British Army ritual on the supposition – often correct – that dawn is the most probable time for an enemy's attack because previous preparatory movements are concealed by darkness. On this parade the roll is called and accoutrements are inspected. The General and staff also 'stand to arms' as a matter of principle, and have difficulty in keeping warm. On dismissing, battalions clean up, are inspected, and breakfast.

The mornings are occupied with military training or route marches, except for the large parties required to repair roads, erect road barricades, find guards on them, and dig trenches on the plateau overlooking the Aisne.

The Brigadier, accompanied by Heywood or me, visits battalions daily.

After dinners there are ordinary duties, working parties and games – chiefly football.

Following teas the battalion guards mount for the night. All men have a cup of soup with bread or biscuits about 9 o'c prior to roll-call. The 'Lights Out' signal goes half an hour later.

On Sundays Church parades are attended by all not on duty.

Office work keeps us busy for a large part of the afternoon, and sometimes after dinner; we generally ride or walk for an hour or two after lunch.

A reliable typewriting machine has arrived at last, to the

relief of our excellent brigade clerk, Sergeant Hodgkinson. Hitherto much of our correspondence has been in manuscript.

Replacements of equipment, etc., are reaching the brigade more regularly since our permanent attachment to the 4th Division. Previous to that, when we were being continually 'switched' from one division to another, I can imagine the delight with which greatcoats and other clothing intended for us were received at the headquarters to which we had ceased to belong. 'Jock! Here are 500 coats for the 19th Brigade. Where have they gone? What shall I do with them?' 'Oh! the 19th will be all right; just send them to the "Loamshires" who are short again.'

According to indents which I handle to make up losses, one might suppose that the men were naked when the Retreat ended. The huge deficiencies (many due to carelessness) have nearly all been remedied.

The men are comfortable, in good heart, well behaved, and properly equipped.

On this our first halt in billets since leaving Valenciennes the accumulation of letters and parcels from Home is almost overwhelming. Our quarters resemble a miniature Harrod's Store, with chocolate, soup squares, cakes, tinned jam, tongues, and other food; pipes, cigarettes, tobacco, socks, underwear, cardigans, electric torches and their refills . . .

We are a happy mess. The Brigadier and Heywood are very able soldiers, the latter being easy-mannered and pleasant.

General Gordon has a fine character, a spare frame, and a very strong sense of duty; but I find him tryingly reserved and hard. Nevertheless, he has told me to come to him when I want help with my work. His tastes are simple, even austere; he sleeps and eats little besides drinking less; he is always up at dawn and works or reads till bedtime. The table in his room is never without a Bible which I often observe him studying. He appreciates seeing my copy of the *Glasgow Herald*, of whose articles he has a high opinion . . .

The weather is generally bright and the nights are cold. My rides on a handsome chestnut charger, through the prettily wooded countryside turning to autumn tints, are a great joy . . .

At Château Ecury my friend Duval is now on duty. He has

shed his becoming helmet and plume, blue tunic and crimson breeches for the new French horizon-blue uniform . . .[1]

THE MOVE TO FLANDERS
(Oct. 5–10)

OCTOBER 10TH: ESTREES ST DENIS
(20.4 MILES N.E. OF PARIS)

. . . on the 5th the brigade received unexpected orders to move. We have been marching steadily westwards ever since then, in clear frosty weather, and by night so as to escape the enemy's observation from aircraft . . .

We understand that the whole of the B.E.F. is being relieved on the Aisne by the French, but we do not know our destination although rumours point Flanders way. The greatest secrecy prevails. One night when Heywood and I were reconnoitring the road and billets by car we were stopped and questioned by an unknown officer as possible spies; our answers, however, especially a hearty curse from the chauffeur at some mishap, assured him of our nationality.

On the 7th I had a 27-mile motor drive to H.Q. at Fère-en-Tardenois for orders regarding entraining. Unfortunately the trains must be of an unalterable French composition for an infantry brigade, and, besides containing extra details, the 19th Brigade is much stronger than nearly all the British brigades which have been fighting on the Aisne. If, therefore, the French cannot spare us another coach or two it seems that we shall have to leave units on the platform when our last train departs.

Other journeys have been undertaken on the luggage-carrier of a motor bicycle, clinging to the despatch-rider. This is a really terrible means of conveyance on the French cobbled roads . . .

At Bethisy when we were wrestling with railway timetables and insufficient train accommodation . . . a number of courts-martial files most inconsiderately arrived for scrutiny.

[1] *This is a very early mention of 'horizon-blue', which was not generally issued to the French Army until 1916. In 1910 there was a proposal to adopt 'mignonette green'.*

The brigade has an average of about one court-martial per week, a trifling list in view of the fact that under Military Law many misdemeanours not otherwise heinous *must* be tried by court-martial.

The chief offence is aggravated insubordination – under circumstances when tempers are easily roused.

Yesterday battalions reached Estrées in the morning but had to squat on the station yard all day – some till late at night – as the French do not appear to be fanatically punctual in the matter of troop trains. Here some of our rascals contrived to get drunk.

Drunkenness is a very rare offence; the penalties are severe and estaminets are carefully watched by our military police. Simple cases of drunkenness normally receive 28 days (or less) 'Field Punishment' – the maximum term awardable by battalion commanders. This punishment is undergone with a man's unit and involves extra duties, deprival of pay and luxuries, the closure of the canteen to the culprit, along with confinement to camp.

Court-martial sentences are carried out in prison at the Base, where the guilty one escapes battle risks.

'Drunk in action' or 'when warned for action' are very grave crimes, punishable by death but generally entailing – as with insubordination – a term of 6 months to 2 years' imprisonment with hard labour, part of which is probably remitted.

The first train, on which the brigadier and Heywood travel, departed at 6.30 yesterday evening; the second at 10.30, and the third later. The fourth battalion and the remainder of the brigade spent a cold night in the yard, all kits having, of course, been stowed away.

Having survived this experience, thanks to some sacking found by my good servant, Bartlam, I see the fourth train off at 6.30 o'c this morning. Part of our Field Ambulance was threatened – as we anticipated – with being marooned on the platform through lack of accommodation, but the French railway staff, now moved to compassion, are adding some extra trucks to the fifth, and last, train which is due to leave at 10.30 a.m. with all remaining details.

The B.E.F. was now taking part in the manoeuvre misleadingly known as the 'Race to the Sea'. In fact, it was an attempt by both sides to act against the enemy's open flank – the remainder of the front, from Soissons to Switzerland, having stuck in trenches. General Foch was appointed to co-ordinate the Allied (French, British and Belgian) forces in Flanders; his object was 'to exploit the last vestige of our victory on the Marne'. General von Falkenhayn (who had now replaced von Moltke) has defined his objects as: depriving the Allies of the Belgian coast in order to facilitate 'drastic action against England and her sea traffic with sub- marines, aeroplanes and airships', avoiding the encirclement of the Ger- man right wing, and, with luck, forcing the Allies into a new retreat. Intelligence about the enemy was defective on both sides; a series of stern encounter battles thus followed.

THE ADVANCE FROM ST OMER TO NEAR LILLE

OCTOBER IITH: ST OMER

. . . Our advanced cavalry report a few Germans in the vicinity.

The 19th Brigade is now attached to the 6th Division,[1] whose 18th Brigade has come up on our right. The 4th Division is on our left.

The billet accommodation is very scanty and the infantry come off worst as usual; any corner is supposed to be good enough for them, but is accepted good-humouredly as a matter of course . . .

OCTOBER 12TH; RENESCURE

. . . It seems that the B.E.F. is to advance eastwards against the right flank of the German Northern Army in the hope of driving it (in conjunction with our Allies) out of Belgium, and anyhow of making secure the Channel Ports still in our hands.

At 6.30 a.m. the brigade, in reserve, marches 10 miles east- wards . . . Many villages ahead are burning; the Middlesex are in touch with the enemy.

The open, cultivated country is studded with villages and farms, and is intersected by numerous streams besides tree-lined

[1] *The 6th Division (Major-General J. L. Keir, C.B.) joined the B.E.F. on Septem- ber 16th and later became part of III Corps.*

61

roads. Three miles south lies the extensive Forest of Nieppe. Five miles north-east and north-west, respectively, stand the prominent blocks of hills at Mont des Cats and Cassel.

This morning, about Hazebrouck, the advanced guards of the 6th and 4th Divisions had a skirmish with German cavalry whom they brushed back without difficulty.[1]

British and German aeroplanes are often overhead . . .

OCTOBER 13TH: BORRE

. . . Our forward companies again entrench on the low-lying sodden land and spend a wretched night . . .

The III Corps is opposed by relatively weak forces.

OCTOBER 14TH: ROUGE CROIX

The 6th and 4th Divisions (from right to left) continue their attack, the enemy retiring about 9 a.m.

At noon our brigade, with a field battery attached, forms one of several columns advancing eastwards, our way being along the Bailleul road in column of route.

When near Bailleul a report arrives to say that the Welch Fusiliers, on advanced guard, are checked by the enemy in the south-eastern outskirts of the town. The column therefore halts and I am sent forward in an open car to find out the situation. From the spasmodic splutter of musketry it appears that hostile rear-guards are at hand.

We drive down the wide main street, loaded rifle in hand, being greeted with frantic enthusiasm by the inhabitants who lean out of the windows of their five-floor tenements cheering, shouting 'Vive l'Angleterre', 'Viva les Ecossais' (on perceiving my Glengarry bonnet), waving handkerchiefs, and even blowing kisses. A thrilling scene! Since it is reported that our advanced guard, as well as the cavalry contact squadrons, are making good progress towards Steenwerck, and that the enemy is not in strength, I return to headquarters.

Suddenly, in the square of Bailleul we hear the clatter of horses approaching at a gallop from a side street; our driver jams on his brakes to avoid being ridden down. In a flash, a superbly-mounted cavalry subaltern with tanned skin, hawklike

[1] *General von der Marwitz's cavalry army of eight divisions, I, II and IV Corps.*

expression under his peaked cap, pistol in hand, and a trooper with drawn sabre on either flank dashes into the square. His glance darts from right to left, and without slackening pace he and his escort are off in the direction of the firing. What a picture – but too excitable!

Our advanced cavalry always ride sword in hand or lance at the 'carry', and charge at sight any hostile mounted bodies within charging distance . . .

On my reporting to General Gordon the brigade proceeds amid the renewed cheers of the populace, through Bailleul, which contains some German wounded, and along the Steenwerck road. The enemy's skirmishers fall back having inflicted three casualties on the Fusiliers.

At dusk we hear a considerable engagement towards the River Lys, and are ordered to select a defensive position for the night about Mont De Lille, which consists of a few bare knolls, overlooking a flat plain, one mile south-east of Bailleul. Here on the Belgian border, battalions spend a disagreeable night, some companies being bedded in wet fields of root crops . . .

The darkness is lit here and there by the glare from burning villages and farms . . .

OCTOBER 15TH: BAILLEUL

. . . At 10 a.m. the brigade marches to the south-east in dull weather, with the Fusiliers again advanced guard since they bivouacked last night as leading battalion and are not unduly fatigued.

Although the country is flat, open and fenceless, advanced guards and patrols, unless in action, must move on the roads because their crossing of the many wide ditches would waste time and cause delay to columns in rear.

The Fusiliers, whom I accompany, are followed by a section of two field guns ready to unlimber instantly and open fire. Steenwerck is occupied after a trifling engagement in which the Welchmen account for an entire German patrol.

Cantering back on 'Ginger' to report this news to headquarters, and leaping ditches on the way to our mutual enjoyment, I am smilingly accosted by Heywood who asks if my message is so urgent that I must gallop. I reply in the negative;

whereupon he quite properly reminds me that save when urgency demands it, our Training Manuals forbid staff officers to ride faster than a trot in order to avoid the risk of unsettling troops.

Following a long halt we are ordered back to billet in Bailleul, so thither the four battalion adjutants, our French interpreter and I proceed (at a trot) to arrange accommodation.

This business is barely accomplished, and the brigade present to take over its quarters, when fresh orders arrive to return to Steenwerck . . . The adjutants and I therefore 'trot' there, and the battalions, marching at 8 o'c, are all in bivouac on the wet fields in drizzling rain by 11 p.m. The transport parks on the roadside to avoid being bogged in the mud. We have had, seemingly, a purposeless day's excursion of 11 miles; all ranks are out of humour.

Crowds of refugees pass through our lines by day; they are not allowed even to approach at night when sentries could not distinguish them from the enemy.

The 6th and 4th Divisions have fairly easily taken Sailly-sur-Lys and Nieppe, respectively . . .

Another 'white flag incident' is reported through our troops leaving cover to 'accept the surrender' of bodies of the enemy, and being quite legitimately fired on by other Germans still in action. Doubtless we shall learn sense in time!

THE BATTLE OF YPRES–
ARMENTIÈRES–LA BASSEE

OCTOBER 18TH: VLAMERTINGHE

On the 16th the Brigade, on transfer as reserve to the newly-formed IV Corps,[1] marched from Steenwerck 14 miles northwards via Neuve-Eglise and tiring pavé roads to billets in Vlamertinghe (2 miles west of Ypres), where it arrived at 5.30 p.m. . . .

Midway on our journey we passed through a block of hilly

[1] *IV Corps, formed on October 9th under Lieut.-General Sir Henry Rawlinson, consisted of the 3rd Cavalry Division and 7th Infantry Division, which had been operating independently towards Antwerp.*

64

country with sharply-broken wooded spurs, all of them clearly out-topped by Kemmel Hill which stands massively alone. Streams, called 'bekes' in this neighbourhood, wind sluggishly along the low ground.

North of this hilly area, which joins the wooded slopes south-east and east of Ypres, we are on a flat plain once more – and in Belgium.

The brigade billets are most comfortable and our headquarters are in a substantial house in the street of this pretty, old township. Our Belgian host is most kind, presenting wine to the mess. The weather has become colder, but a good stove in the office and a tray of liqueurs sent in by our host each morning pleasantly ameliorate the rigours of the climate.

Battalions are resting, cleaning up and hair-cutting. They all held Church parade this morning.

The British advance continues slowly. German resistance has stiffened very much in the last two days . . .

In the afternoon the French interpreter and I, armed to the teeth, motor to reconnoitre the Kemmel road. We run no danger, of course, but I cannot resist the temptation of trying to 'pull the leg' of my timid-looking companion by suggesting that we must be prepared for anything. However, he is not to be 'drawn', saying he is as ready to die for France as I may be for Scotland!

We return from our tour via the fascinating old town of Ypres, passing over the moat through Vauban's 17th century ramparts by the Lille Gate. The large cobbled square is full of British and Belgian troops, besides people of all sorts. We pay a too-brief visit to the wonderful Flemish Cloth Hall and St Martin's Church. It is a gem of a town with its lovely old-world gabled houses, red-tiled roofs, and no factories visible to spoil the charm.

OCTOBER 19TH

Our short pleasant stay in Vlamertinghe ends, and I motor to Laventie, five miles south-west of Armentières, to settle about billets there. The 19th Brigade has been reposted to the III Corps.

At 1.30 p.m. the brigade begins its march of 22 miles southwards and arrives at Laventie about 11 o'c. The Cameronians travel in 40 motor buses bearing their homely London labels and advertisements, including 'Pears' Soap' and (I think rather callously under the circumstances) 'Dewar's Whisky'.

Large bodies of French cavalry, Algerian Turcos, artillery, armoured cars and transport are assembled in the towns close behind us.

The II Corps is heavily engaged in the La Bassée sector. The battle is extending northwards.

The Germans have been greatly reinforced and hard fighting has developed east of Ypres . . .

THE ACTION OF FROMELLES – LE MAISNIL

OCTOBER 20TH: LAVENTIE

At 7 a.m. the Welch Fusiliers and the Cameronians commence to entrench on the line Fauquissart – Croix Blanche. This work is, however, cancelled at noon, when the brigade is sent forward to Vert-Touquet, five miles south-east of Laventie.

Two hours later the Fusiliers and half the Middlesex are moved up to the line Fromelles – Pont-de-Pierre, where they are slightly behind, although in touch with, dismounted French cavalry and cyclists holding the three-mile gap between the left of the II corps at Aubers and the right of the 6th Division at Radinghem . . .

The showy clothing of the French dragoons looks rather out of place at this time compared with our inconspicuous khaki uniforms.

About one mile in front of Vert-Touquet, in the direction of Lille which is about eight miles away, a low distinct ridge runs via Aubers, Fromelles, Le Maisnil and Radinghem.[1] The country is open except at the villages and farms where there are orchards and other trees. The ditches on the low ground are lined with willows, most of them 'topped', while three-quarters of a mile to our rear the sluggish Layes brook flows parallel to the ridge.

The Germans, who all the time have been trying to drive

[1] *The B.E.F. was now becoming acquainted with place-names which would become historic during the next four years.*

back the French cavalry, commence attacking the 6th Division in the early afternoon; and from this hour fighting is in progress everywhere along the ridge, where we see shells bursting incessantly.

The battle has become general throughout the British front from La Bassée as far north as Zonnebeke, a distance of 25 miles as the crow flies and much farther as the troops' lines run . . .

During this very anxious, sleepless, cold wet night we continually hear tremendous crashes of rifle fire from the ridge. We are, therefore, most concerned for the safety of the Fusiliers and the Middlesex although they are in company with stout-hearted Frenchmen . . .

OCTOBER 21ST: VERT-TOUQUET

The whole brigade spent an abominably disturbed night and all ranks are pretty wet . . .

At 4 a.m. . . . the Argyll and Sutherland move up the ridge and relieve the French cavalry at Le Maisnil, the Fusiliers at Fromelles and the Middlesex at Pont-de-Pierre doing likewise.

About 7 a.m., just as the Cameronians, the remaining two Middlesex companies, and Brigade Headquarters are on the point of marching to Bas-Maisnil, at the foot of the ridge in rear of the Argylls, we see a column, not British, approaching down a sunken road 400 yards away from the direction of Radinghem lying behind our left flank and probably now in the enemy's hands. As we are not sure in the mist whether it is French or German, these battalions deploy at once, lie down, fix bayonets and prepare to open fire. Being mounted, I canter across the fields pistol in hand, and identify the column as French cavalry withdrawing as ordered.

During the morning the action becomes very hot. I am sent in a car to the commander of some French batteries, supporting us from three-quarters of a mile in rear, with a message giving our positions and asking him to open fire on the enemy's concentrations in front of them. The French guns are not 'dug in', but concealed from the ridge by hedges and the trees of orchards. The commander of the batteries, a fiery little man,

67

shouts out orders and is quickly surrounded by the necessary subordinates. In a few moments the 'soixante-quinze' field guns are blazing away by map direction at targets out of their view but described on the written message delivered by me.

On returning to Bas-Maisnil I find that reports from battalions are not good. The German shell and machine gun fire have increased (the usual preliminary to an infantry advance) and the left of our line is suffering considerably although units entrenched as well as they could on reaching their positions.

At noon the remaining two Middlesex companies are sent to support the Argylls.

In the afternoon I ride forward to get the latest information from the Middlesex and Argylls, whose headquarters are in ditches just behind the rest of the ridge now being heavily shelled. Some machine gun bullets are whistling past; bursts of rapid rifle are continually breaking out from the front companies; and the German infantry, in strength, are pressing gradually nearer, particularly on Le Maisnil.

The situation is growing acute. Colonel Ward says he thinks that the Middlesex can hold on although his only reserves have been taken away to help the Argylls; Colonel Moulton-Barrett is more doubtful. Heywood has a satisfactory report from the Fusiliers.

Dusk is now approaching, and I am ordered to guide Lee's company ('B') of the Cameronians forward to assist the Argylls at Le Maisnil. It sets off in column of platoons in single extended ranks, and we are soon under negligible shell and machine gun fire . . . Presently Lee goes ahead towards the village with one of his platoons to reconnoitre . . .

Le Maisnil is burning. Following Lee, I am horrified to meet two companies of the Argylls retiring down the slope, their positions having become untenable – especially through French cyclists on their left having been forced to give way – and their advanced companies decimated. I am informed that owing to the Highlanders' retirement the Middlesex are also vacating their positions, and that Colonel Ward, always so kind to me, has been killed . . .

I 'gallop' back to report – this being plainly an emergency. Since the right of the brigade is now compromised and the three remaining Cameronian companies are insufficient to restore the situation by a counter-attack, General Gordon orders his command to fall back forthwith . . .

The very last of the Argylls and some Middlesex pass me in the semi-darkness, but the whereabouts of Lee and his platoon are unknown . . . [Ritchie] wants to go and look for them. Saying, however, that his proper place is with his company, I dismount, and drawing my revolver scout carefully along a line of trees a short distance towards the orchards of Le Maisnil, calling out Lee's name.

There is no reply, and the firing has died down. One's nerves are rather 'on edge' until tightened by the approach of a small party. Friend or foe? A Scots accent reassures me; they are wounded stumbling back with their helpers. Nearby are two Cameronians, Sergeant Staines dead, and Company-Sergeant-Major Cox just leaving the body. Cox says he is practically certain that all our troops have retired. So, assuming that Lee and his men are either casualties or have retired by another route, I rejoin Ritchie and accompany him and his platoons for the mile to La Boutillerie.

Here the brigade, rather mixed up and in little more than one single extended rank, lies lining the road and buildings, rifles ready and bayonets fixed, expecting the Germans at any minute.

After reporting to General Gordon that I believe all our units have come back, I proceed to find and bring up the ammunition carts and ration limbers, while Heywood attends to the brigadier's orders allotting sectors of defence, and Churchill arranges his telephone cables.

A very tense, sleepless night with a good deal of firing.

OCTOBER 22ND: LA BOUTILLERIE

Yesterday the brigade lost 8 officers and 300 other ranks, chiefly Argyll and Sutherland . . .

. . . entrenching is carried out under some shelling, and therefore promptly. The covering companies, although close to the Germans and rather pressed by them, succeed in holding their ground until retiring on their battalions at nightfall as arranged . . .

The Lahore Division[1] and a brigade from the II Corps are behind us at Estaires, ready to give help if necessary.

Since the 23rd the Germans also have been entrenching,[2] 500 to 700 yards from us; their earthworks are visible here and there.

The two-mile front held by the brigade is so extensive that the advanced battalions form practically a single line, with gaps between them and most of their companies. Scarcely any men can be spared for local supports. At night the gaps are guarded by standing posts or patrols.

Where the trim, deep, willow-lined ditches of the country are suitably placed they have been adopted as trenches in order quickly to provide cover from fire, and are being widened and improved. The 'field of fire' from them is only some 200 to 400 yards on account of trees, buildings and haystacks; but even the smaller figure is considered to give sufficient field of fire in this war although our teaching of 1913 insisted on 500 yards at least.

Battalions are by now well dug in; their headquarters are in inconspicuous houses about the La Boutillerie road, 300 to 400 yards from the trenches.

A few rolls of barbed wire, made up on wooden reels in one-man loads, are arriving for battalions nightly. They are pegged out after dark 25 yards ahead of the trenches so as to trip an oncoming enemy. No work is possible in close view of the Germans in daylight.

Our own and the hostile sniping are getting sharper. The marksmen of both armies hide in trees and buildings waiting for the chance of a shot. Through this annoyance I had a disagreeable ride on a 'push' bicycle along the road to the next brigade in Le Touquet, where our neighbours seem none too happy about the situation.

---

[1] *The Lahore Division (Indian Corps), less one brigade, arrived at Marseilles on September 26th; it lacked much vital equipment.*
[2] *A German officer of the same rank as Jack, Captain Rudolph Binding, also fighting at Ypres, wrote on October 23rd: 'Slow progress, if it can be called progress.'*

The Germans pound our trenches daily for about three hours in the mornings and three in the evenings with heavy howitzers. Our artillery reply is relatively feeble since we have few howitzers and not enough shells for them. Field gun shrapnel and high explosive shells, while effective against troops in the open, are useless for dealing with men in good trenches.

Most of the houses in La Boutillerie and others close to the front are alight from shells, but the area in rear has not been much disturbed so far.

We are expending a good deal of rifle ammunition. This is replaced from the 2-horse battalion ammunition carts which, disregarding a few shells, trot singly up the road to their battalion headquarters during the middle of the day; at this time things are at their quietest, the Germans being probably at dinner. Rations and other stores are delivered in the same way after nightfall; if, however, the shell fire on the roads is too severe infantry carrying parties fetch them over the fields from Croix-Maréchal.

The other day, when I was on the roof of a house trying to locate a boldly handled enemy forward battery, a dozen shrapnel shells burst at intervals close at hand. Although safe enough by lowering the body to arm's length behind the peak of the roof on seeing each explosion, I was, nevertheless, glad enough to get down and take my notes to Heywood.

Today I made a stupid mistake. When motoring a French artillery officer from near Rouge-de-Bout to discuss matters with the brigadier, I missed the proper road turning, and we were almost in La Boutillerie before I discovered the error. I said nothing; it was better to go on than to turn. We were then concealed from the enemy's view by the convent wall beside the trenches, buildings and trees, but when clear of them our car was fully exposed. Acting on my advice, the chauffeur opened the throttle, skidded us round the corner, and we shot up the Fleurbaix road, chased by one or two remarkably accurate shells. My 'fare' politely made no remark, and I deposited him some way from our headquarters to avoid getting them marked down by the Germans – in addition to a 'raspberry' from Heywood. His business over, I returned the gallant gunner by a less exciting route while remaining dumb to all about the incident.

Every night the Germans persistently crawl along ditches and behind trees right up to our very thin line. They may be merely seeking for gaps or testing our strength; but as their numbers and purpose are unknown to us, and our men's nerves rather strained from long exposure, these hostile approaches cause the most terrific outbreaks of musketry from the threatened points. The pandemonium, which is increased by our artillery joining in, keeps Brigade Headquarters anxious till dawn as we do not know what is happening on account of telephone cables to battalions being often cut by shells, and the long time taken for messages to reach us by orderly.[1]

Following their minor attacks of the last three days the Germans last night opened a heavy bombardment on the brigade front and seem to have made a more genuine, but unsuccessful, attempt to penetrate our defences.

Ritchie says that his battalion takes a pride in not firing unnecessarily, and is not easily drawn into 'wind-ups'. He expresses the greatest admiration for the courage, enterprise and coolness of our foes, whom he considers to be 'not better soldiers than we are, but with a more soldierly manner of carrying out their duties'. His company has buried a party of them who tried to break through his lines, placing on their graves a rough wooden cross inscribed 'Here lie twenty brave Germans.' He also remarks that our 'listening posts' in front of the trenches get very jumpy at times since hostile patrols crawl boldly up to them.

The brigade has had 2 officer and 74 other casualties since the 22nd . . .

All idea of our advancing further must be out of the question at present as the Germans have assumed the offensive on the entire British front . . .

OCTOBER 29TH: CROIX-MARECHAL

There is little change in the local situation; the brigade has not been seriously attacked, but apart from definite actions the daily German shelling and sniping continue to be severe . . .

[1] *Brigade Headquarters were three quarters of a mile behind the trenches.*

Battalions continue to put out more wire, and higher, so as to form a fence which will prevent the enemy from rushing them in the dark. They are also improving their defences, and digging short communication trenches to enable men to pass to and from the fire trenches in greater safety. Further work is on shelters, for the construction of which damaged buildings are being stripped of timber.

Thin streams of wounded keep walking back to the Dressing Station near Croix-Maréchal. Those who cannot walk are collected near the Boutillerie road at night by horse-drawn ambulances.

The weather has rather broken down, and all men coming from the trenches are plastered in mud from head to foot.

More hostile aeroplanes than usual are flying over our lines. They generally keep out of rifle range, but are enveloped in the white puffs of smoke from our anti-aircraft shells, which seldom succeed in bringing any of them down . . .

Ritchie's company (my old company), holding 'Ritchie's Farm'[1] on the left of the brigade, has received the divisional commander's (6th Division) congratulations for its enterprise against the enemy.

The 2/Cameronian machine guns are with this company. According to prisoners the Germans estimate their number about the farm to be six. This miscalculation is due, no doubt, to the skill with which their very wide-awake and capable commander Robin Money, frequently changes the gun positions, and to the excellence of their crews; as well as to the volume of rifle fire which British infantry can produce.

Some nights ago the Cameronians set fire to haystacks in front of their trenches so as to show up any enemy approaching. Our inventive Royal Engineers are making flares for the same purpose[2] . . .

We have had to change our residence twice. On the 26th several shells exploded close to the house, one of them smash-

---

[1] *The initiation of the practice of naming trenches and posts is credited to Brigadier-General Hunter-Weston on the Aisne.*

[2] *The Germans, anticipating difficult sieges, were better equipped than the B.E.F. for trench warfare; besides flares, hand-grenades, periscopes, trench mortars, sandbags, even picks and spades were in short supply or non-existent.*

ing a door, a window and some china, without doing any more harm.

At our second headquarters on the following day three shells burst in the yard, wrecking part of the farm walls and roof, but again wounding neither man nor beast. All the same, we packed up and departed forthwith, grooms, horses and carts, servants with kits, orderlies with documents, Hodgkinson clasping his typewriter, the General and staff laden with despatch-cases, swords, accoutrements and mackintoshes. A quaint flitting! Stumbling rearwards we settled in the quietest looking of a row of small houses one and a quarter miles from the line.

After dark today there is the normal din of rifle fire from the front. Anxiety at night about our line holding is often increased by reports from battalions that many rifle bolts have jammed from mud (besides excessive rapid firing), and that a larger issue of oil and flannelette is required for cleaning them. The difficulty of preserving weapons in proper order in this mud is recognised, but it might be reduced by the exercise of more care and stricter fire-discipline.

I have been feeling rather unwell. Wrapped in two coats against the cold I try to get a sleep in the orchard during a lull in the afternoon's work. It is useless. An orderly with papers for signature hunts me down in no time.

A FORMIDABLE ATTACK ON THE 19TH BRIGADE

OCTOBER 30TH

The Battle of Ypres was now swelling to its first great crisis, which occurred on the front of I Corps on October 31st, when the village of Gheluvelt was lost, and then retaken by the 2/Worcestershires. The remainder of the British line was also severely pressed. Rudolph Binding, on the other side of the line, wrote: 'This is the thirteenth day of uninterrupted fighting at the same place . . . I can see no strategy in this manner of conducting operations . . . I don't call it a success when a trench, a few hundred prisoners, are taken. They have always cost more blood than they are worth.' Jack's narrative now illustrates what he meant.

74

Last night, just after midnight, the enemy suddenly opens intense shell and machine gun fire on the brigade front. Our battalions reply immediately in order to stop an infantry assault.

We are all awake and up in a moment, Heywood going outside the house to see from the 'direction board' (on which white chalked lines point to the various sectors) where the firing is. He returns at once saying to General Gordon, 'Seems to be on the whole of our front, sir.' The brigadier turns to me; 'Inform the artillery, and ask them to open fire.' (Their targets . . . having already been arranged in case of such emergencies.)

In two minutes, or less, from the commencement of the bombardment, the couple of 18-pounder batteries supporting the brigade are hard in action; a few seconds later these are joined by the 4.5 howitzer battery and the two 6-inch howitzers further away. Their shells whistle over the trees by our headquarters, the flash of their explosions fitfully lighting up the front; the clamour of all arms is deafening.

Headquarters 6th Division are informed by telephone and by motor cyclist that this seems to be a real attack, the sectors involved, and that the Argyll and Sutherland, in reserve near Croix-Maréchal, are being moved up to . . . our second line of defence.

Momentary lulls occur in the hurricane; then the crash of rifle fire breaks out afresh, sometimes in one quarter then in another.

The Argylls, a mere handful, 200 to 300 men, are soon on the way to their position of readiness.

Although outside the blast, Brigade Headquarters are without reports and in a state of suspense for almost an hour, as the telephone cables, laid forward on the ground, have all been cut by shells. Then written messages, confirming the extent of the bombardment and giving other details, commence to arrive.

About 2 a.m. the enemy's guns lift on to our support line; their machine guns redouble their fire for a minute or two before stopping abruptly. At once the German infantry advance with consummate courage, cheering and bugles blowing, the survivors getting right up to the trenches.

A little later reports from battalions say that they are hard

75

pressed and want reinforcements. Then word comes that the enemy has penetrated a gap in the Middlesex line. The Argylls are therefore ordered to turn them out, the 1/Leicestershire, about 200 strong, sent from the 6th Division, taking their place in reserve.

I am now despatched to discover and report on the situation. An orderly with loaded rifle and fixed bayonet accompanies me as we hurry forward to La Boutillerie. There we learn that the Highlanders, under Captain Henderson, have restored the position with great promptitude, bayoneting or capturing about 50 of the enemy. I report this news by orderly to Head-quarters, where I myself shortly return with a fuller account of the satisfactory state of affairs.

The attacks cease at dawn. They have been a total failure. Three hundred German bodies, mostly 223rd and 224th Infantry Regiments,[1] are counted lying in front of our trenches.

The Brigade casualties amount to 4 officers and 70 other ranks, among those of my old Cameronian company being Ritchie wounded and Sergeant Amos killed.

In the afternoon a telegram . . . conveys the Commander-in-Chief's congratulations to the Brigade, and adds to the pride felt by all ranks at the outcome of the action.

NOVEMBER 1ST

There have been no further attacks, but the German daily cannonade, machine gun fire and sniping remain severe, while their infantry are commencing to sap closer to our trenches . . .

I must again express my confidence in General Gordon and Heywood. They are always so calm, clear-headed, sound; and appear to be tireless . . .

The weather is raw and cold. I have a touch of fever and again fail to get a little sleep in the orchard this afternoon as papers arrive for attention. I feel about at the end of my tether and must have a rest.

---

[1] *Of the XXIV Reserve Corps, one of the new formations of young volunteers specially raised in August 1914. The British Official History gives their losses on Oct. 29/30th as over 200 dead and 40 prisoners.*

HOSPITAL, SICK LEAVE AND
HOME DUTY

NOVEMBER 1914

After lying on a mattress on the floor of Brigade Headquarters for the previous two days, during which the next house was shelled, I was sent on 4th November to No. 7 Stationary Hospital, Boulogne, suffering from an acute feverish chill which a good sleep had not removed.

Before departing I asked General Gordon to allow me to return to duty with my regiment when I had had a little rest; but he said I must first take a month's leave and get quite strong again.

I had had, perhaps, an unduly wearing task. The 19th Brigade was formed practically on the battlefield and short of equipment; was (like others) constantly on the move or in action; was attached seven times to different headquarters, which greatly increased the Staff Captain's administrative duties. It had three changes of commander and three of Brigade Major, thus adding a considerable amount of General Staff work to my own.[1] (And I was not suited for staff employment.)[2]

Tom Riddell-Webster (Cameronians), an exceptionally level-headed subaltern with sound judgment and marked ability, succeeded me as Staff Captain and did splendidly.

On 7th November I reached Miss Pollock's Hospital in London, where the peace, rest, good food, baths, linen sheets on the bed, and clean clothing were like a foretaste of Heaven after such a trying time.

Two days later I appeared before a medical board, declined the month's leave offered and proceeded to Scotland on fifteen days' furlough . . .

*   *   *

So ended Jack's part in the First Battle of Ypres. The last dangerous crisis of the battle came on November 11th when the Prussian Guard attacked down the Menin Road, and were repelled by a charge of the 2/Oxford and Buckinghamshire Light Infantry, whose forbears (52nd

[1] *I.e., Operations, as well as Administrative duties.*
[2] *Added by Jack in manuscript after first typing of his text.*

*Foot), on June 18th 1815, had led the counter-attack upon Napoleons'
Imperial Guard at Waterloo. By November 30th the battle was over. 'We
may be stuck for good and all,' wrote Rudolph Binding prophetically.*

*The cost to the B.E.F. had been terribly high. The grand total,
between October 14th and November 30th, was 58,155. This brought
the total from the beginning of the War to 3,627 officers and 86,237
other ranks. By far the largest proportion of these were infantry, and
the infantry of the first seven divisions numbered only 84,000. 'The
old British Army was gone past recall,' says the Official History.
Worse still, 'By the end of the year practically all the Army Reservists
and the pre-war Special Reservists had been used up . . .'*

*After Ypres, it would evidently have to be a different kind of Army
which continued the War; the few survivors of the old Regulars, and
officers like Jack, would be at a rare premium.*

*   *   *

II

Commanding "C" Company

1/Cameronians

Armentières Sector

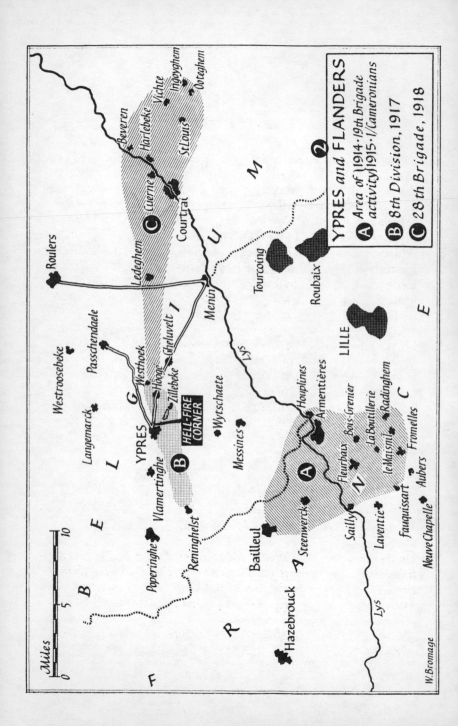

YPRES and FLANDERS

A Area of } 1914 · 19th Brigade
B activity }1915 · 1/Cameronians

Ⓐ 8th Division, 1917
Ⓑ
Ⓒ 28th Brigade, 1918

Miles
0   5   10

W. Bromage

LEAVE AND HOME DUTY

I found affairs at Home quiet yet very busy. The public – hitherto accustomed to regard war as the affair of the Regular Forces – had been roused to take part in it by the enemy's successes. Several hundred-thousands of men were *voluntarily* enlisting to form the New Armies, or to join the Navy and the Flying Corps . . .

Since my regiment in France was now very short of officers I intended to rejoin it as soon as possible, and so obtained a medical board in Glasgow on 23rd November. Asked if I felt fit again I said 'yes', and the matter ended except for a short stethoscopic examination.

On 25th November I reported to the 3rd (Reserve) Battalion of my regiment at Nigg, one of the garrisons guarding our Naval Base on the Cromarty Firth. There I remained on duty till warned at 11 p.m. on 5th December to return to France at 7.30 o'c the following morning . . .

The spirit of the 3rd Battalion was excellent. Those not included in the next drafts for France grumbled profusely in spite of knowing conditions at the Front where many of them had been wounded . . .

GENERAL CONDITIONS ON THE BRITISH FRONT IN LOW FLANDERS DURING THE WINTER OF 1914–1915

On the Western Front a strange and novel form of war had now established itself: the opponents faced each other in almost unbroken lines of trenches, stretching from the shore of the North Sea to Switzerland. On both sides the trenches were protected against sudden assault by ever-thickening belts of barbed-wire entanglements. The space between them (No Man's Land) varied in breadth from as little as 20 yards to over half a mile. The configuration of the trench-lines was entirely haphazard, according to the positions taken up in haste during the battles of en-counter; this led to the occupation (by both sides) of many 'untenable' angles and salients. The Germans were at an advantage here: standing on enemy ground, which they had lavishly conquered, they could always afford to rationalise their situation by small tactical withdrawals and adjustments. The Allies, on the other hand, conscious of lost territories, developed cramping inhibitions about giving up even a few yards. The French High Command, in particular, allowed itself to be obsessed with considerations of the 'sacred soil' of France; the Belgians, who only retained a tiny corner of their country from Ypres to Nieuport, were simi-larly affected; and the British Expeditionary Force found itself com-pelled to respect the sentiments of its Allies, to the great danger and dis-comfort of the soldiers.

. . . Of the four battalions in each brigade, two normally manned the trenches; the other two, in reserve, were billeted in villages one to a couple of miles in rear, both with a forward company in close support to the trench battalions. Every four or eight days the rear and the advanced battalions changed places.

Battalions in the trenches generally held from 1,200 to 1,500 yards of front, with all four companies in the line, there being no men to spare for local supports.[1]

The duties were very heavy. Construction and maintenance of wire entanglements as well as earthworks, the finding of sen-tries and parties to carry up rations besides other stores, engaged fully two-thirds of all ranks throughout every night. Half the trench garrison performed repair work for at least three hours during daylight. Officers and men in the line were lucky if they got six hours' rest in the twenty-four. The average casualties per battalion were from five to fifteen during each tour even if no actual operations had taken place.

The two reserve battalions provided large working parties near the front nightly.

In the low-lying parts of Flanders nearly all the trenches be-

[1] *Owing to the shortage of reserves, Jack tells us, 'The 1/Cameronians occupied their La Boutillerie trenches for thirty days on end with only one break of 24 hours a few miles in rear . . ."*

came almost knee-deep, or deeper, in water and mud during the winter, despite the diligent use of hand-pumps and the digging of pits for draining purposes. Dug-outs were therefore out of the question, and the men had no protection from the weather apart from their waterproof capes rigged up as shelters behind the parapets. Mud rendered the communication trenches, giving covered access to the front line, impassable for laden men, so the nightly delivery of rations and stores had to take place across the open, often under shell and machine gun fire.

By January 1915 the flooding of the trenches had become insupportable and necessitated the throwing up of 'breastworks', roughly six feet high and eight feet thick, on the top of the ground. This task entailed an enormous amount of labour for several months, but behind the breastworks the troops got less wet, although they were more exposed to the enemy . . .

Under these disagreeable conditions the winter passsed fairly quietly (except for sniping) on the British front . . . shell-fire having not yet become severe, as it did later.

The strength of the battalions was maintained at about 600 to 700 men. Although often wet, tired, cold, overworked and covered with mud, all ranks kept cheery and remarkably free from sickness. The issue of leather jerkins to wear over their tunics was a great comfort. The rations were sufficient and the supply regular. Baths and Field Force Canteens[1] were soon established in the reserve areas, the latter catering for all minor wants of the troops.

In spite of temptations in the village estaminets the conduct of the Army remained excellent . . .

DECEMBER 14TH: HOUPLINES (NEAR ARMENTIÈRES)

On the 11th I was happy to receive orders to rejoin my own battalion; one had rather dreaded being sent to a strange regiment . . .

Today I have been reading back orders and studying 'Trench Warfare', which is new to me, at Battalion Headquarters in a damaged house here.

Although my battalion has not been in the centre of any

---

[1] *No Canteen was authorised until early 1915, Lord Kitchener having stated, in August 1914: 'This war is not going to be a picnic.'*

battles, it has lost since arriving in France in August over 500 of its original 1,022 officers and other ranks, a small figure compared with that of most other battalions.

Ritchie died on 22nd November of his wounds. In his brave last letter, of 2nd November, he wrote of the action on 30th October, 'I thought I was dying, but when I came to my senses again the fight was still going on. They had put me under shelter; my subaltern was holding my hand and shouting orders. It was all very jolly, but only a little bit of a thing.'

Tetanus is a great danger in this highly cultivated land. All casualties, however slight, are now immediately inoculated against it . . .

A TOUR IN THE TRENCHES
(Dec. 14th–19th)

DECEMBER 21ST: HOUPLINES

After dusk on the 14th an orderly guided me three-quarters of a mile eastwards to 'C' Company's Headquarters in the trenches, where I took over command of my old company from 'Jock' Stirling.

Three of our companies, with all four platoons in the line, each hold about 400 yards of front with section posts (1 N.C.O. and 6 men) some 25 yards apart; their only immediate supports consist of a few orderlies, storemen and signallers. The trench between the posts is over ankle-deep in mud and water . . .
. . . The company headquarters are situated in small thinly-roofed shelters in the support trench, about eighty yards behind the front trench; there the officers and Company-Sergeant-Major recline on planks for a couple of hours' sleep by day and the same by night . . .

Besides other duties, constant work is required on the trench walls which keep falling in in bad weather.

When off duty for their short, broken rest the men sleep huddled on the fire-step of the trench or in small recesses excavated in the side; their feet tucked up out of the slime, bodies covered with waterproof sheets, jerkins, any sacks or sandbags available.

Greatcoats and spare kits are stowed with the transport so

as to be dry and clean when companies come out of the line soaked from thigh to heel and covered with glue-like mud.

The Colonel, adjutant, machine gun officer and medical officer visit some of the companies daily, usually about dawn or dusk, as their route is exposed to the enemy and the half-light minimises the risk of their being shot.

Rations and other stores arrive in the trenches every night. They are carried up by the company parties from the transport rendezvous on the road half a mile in rear. The rations consist of Quaker Oats or bacon, tinned bully-beef or Maconachie stew, potatoes, bread, butter, jam or cheese, tinned milk, sugar, tea or cocoa, and half a gill of rum per man . . .[1]

Fires, whose smoke by day or glare by night might be seen by the Germans, are forbidden; the little cooking possible is performed by sections on coke braziers, or on tiny fires made from dry chips of ration boxes.

The German trenches are 150 to 250 yards distant. His shell fire is trivial, but the least exposure draws a sniper's bullet, and infinite care is necessary when examining his lines through binoculars. For this purpose one wears a brown woolly cap instead of our too-conspicuous black Glengarry bonnet, and the head must be raised ever so slowly into a niche in the sandbags on the top of the trench.

Across the level stretch of rank grass in No Man's Land one sees the enemy's rust-brown wire, the irregular line of sandbags on his parapet, and polled willows marking some of the ditches . . .

However intently one may gaze there is scarcely ever a German to be seen. Perhaps one or two figures may momentarily appear at dawn or dusk, or a glimpse may be had for a second during the day of a blue cap amid the sandbags of their advanced trench.

From the higher ground an enemy's searchlight plays in our direction at night; when in its beams our ration and working parties lie flat till it has passed over . . .

On the 19th at 11 a.m., 1 o'c and 3 p.m. our battalion, besides

[1] *The rum, Jack adds, 'must be drunk before an officer to ensure that no one, by barter or otherwise, gets more than that amount. It is in no sense a "battle dope".'*

others nearby, manned their trenches and opened three rounds rapid fire at the German parapet as directed. This demonstration was intended – so we suppose – to simulate preparation for an immediate attack and thus cause the enemy to expose supporting troops to our artillery. But although the special observers and I watched most carefully we did not see a single Prussian, their only reply being derisive cheers, 'cat-calls', flags waved, and a shower of turnips, newspapers and rubbish cast into the air.

The Teutons are far too tough to be so easily 'bamboozled'.

On the evening following, Stirling had a rash adventure which I stupidly allowed. He came to tell me that he had just seen a message-container from a German aeroplane fall a little way in front of our trench; that he knew its exact position which he could reach by crawling along a ditch, and begged permission to try to recover it. Thinking that the message might be of importance to us, I finally assented to his request, warned the next companies of our intention, arranged for increased sniping at dusk on the flank furthest from his exit forward, and for a few men there to show the crowns only of their bonnets raised on sticks. I hoped that this display would draw the enemy's eyes away from the enterprise.

With our posts ready to open covering fire 'Jock' wormed his way through a cleft in the parapet and crawled into No Man's Land, leaving me in an agony of apprehension till, after what seemed an age, he returned without having found the message and having been fired at. I cannot describe my thankfulness for his safety . . .

This episode illustrates all the naïveté of early days. Why on earth should the Germans want to drop a message in this way? No battle was in progress; their normal communications were ample and intact. Whatever Stirling saw, it is most unlikely that it was any kind of 'message'. At the same time, the incident also shows the tremendous care which Jack always took over any enterprise, and this habit will be seen time and again.

DECEMBER 23RD: HOUPLINES: IN BATTALION SUPPORT

. . . Our sector of the front is quiet. This village is seldom shelled; consequently many French inhabitants are still in the neighbourhood.

We have passed three pleasant days, are comfortable, rested and washed. Much of our spare time in billets is spent in acknowledging parcels and letters from Home. The Press is studied for news of the War outside our tiny cockpit.

I am lucky in my officers and the company is in a good state. Some of the middle-aged reservists, however, are feeling the strain of these months of great exposure . . .

My subalterns, Harry Becher, 'Frankie' Rooke and Darrell Hill, have come through all the engagements from Mons without a scratch, or sickness or broken nerves. They are a tough trio of first-class, cool-headed, cheery young officers . . . Company-Sergeant-Major Malins is an old friend of mine.

When out of the line we trim up and parade for an hour's drill daily. At night most of the company is at work repairing roads or carrying stores to the trenches.

Last night I received a disagreeable shock. At 11 p.m., when I had just lain down in my valise to sleep, with boots, belts and tunic beside me ready to slip on in an instant, a horseman galloping along the cobbled street roused me. What can so unusual and hurried a messenger want at this hour? Presently an order arrives from Sam Darling (adjutant): 'Test all company wire-cutters (hand pliers) and report forthwith.' An ill-omened instruction, this, suggesting our making an attack. I rise, consult my Quartermaster-Sergeant, besides others concerned, and am happy to reply that many of our wire-cutters have been lost or damaged without being yet replaced. The excuse is of no avail. Another note from Sam says that the Quartermaster is making up these deficiencies to all companies at once, and repeats: 'Test and report forthwith.' What with this occupation and the stir of orderlies and motor messengers in the village there is no sleep for some of us. I keep nervously wondering for what exploit we are bound. So far I have heard no more on the subject . . .

87

IN THE TRENCHES
(Dec. 23rd–25th)

DECEMBER 24TH

. . . The lines are in a terrible state. The incessant rain has caused large portions of the trench walls to subside. We are hard at work revetting the broken edges and filling sandbags to stop the breaches after dark.

Except at the posts, where the parapets have been built higher than at other parts of the line and the men stand fairly dry on wooden gratings,[1] the trenches are knee-deep in water and mud. Two hand-pumps – when not clogged up – are constantly at work in the company, but the men are convinced that their exertions are fruitless and that the bottom of the trench is below sea-level!

CHRISTMAS DAY

The weather has suddenly changed. Hard frost replaces the rain, rendering digging easier, the parapets firmer, and the blocking of drains which run into the trenches possible.

Notwithstanding the Day, the ordinary round of duties, sniping and shelling is carried out.

At night there are sounds of revelry in the Prussian lines. We are astonished to hear from them the strains of our National Anthem played on a cornet and accompanied by a chorus. (A German hymn has the same air.) 'C' Company gives three hearty cheers on hearing the familiar tune. These are followed by a Teutonic burst of 'Hoch der Kaiser', which is promptly answered by a united and fervent shout, 'Curse the Kaiser'. Later a voice from the enemy's trench calls out: 'When are you going back to Maryhill Barracks?' and a short exchange of badinage take place, some German from Glasgow having evidently recognised our bonnets. Their merry-making continues till the small hours of the morning, but 'C' Company, physically cold and mentally dour, maintains a stiff reserve except when, as with the Imperial Toast, particularly irritating remarks are made by the Huns.

[1] *'Duck-boards'; they made their first appearance in Ploegsteert Wood in December 1914.*

So passes the first Christmas of the War, far away from the original 'Peace and Goodwill to all men' – or is the true message 'I came not to bring peace, but a sword'?

DECEMBER 26TH

Snow and frost. The ground has become too hard to dig, rendering visits to the company posts much easier . . .

All ranks have received a much appreciated Christmas card with its kind message from King George and Queen Mary.

Sergeant Buss and Lance-corporal Gibb of 'A' Company set out last night, of their own free-will, to try and capture a German machine gun. Neither has returned. (Gibb was killed.) . . .

IN RESERVE
(Dec. 26th – Jan. 1st)

JANUARY 2ND 1915: BILLETS, ARMENTIÈRES

. . . My Company had only one casualty during our last tour in the trenches . . .

Princess Mary has generously sent to each officer and man a pretty embossed brass box containing tobacco, and a pipe.

The number of Christmas letters, plum puddings, mince pies, cakes, tobacco, socks, mufflers, wool vests, and electric torches received by us on coming out of the line was really immense. My parcels included oatcakes and shortbread from my brother besides pâté de foie gras . . . Ordinarily, mails from Home are delivered to us daily, even in the trenches, in from two to four days after posting, a wonderful performance on the part of the Postal Authorities, considering that our only address is the name of one's regiment followed by the initials 'B.E.F.'

It is said that the 'wire-cutter test' on the 22nd of last month was connected with a very disagreeable adventure actually staged for the next afternoon.

Briefly, the plan was for my battalion (possibly others also) to 'surprise' the Germans by dashing across No Man's Land at dusk, cut their wire with pliers, kill or capture the front trench garrison, then return to our lines with what prisoners, machine guns and other booty we could collect.

I am unaware what role our artillery and machine guns were to play; in any case they were too few in number to support us effectively. Anyhow, the attack was cancelled owing to the strenuous opposition of General Gordon and Colonel Robertson.

Coldly reviewed, the chances were that my battalion would have lost from 250 to 400 men; that it would have failed to penetrate the enemy's wire; that if we had succeeded in doing so we might have accounted for 100 to 150 Germans and captured three or four machine guns. The exploit would probably have badly shaken the nerves of the survivors, also their faith in the judgment of High Command. The Germans are far too resolute, well-entrenched and wired to be defeated by perfunctory means . . .

The Battalion is billeted in a large factory, the men sleeping between the looms . . .

'C' Company's happy little party is in a house with comfortable beds – a rare luxury – and a bath, which seems to be a scarcity in these regions . . .

At our plain little 7 o'c dinners out of the line, we hold to the old custom of the 1/Cameronians of nightly proposing the King's health in the following manner: when the port-wine bottle (decanters at Home) has been placed on the table, and before glasses have been filled, the president calls 'Mr Vice, the King', to which the vice-president at the other end of the table replies 'God bless him', thus finishing the toast. The 1/Cameronians do not rise nor drink the toast *at their own table*, but of course conform to the usual practice at all other times. The custom is said to have originated with the Scottish Covenanters, our regimental forbears, rabid teetotallers.

The companies are pretty well cleaned up. Each has been once to the divisional baths here to have a proper wash and their clothes fumigated against vermin – deloused in fact!

The pre-war daily routine is carried out . . . It includes two or three hours of close order drill, musketry, bayonet exercise, and tactical training or route marching. All companies mount guards at nightfall . . . Bugle calls are dispensed with on active service lest the enemy should use our calls to his advantage, particularly the call to retire. The men are warned for duties by the orderly sergeants and corporals, or by a piper – it being understood that the enemy has no bagpipes! The only musicians left to us are a few pipers, as the band became stretcher-bearers on mobilisation; so the mouth-organ has come into its own . . . In the trenches it is hoped to have the 'Hunting Chorus' rendered during the rum issue at dawn daily; I continually whistle the air . . .

The weather remains raw and damp, but apart from colds the health of all ranks is very good. Games, mainly football, in the afternoons keep them fit and cheery . . . however tired the rascals may be for parades they have always energy enough for football . . .[1]

My old Battalion is in good form. Colonel Robertson, aged about 50, Oakley and the senior company commanders . . . all about 40 years old or more, have stood the strain and exposure of the past four and a half months without a sign of breaking down. Sam Darling's clearheadedness and exactitude have never varied. The only officers to 'crack up' mentally or in health have been a few youths like myself; the rest have become hardened soldiers. The other ranks maintain their imperturbable good humour. The War seems to have affected their spirits little more than uncomfortable manoeuvres in Peace-time. Although war-worn, shorn of nearly all polish, and considerably short of numerical establishment, the 1/Cameronians, now veterans, are a soldierly, useful and well-behaved body of warriors . . .

IN THE TRENCHES
(Jan. 2nd–7th)

JANUARY 3RD: BOIS-GRENIER

Yesterday at dusk the battalion filed by companies five miles southwards in foul weather and took over the Cordonnerie Farm sector near Bois-Grenier. One guide per company of the

[1] *In July 1915 General Haig (commanding First Army) noted an increase in the number of cases of men asleep on sentry duty (a crime punishable by death, though only two soldiers were actually shot for this). Haig wrote in his diary: 'Men should rest' during the day when they know they will be on sentry duty at night. Instead of resting they run about and play football.'*

battalion we relieved met us on the road short of the village, and one guide per platoon near the trenches to lead us across the open ground, under desultory machine gun fire, to our posts. The relief passes quietly although many of us were kept floundering about in the mud till late at night seeing that everything was correct.

Soon after reaching my company headquarters shelter I was intensely shocked to learn that 'Jock' Stirling (with 'B' Company) had just been killed, after five weeks of active service . . .[1]

The rain is terrible. Much of the parapet is subsiding; sections of the trenches are nearly thigh-deep in water, and we can scarcely drag our legs through the mud when visiting the lines . . .

JANUARY 5TH

Allowing for windings, the battalion holds about 1,500 yards of front with all four companies in line . . .

One other battalion of the Brigade and two companies of the 5/Cameronians (T.A., attached to the brigade) are also in the trenches . . .

The Prussian trenches, one to two hundred yards from ours, must also be flooded as we are delighted to see buckets of water being thrown over their parapet.

JANUARY 6TH

'Frankie' Rooke was badly wounded this morning by a bullet in the groin. With just a field dressing bandaged on by the company stretcher-bearers, he had to lie in our shelter all day in considerable pain until he could be carried back safely at dusk to the ambulance . . .

The men are great-hearted fellows. Their legs, capes and jerkins are habitually sodden with wet clay. Where there is a small patch of fairly solid ground the lucky ones off duty huddle round a coke brazier, of which each company has five.

---

[1] *'What a family' says Jack. One of Stirling's brothers went down in H.M.S. 'Monmouth' at Coronel. Another was awarded the D.S.O., M.C. and bar, and four mentions in Despatches; wounded at Passchendaele, he was mortally wounded in March 1918, commanding a battalion at the age of 24. Their father, Brig.-General Stirling, C.B., C.M.G., Croix de Guerre (Royal Artillery), was mentioned five times in Despatches.*

In spite of extremely long hours on duty in great discomfort, hard labour repairing the parapets and other defences, besides no proper meals in the trenches, there is little grumbling and never a whine from their lips whatever they may think of the business in hand . . .

JANUARY 7TH

It is raining hard and the trenches are in an indescribable state, necessitating our having to be dragged out of bogs at times when on rounds. The enemy appear to be in a similar way, to judge by their baling.

The parapets have fallen dangerously low, and the men are confined to their posts which are like islands in a morass . . .

Both we and the Germans are far too busy trying to improve conditions to bother each other much; so the front is quiet and the shell fire trivial . . .

The enemy's snipers are active. This morning one of them put a bullet into the parapet a few inches from the Colonel's nose and mine. Being chaffingly blamed by the Colonel as the cause of the shot I respectfully suggested that his bald head had caught the German eye . . .

IN BRIGADE RESERVE
(Jan. 8th–12th)

JANUARY 13TH: L'ARMEE

The 8th was another miserable wet day in the trenches.

That night the battalion, on relief by the 2/R. Welch Fusiliers, marched three and a half miles . . . to billets in L'Armée two miles south of Armentières . . .

Next morning all ranks were pretty fresh again – a long sleep and a square meal perform miracles. I confess to having felt exhausted on the previous night.

The billets are well warmed by metal stoves which, being placed towards the centre of the rooms, give the maximum amount of heat . . .

Although we are such a short distance from the front, the War does not trouble us here. The peace and comfort are Heavenly . . .

There are extraordinary stories of unofficial Christmas truces with the enemy.

It seems that on Christmas Day the 2/Argyll and Sutherland Highlanders (in trenches next to ours) actually arranged to play a football match versus the Saxons – whom we consider to be more human than other Teutons – in No Man's Land that afternoon. Indeed, someone in my trench told me of the proposal at the time, but I scouted so wild an idea. In any case, shelling prevented the fixture.

In the sector of the Buffs, however, it is said that a truce existed for some days . . .

It is further reported that a certain British officer dined in the German trenches on or about Christmas night.

There was no truce on the front of my battalion. It is interesting to visualise the close of a campaign owing to the opposing armies – neither of them defeated – having become too friendly to continue the fight. Anyhow, these incidents seem to suggest that, except in the temper of battle or some great grievance, educated men have no desire to kill one another; and that were it not for aggressive National Policies, or the fear of them by others, war between civilised peoples would seldom take place.

An affair of a different nature was enacted in 'A' Company's sector to bring in the New Year.

The storeman of that company having become a casualty, the Company-Sergeant Major . . . selected Private McN. to replace him.

That night McN. duly took charge of the rations, water and other stores, including the company jar of rum . . .

Nothing abnormal was noticed till dawn next day, when the posts of 'A' Company were petrified to see a very drunken soldier, minus his equipment, lurching along in No Man's Land to the cheers and laughter of the Germans who sportingly did not fire. The entreaties and orders of friends passed unheeded, the delinquent merely pausing occasionally to take a mouthful of rum from the jar he was carrying. Pursuing his unsteady way, McN. came opposite the trenches of the adjacent battalion, where he received a peremptory warning to come in, or *he would be arrested.* This last being too much for our storeman's dignity, he turned towards his threatener, took another 'swig' and coolly remarked 'Come oot and fetch us' – an offer which was, needless to say, declined.

Eventually, having caused great excitement to friend as well as foe, the craving for sleep overcame him and he subsided into the British line – by chance, not, under the circumstances, from preference . . .

IN THE TRENCHES
(Jan. 15th–23rd)

JANUARY 17TH: GRANDE FLAMENGRIE FARM

. . . Since the trenches have been practically untenable through flooding for some time, and the sick rate consequently considerable, High Command have ordered the construction of a line of Breastworks, a hundred yards in rear[1] of them, to take their place ultimately . . .

'C' Company's headquarters are in the vaulted cellar of this derelict farm, 250 yards from the front trench . . . The floor is awash with water which leaks in from the moat, and a hand-pump is at work day and night. A small concrete platform in the corner, covered with damp straw, sacks and mackintosh coats, provides us with a dryish place on which to lie; a coke brazier maintains a moderate degree of warmth. The cellar roof is cracked and shaky from the concussion of shells, and we think that a direct hit from a howitzer gun would likely turn this sanctuary into our tomb. Although safe from bullets, we frequently hear them 'pinging' through the empty doorways above or sputtering into the walls. Nevertheless, the cellar is a palace compared with the trenches, and needless to say, no-one is allowed to show his nose outside in daylight . . .

JANUARY 19TH

. . . It has been raining hard for several days, and we have a severe struggle in places to get through the mud to visit the posts . . .

The other night I fell into a ditch when on rounds, and Oakley, with his habitual thoughtfulness, sent me back to the support company to dry myself . . .

[1] *N.B. 'in rear' – i.e. a tactical (and practical) withdrawal; a rare occurrence.*

There is so little cover from the enemy that we can seldom use our electric torches to pick the way, with the result that I again stumble into a ditch and am sorry to confess that my curses must have been heard afar. A little later, as if in reproof for them, I sink, *speechless* with anger, through what appears to be a firm surface, up to the waist in a cess-pool. At 2. a.m. I reach my trench shelter. It is too cold to sleep and the coke embers have almost died out. Sitting tired and annoyed on a broken chair, with feet on a ration box to keep them out of the water, my eye catches a lantern, pistol, some tin mugs, and an empty rum jar hung on the wall. How closely the scene resembles a smugglers' cabin, and with what delight we, when boys, would have revelled in it – for an hour or two! . . .

JANUARY 23RD

It is very cold and a sharp frost has made the narrow paths trodden in the trenches hard and level. This change in the weather immensely lightens our tasks and discomforts . . .

Feeling very unwell and huddling into the corner of a traverse to escape the wind and sleet, I was greatly touched by the kindness of Private Rose and another oldish man of my company. Although with none too much tea or fuel for themselves, one or other of these two angels kept coming round my traverse at intervals all day, sometimes with a drop of hot tea and a piece of biscuit, or with a few sticks for my brazier.

Our artillery fire on the German trenches has recently slightly increased; it consists of a few minutes' sharp bombardment two or three times in the twenty-four hours. We think that it is probably more irritating than damaging to the enemy; but it seems to imply that the Home Government is remedying the shortage of shells, guns and howitzers which was the subject of bitter complaint during the October-November battles. The German reply is insignificant and we hope that they are short of munitions . . .

JANUARY 24TH

On 'C' Company's front the German trenches are some 200 yards distant, and a report is required by High Command as to how much a ditch midway between the lines would hinder an enemy attack. After dusk, therefore, a strong-nerved Lance-Corporal and I steal forward, revolver in hand, I with a long measuring stick in addition. The night is bright yet cloudy and so is most suitable for such errands. One has the faint light to see where to go, and darkness for the movement; besides, the enemy is quieter and sends up fewer rockets on fairly light nights than he does when it is very dark. The only risk is from a chance bullet or a hostile patrol.

When close to the ditch we see a low indistinct object and, instantly lying flat down, cover it with our pistols; but after one or two tense seconds we realise that it is only a bush. The measurements of the ditch are taken without further concern – a stationary party is much safer than one on the move – and we return to our lines.

Where No Man's Land is wide and contains no identifiable features it is quite possible for even experienced men to lose direction at night through their turnings, and to become uncertain which are their own lines and which the enemy's. The ordinary British and German rockets appear to shoot up all round, and, on account of the windings of the trench lines, even the unmistakably slow 'rat-tat-tat' of the hostile machine guns is not an infallible guide unless it is nearly opposite. For these reasons patrols should carry luminous compasses and know the bearing back to their sector; or a special signal may be lit – a call might not be heard . . .

1/Cameronians were in brigade support from January 24th – 28th.

JANUARY 30TH; FRONT TRENCHES NEAR
BOIS-GRENIER

Last night the Battalion relieved the 2/R. Welch Fusiliers in our late sector in fine frosty weather and without incident. Reliefs take far less time when the units concerned are accustomed to working together than they do otherwise . . .

This afternoon half-a-dozen howitzer shells fall at short intervals close to company headquarters; the first some 40 yards over, the second 50 short, so we expect the next on the top of our shelter and are happily disappointed. The remainder explode within 15 – 30 yards of us, blowing in part of the parapet and covering those present with clods of earth.

During this episode our stouthearted comedian, Darrell,
amuses the men at hand . . . by opening an old torn umbrella
for cover on each burst, calling on St Mungo for protection, and
finally falling down and kicking as no wounded man could
do . . .

Tonight my lance-corporal and I perform another minor reconnaissance.

When the nights are suitable the company sends a small
patrol into No Man's Land, always with a definite, even if
unimportant, mission. The main object of the practice, however, is to prevent morale from deteriorating through our remaining always behind parapets and so leaving the Germans in
undisputed possession of No Man's Land.

We have lost no-one on this duty to date.

*An active raiding policy was ordered by G.H.Q. in February 1915 in
order to counteract the depressing effects of a perpetual defensive posture,
enforced by the shortage of men and munitions. It is interesting to note
from Jack's account that the practice was originated by lower formations.*

*'These minor operations', said G.H.Q., 'should, of course, not be of an
aimless character but should be based on a specific object, have a reasonable chance of success, and be commensurate with the losses likely to be
entailed. They should be methodically initiated in accordance with the
instructions of the Army Commanders, and must invariably be well
thought out beforehand, and careful preliminary arrangements made for
their execution.'*

*Successes and resulting congratulations, promotions or awards would,
it was hoped, stimulate a 'keen spirit of rivalry and emulation'. This was a
laudable object, and with battalions like 1/Cameronians, which still
possessed a high proportion of fully-trained soldiers, the results were excellent. With newer formations, sometimes containing many townsmen
who knew nothing of fieldcraft, against the admirable German infantry
of this period, there were many costly failures. These had a damaging
effect on the morale they were intended to maintain. Yet the need to
dominate No Man's Land remained, and was never greater than during
this 'early-middle' period of the War, with its murderous crater fighting.*

JANUARY 31ST

. . . We are having difficulty in getting all the stores indented

98

for; timber to shore up the parapets, knife-rests on which to fix barbed wire, and trench-gratings. The delay in their delivery is not surprising since all units are shouting for the same bulky material and the transport is overloaded already. Considering the conditions, infantry requirements of all kinds are met really admirably . . .

FEBRUARY 2ND

. . . Bad weather naturally increases the sick list – chiefly colds, fever and rheumatism – but practically all 'stick it out' as long as they can before reporting to the Medical Officer.

Yesterday three of my men were wounded in the head by the splinters of one shell, none of them seriously, thank Heaven; one, however, made a fearful fuss about his broken tooth, which he might have lost with a quarter of the din playing football . . .

Private Amos was sniped dead today, through taking too little care, I am told. Although one cannot keep up meticulous regard for one's safety all the time, few things annoy me more than men running unwarranted risks. We are paid to beat the Germans, not to fill graves and hospitals needlessly . . .

FEBRUARY 3RD

. . . In the evening we watch half an hour's intense bombardment of the enemy's trenches by our artillery. It is a great joy to see fragments of their shelters flying into the air and holes blown in their parapet; but although the company 'stands to' ready to fire no targets appear . . . In these days we shell the Germans more than they do us . . .

IN BRIGADE RESERVE
(Feb. 3rd–7th)

FEBRUARY 5TH: CHAPELLE D'ARMENTIÈRES

Yesterday was quiet till evening when the enemy, turning searchlights on to the front, opened a very heavy bombardment. The rifles and machine guns in the trenches replied at once to stop a possible infantry attack. In a couple of minutes the artillery joining in brought the clamour to its height. Our battalion besides other troops in reserve stood to arms forthwith fully equipped.

I confess to having felt damned frightened. The prospect of having to counter-attack in the dark, through severe fire, to restore an imperfectly known situation is always most disagreeable . . .

The affair subsided about 8 p.m. . . .

FEBRUARY 7TH

I cannot throw off a chill caught some days ago, and have therefore stayed in bed since the conclusion of yesterday's parades, with a slight temperature and some pain in the chest. Davidson (Medical Officer) has advised me to report sick but I declined to do so. He then sent a message saying that the Commanding Officer concurs with his opinion, and asking what hour will suit for the mess cart to take me to hospital on handing over my company. I replied that 'No time would suit.' The kindest of colonels then called to see me and accepted my assurance that I felt much better and would be fit to go to the trenches tomorrow. How often I wish that my duties were all finished!

IN THE TRENCHES
(Feb. 8th–12th)

FEBRUARY 10TH

. . . the trenches . . . are a quagmire . . .

Last night the enemy kept opening bursts of machine gun fire, hoping to catch our working parties, who promptly jumped into shell holes. Incredible as it may seem nobody was hit.

The nights are pitch dark and work is carried out under great difficulties . . .

FEBRUARY 13TH

. . . We shall be glad when the breastworks are ready for occupation as the trenches have become almost impassable. The posts are practically isolated in daytime.

The German shelling has slightly increased, while his sniping by day and machine gun fire by night are now much hotter. These changes betoken a relief of the battalion opposite us . . .

The chill has not left me in spite of large doses of quinine and the warmth afforded by two Burberry coats, cardigans and mufflers.

Jack was by now a very sick man. On February 14th he was ordered to hospital with severe influenza. He wrote:

'It was a terrible trial to be, for the second time so soon, in hospital unwounded. Before the War I was as strong as any, and to be again beaten for stamina by all save three or four of my officer comrades, many of them much older than I, was a severe blow. Even the kind remarks of the Colonel . . . did not remove the sting. I could, however, hold out no longer.

'I am happy to state that my subsequent record improved. From resuming duty in May 1915 till finally invalided Home as the result of a steeplechase accident near Cologne in May 1919, I was only off duty twice for six days each through illness, once for ten months (wounded) and six times on ordinary leave.'

On this occasion in 1915 he was brought back to England on February 25th; he remained in hospital at Torquay until March 2nd, when a Medical Board ordered him on a month's leave; this was extended for another month by a second Board. He returned to Home Duty on May 4th.

During Jack's sick leave, his old company, 'C' Company 1/Cameronians, suffered severe losses: Lieutenant Becher was killed on March 13th; Lieutenant Rooke was killed on patrol on June 19th; his body was brought in by Lieutenant Gray, who was killed in turn two days later. 'So three of my four gay young "C" Company officers . . . were no more.'

At the same time, the 2/Cameronians (23rd Brigade, 8th Division) was also undergoing grim experiences. At Neuve Chapelle (March 10th) the battalion had 14 officers killed and 9 wounded, out of 24 engaged. The 23rd Brigade incurred 1,241 casualties during its assault, mostly Middlesex and Cameronians. At Aubers Ridge on May 9th this battalion lost a further 12 officers and 156 other ranks. The proportion of officer casualties rose steeply at this stage, as more and more untrained soldiers entered the field, requiring ever-greater exertions and example from their leaders.

*　　　*　　　*

III

Company Commander and
Second-in-Command
2/Cameronians

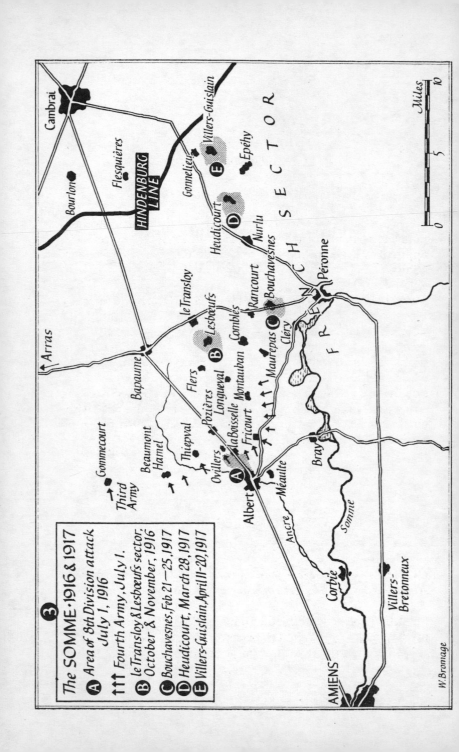

The SOMME · 1916 & 1917

Ⓐ Area of 8th Division attack
  July 1, 1916
↑↑↑ Fourth Army, July 1.
  le Transloy & Lesbœufs sector.
Ⓑ October & November, 1916
Ⓒ Bouchavesnes, Feb 21—25, 1917
Ⓓ Heudicourt, March 28, 1917
Ⓔ Villers-Guislain, April 11-20, 1917

Miles
0   5   10

W. Bromage

SICK LEAVE IN THE U.K.
(Mar. 2nd–May 4th 1915)

On March 18th Jack was dining in London with an old friend.

. . . we were both shocked at the unsoldierly appearance and manners of many of the new officers in London before a disapproving Provost Marshal and staff changed this state of affairs.

. . . About this time strikes in the U.K., bitterly resented by the troops, caused trouble . . . It seems monstrous that, in the same desperate struggle, men volunteering as soldiers, undergoing great risks and hardships for about two shillings a day, should be liable to be shot for disobeying orders in the field, while munition workers, miners and other civilians, well paid, safe at home and engaged on work vital to the needs of the Army, should be at liberty to 'down tools' when they like without incurring any penalty. The strikers were, unwittingly no doubt, committing manslaughter, just as artillerymen would be doing by quitting their guns in action, their fire being required to cover an attack. In war some kind of discipline is as necessary for the public as for the Fighting Services . . .

HOME DUTY
(May 4th–June 26th)

On May 20th Jack again found himself with the 3/Cameronians at Nigg; this time he was less approving of the Reserve Battalion.

. . . I thought little of the discipline of the 3rd, although doing my best for No. 3 Company placed under my command . . .

On the 31st a draft – 40 from my company – left for France

in grand form. On 5th June, 300 men from the cavalry and other units arrived for training as infantry, and seemed none too pleased at the change. Four days later 84 volunteers from the R.A.M.C. reached us for the same purpose . . .

On 26 June I gladly received a telegram ordering me to rejoin the B.E.F. in France forthwith . . .

DUTY AT A FRENCH BASE
(June 29th–Aug. 24th)

JULY 4TH: HARFLEUR: NO. 8 INFANTRY BASE DEPOT

. . . This depot holds reserves for the 8th Division and I command 93 men of the 2nd Battalion of my regiment . . .

The mess is crowded with inexperienced young gentlemen whose manners might be improved were some of the senior officers to dine with us instead of always in town or in their own quarters.

Parades are held daily from 8.15 a.m. till 12.30 p.m. and from 2 o'c till 3.30 in the afternoons. On the top of the hill there is a good level training ground with practice trenches, assault courses, and a rifle range. In addition to tactical exercises, route marches, lectures and other training we carry out daily a little close-order drill, in which I firmly believe as a solid foundation for making soldiers. Detachments of the Guards are continually at drill, performed, as are all their duties, with the thoroughness that places them, perhaps, the first soldiers in the world. They are not merely 'show' troops, as some of the public imagine. I would rather have the Guards alongside in battle than any others . . .

JULY 11TH

. . . Except for occasional heavy showers the weather is fine; so we are able the better to enjoy the Thursday evening concerts provided by an excellent string quartette composed of staff sergeants, the instruments and musical scores having been kindly presented by Messrs. Boosey & Co. . .

JULY 25TH

. . . We have all been inoculated against enteric fever . . .

On July 27th there arrived a smart draft composed mostly of our riflemen recovered from wounds received at Neuve Chapelle in March. Three days later, one of 60 reached us from the 12th (New Army) Battalion, splendid material but insufficiently trained . . .

I read a good deal in the seclusion of my tent. One book of interest is *Rome* by Zola; another *Ordeal By Battle* by Oliver,[1] in which the author quotes the nonsense publicly delivered by two eminent politicians who declared that 'one volunteer is worth six (the other said three) pressed men.' Is it seriously suggested that one British soldier, a volunteer, is equal in battle to six, or even three, conscript soldiers of the magnificent German Army? Pure rubbish! . . .

WITH THE 2/CAMERONIANS (SCOTTISH RIFLES): ARMENTIÈRES FRONT
(Aug. 26th 1915–Mar. 27th 1916)

AUGUST 31ST: CROIX BLANCHE: IN BRIGADE SUPPORT

. . . In this area I spent all last winter . . .

The Battalion is housed in brigade support 3 miles behind the front line, each company finding two platoon posts in redoubts beside farms about a mile in advance, each post with two days' water, rations and plenty of ammunition in case of being cut off by a German attack. All available men are daily or nightly on fatigues, mending roads, building redoubts, improving accommodation, etc., as well as furnishing guards. Save for occasional shells the sector is quiet . . .

The usual routine and parades, when the battalion is out of the line, are: 6 a.m., Reveille; 7, Roll-call, wash, clean arms and equipment; 8, Breakfast; 9-12 noon, Orderly Room, inspection of arms, equipment and quarters, then drill or other training; 1 p.m., Dinner; afternoon, Office work and games; 4, Tea; 5, Guard-mounting; 7, Officers' dinner; 9.30, Lights Out; companies reported present or otherwise by one officer per company to the lieut-colonel.

The only notable changes of infantry weapons since I was

[1] *F. S. Oliver, 'Ordeal by Battle' (Macmillan, 1915).*

last at the front are the increase of the battalion Vickers machine guns from two to four, and of Lewis guns to two per platoon, or eight for each of the four companies, greatly augmenting our fire-power.[1]

Lieut-Colonel G. T. Carter-Campbell, an exceptionally able officer, twice wounded at Neuve Chapelle, commands the Battalion. Major V. Sandilands, a cheery former company commander of mine, is second-in-command. Major Hyde Smith, another first-class soldier . . . is also present. The adjutant is Colin Stirling, a splendid little lad whose brother 'Jock', of my company, was killed near here last January . . .

The subalterns of my company, 'B', Rodgers, McHarg, Connal and Burt, all New Army, appear to be a toughish lot . . .

Another friend I must mention, Regimental-Sergeant-Major Chalmers, M.C., D.C.M., the first to instruct me in rifle drill on my joining the Regiment in 1903 . . .

All ranks here, some 700, of the 90th Light Infantry, the old 'Perthshire Grey Breeks' . . . are in fine fettle. What else could they be with such a Commanding Officer? I do not believe that a better battalion landed in France.

IN THE LINE
(Sept. 1st–5th)

SEPTEMBER 5TH: CORDONNERIE FARM

. . . The 1914 trenches in this area had to be abandoned last winter as they became waterlogged. In their stead we hold a line of breastworks, on the top of the ground, which we were building in February. There were then no communication trenches; the front line could only be reached across the open; this has been remedied.

The breastworks are some 7 feet high, 7 feet wide at the top and 18 at the bottom. About 6 feet behind the front wall there is a similar wall, with a trench 2 foot deep between the two. The inner face of both walls is revetted with sandbags, and solid traverses every ten yards protect the men in the bays from

[1] *This is incorrect; in 1915, infantry battalions received 8 Lewis guns each; for the Somme (1916), 16; in July 1918, 36.*

enfilade fire as well as localising shell bursts. Small recesses, shored up with timber, in the parapet give shelter to officers and men. On the enemy's side of the parapet a wide ditch, boggy in wet weather, and a thick belt of barbed wire serve to prevent a surprise attack. There is practically no support line, redoubts taking its place.

One feels less confined behind breastworks than one did in the trenches, and the range of view, although little enough, is better . . .

At 4.10 a.m., one hour before dawn, all companies stand to arms at their battle posts fully equipped. When the enemy's parapet can be clearly seen, Day Duties mount, i.e. one sentry per platoon, the remainder of the men dismissing . . .

Arms and the lines are next inspected by the company officers. Reports on the enemy's activities during the night, damage done to our parapet and wire, work and patrols performed by our men, casualties, etc., are collected from platoons and embodied in the company commander's report on the situation sent to Battalion Headquarters . . .

The Colonel visits some companies every day . . .

At dusk (8.50 p.m.) the company falls in fully dressed at its battle posts for officers' inspection. One-third of the men then remain, in two-hour reliefs, as sentries throughout the night. Another third proceed down the communication trench to the rendezvous on the road about half a mile in rear to draw from the Quartermaster's limbers rations, water in sterilised petrol tins, empty sandbags, coils of barbed wire to strengthen the protective entanglements, other stores and the mails from home. These parties are sometimes shelled. The remaining third rest – officially – but are often called upon to find patrols and wiring parties in No Man's Land, frequently under machine gun fire and constantly in the beams of Very rockets shot up by both sides to disclose an enemy's approach. The second of these duties lasts for a large part of each night.

Meanwhile half the officers in turn are going round the company posts till dawn, when one only is on duty; the others snatch an hour or two of sleep in one of the shelters. A full day's work it is; all so familiar to me last winter, albeit now in far less discomfort, no battle strain and better weather.

The enemy's sandbagged parapet, clearly visible through clefts in our wall, and also protected by thick entanglements, is about 120 yards away, part of it 60, some posts in mine craters much less, one of them only 30 yards. Not a sign of a German, however, can be seen at any time . . .

According to Royal Engineer reports the Germans are still mining close to our parapet; one crater touches it. Therefore, after visiting my post 30 yards from one of the enemy's posts, I withdraw it from the forward to the rear lip of the crater, which we have wired so as to 'net' any Huns coming along. One or two other posts have also been retired slightly from dangerous positions since we never know when mines will be blown and cause a lot of damage . . .

IN DIVISIONAL RESERVE
(Sept. 6th–24th)

SEPTEMBER 12TH: BILLETS NEAR SAILLY-SUR-LYS

. . . The company marched to the divisional baths close to Armentières the day after leaving the line for a much-needed wash. Concerts are occasionally arranged for the men; that in my company last night finished ten minutes later than the authorised closing time, earning me a 'raspberry' from the Colonel owing to two rascals attending it from another company getting drunk . . .

The other battalions in the Brigade are; 2/Devonshire, 2/West Yorkshire, 2/Middlesex and 1/7/Middlesex (Territorial Army).[1]

Company commanders have just been told Secretly and Personally to prepare for an early attack on the enemy. This news is not communicated to any others here, and we hope that loose tongues elsewhere will be silenced . . .

There is an immediate tuning up for action, the sharpening of 'swords' – as bayonets are called by rifle regiments – the

---

[1] *Territorial battalions were attached to Regular brigades in 1915 for training. The first Territorial Division to cross to France as a unit was the 46th (North Midland) in February 1915. Other divisions were reassembled as their battalions finished spells with the Regulars – spells during which they were quite likely to see heavy fighting, and sustain casualties.*

practising of assaults, inspection of gas masks and special equipment, and all the other horrid ritual for battle, from which all ranks may draw their own conclusions . . .

We are busy putting finishing touches to training: musketry, route marching to get fit, and practising our old pre-War methods of attack, i.e., deploying rapidly from advancing platoon and section columns into extended firing line and supports to close with the enemy. These formations, with emphasis laid on the vital importance of section initiative, were successfully applied in the early battles of the War.

On several nights, too, the company has been practising crawling up to an imaginary enemy, with the bombers and wire-cutters rehearsing their roles . . .

The men have had another good wash at the divisional baths.
. . . On the 17th we were all out at 5 a.m. to say good-bye to Colonel Carter-Campbell who has been promoted to command a brigade . . . He is a very strict disciplinarian as the following incident shows.

One night a party of his battalion on wiring duty in No Man's Land ran back to their trenches in disorder for what the Colonel considered an inadequate reason – the approach of an enemy patrol or something like that. In order to steady their nerves as well as to provide an example for others, the culprits had to parade and march for half an hour on three successive nights to and fro in front of their parapet, an N.C.O. calling out 'About turn' at the end of each beat. Since this lesson duties in No Man's Land have been as steady as rocks.

My old friend, Victor Sandilands . . . has become our lieut-colonel . . . It is said that none displayed greater courage and coolness on Aubers Ridge last May than he did . . .

THE ATTACK BY THE 8TH DIVISION
NEAR BOIS GRENIER
(Sept. 25th)

(This action coincided with a great French offensive in Champagne and a smaller French attack on Vimy Ridge, together with the main British offensive at Loos and lesser British attacks at Givenchy, Aubers Ridge, Bois-Grenier and Ypres. —J.L.J.)

The ill-fated Battle of Loos on September 25th 1915 was dictated by two factors: the danger of Russian collapse after the terrible losses sustained during the Gorlice-Tarnow fighting, and the growing weakness of France after the costly offensives in the West throughout the year. The British commanders had little taste for the battle, but no option. It marked, however, the first large-scale British participation in a major Allied attack. General Haig wrote in his diary on the 25th: 'The greatest battle in the world's history begins today. Some 800,000 French and British troops will actually attack today.'

The subsidiary attack by the 8th Division was carried out by the 25th Brigade, 23rd Brigade being in reserve.

OCTOBER 3RD: BILLETS, RUE BIACHE

. . . At 2.30 a.m. on the 25th all companies stood to arms and ate a light breakfast.

Two hours later our artillery, the fire of which was reported to have severely damaged the enemy's trenches and wire during the previous four days, opened an intense bombardment on the German parapets. This cannonade was supplemented by a battery of 18-pounder field guns which had been man-handled up to embrasures in our front parapet.

Instantly three battalions of the 25th Brigade, 2/Rifle Brigade, 2/Royal Berkshire and 2/Lincolnshire (from right to left) advanced in the mist and rain from their 'jumping off line', a dry ditch joining the horns of a deep re-entrant in our line, to carry the German trenches . . . The frontage of the attack was some 1,200 yards and the distance of the advance about 250.

Word soon reached us that the attack had been successful, to the extent even that portions of the German second line had fallen. Then that only partial success had been achieved and that our men were fighting hard against reinforcements of the enemy's bombers . . .

In fact, like all the British subsidiary attacks, Bois-Grenier was a costly failure. The ground won was abandoned at 3.30 that afternoon; the three battalions concerned took 123 prisoners at a cost of 52 officers and 1,283 other ranks. Among other difficulties which they had to contend with, Jack relates: 'The fuses of their bombs became damp from rain and would not light . . . there were 12 patterns of hand bomb in British use and few had mastered completely the mechanism of all of them.'

As to the day's events affecting my battalion:

Amid the crack of the field guns near us and the booming of the cannonade at Loos, fifteen miles southwards, we in the undisturbed trenches at Barlette Farm were constantly regaled with official messages telling of the wonderful success of our arms at Loos, of French arms in Champagne; their seizure of place after place; that two of our divisions at Loos had broken right through the enemy. The War seemed almost over bar the shouting.

Later in the morning news became scanty; then there were hints of checks and German counter-attacks; after that there was an ominous silence . . .

'It would be idle to pretend that the outcome of the battle of Loos was not a bitter disappointment,' says the British Official History. Casualties (Sept. 25th–Oct. 13th), for very small gains, were: 2,466 officers and 59,247 other ranks. The French Champagne offensive was also a costly failure.

On the 26th we kept expecting a German counter-attack but nothing of the kind happened . . .

During the day we witnessed much air fighting and heard the rumble of artillery at Loos without learning of progress. Many dead of the Rifle Brigade were seen lying close up to the enemy's parapet, among them one who had helped me at Harfleur was recognised. Shall I ever become accustomed to these sights? . . .

('Side shows', such as that at Bois-Grenier, are always disliked by the troops taking part in them. Often with limited means, and intended to do little more than bait the enemy, they are as dangerous to the actors as 'headline' battles, and the glory is less.—J.L.J.)

Next morning . . . when going round the company I found one of the men amusing himself by throwing three live bombs in the air, one after another, and catching them with his disengaged hand; sometimes a bomb would fall to the ground. I asked the 'conjuror' if he understood bombs; since he said he did not, I begged him to cease his tricks till I had got well away.

IN THE LINE
(Sept. 27th–Oct. 1st)

. . . .The Brigadier[1] went round my lines at dawn on the 29th and appeared to be satisfied with them.

Before sunrise on the 28th a German patrol audaciously crept right up to our parapet and got away safely; too bad! my men must sharpen up.

The enemy's minenwerfer (heavy trench mortars) bothered us considerably during the tour . . . One can see these bombs coming high in the air, and dodge them if there is room and one keeps cool.

We were busy wiring craters during the tour, and thickening the wire belt in front of the parapet. Our parties on the latter duty were much harassed by a hostile machine gun until we put a spoke in its wheel. I asked Sergeant Snowdon, an excellent N.C.O., to get his two Vickers machine guns aligned as well as possible in the dark on the enemy's piece when it next fired; to re-check on the second and third bursts; and then to let rip when I blew my whistle on the fourth burst. Thereafter we had no more trouble . . . .

[1] *Brig.-General H. D. Tuson,* c.m.g.

IN BRIGADE SUPPORT
(Oct. 2nd–7th)

OCTOBER 7TH: BILLETS, RUE BIACHE

... Hyde Smith having left us to command the 10th Battalion[1]
I have succeeded him as Second-in-Command with, no doubt,
the rank of temporary major if the appointment is confirmed. I
therefore handed over command of 'B' Company three days ago
and repaired with my belongings to the more comfortable sur-
roundings of Battalion Headquarters, to the cheery company of
'Sandy' and 'Mickie' Stirling. My first duty in this exalted
position was as president of a Field General Court-Martial,
a duty undertaken as soon as I had time to put on my spurs.

IN THE LINE
(Oct. 7th–10th)

OCTOBER 10TH: CORDONNERIE FARM

... Our headquarters are at the farm, a full half-mile from the
breastworks ... since one or two shells have cracked the cellar
roof to the point of collapse we stay in shelters above ground
some fifty yards behind the walls ...

Since 'Sandy' does everything for himself – with the assistance
of his underlings – my role appears to be confined merely to
keeping the body alive and the mind fresh. So I live like a
gentleman, hoping that the Commanding Officer will meet
with no mishap ...

IN DIVISIONAL RESERVE
(Oct. 11th–17th)

OCTOBER 17TH: BILLETS, SAILLY-SUR-LYS

... The cannonade southwards faded out some days ago. I
always hated to hear it, realising what strain it meant for those
engaged. Happily most soldiers are not greatly concerned with
the happenings to those at a distance, and so are better able to
await their own turn with equanimity. 'Sufficient unto the day
is the evil thereof.'

[1] *10/Cameronians (15th Div.) lost 21 officers and 464 other ranks at Loos on Sept.
25th/26th.*

I have been president of another court-martial, on 'absence without leave', for which the culprit was awarded three months imprisonment . . .

Having suffered of late from severe and constant headaches I rode to Dulieu to consult an Army specialist about my eyes. He said they had been strained and prescribed glasses for reading and writing, ornaments now on my nose for the first time. Out here much of our reading and writing has to be performed in ill-lit rooms, cellars or windowless shelters – in the two last-named by the rays from a candle stump . . .

Today I attended church parade – as an example to those whose Faith is still intact. Besides, the practice helps to screw up one's sense of duty.

IN BRIGADE SUPPORT
(Oct. 18th–22nd)

OCTOBER 22ND; BILLETS NEAR FLEURBAIX

[On the 18th] at 11 p.m. we were suddenly ordered to stand to our alarm posts. This order, however, turned out to be due to a staff error and was soon cancelled. Mistakes will happen, of course, from time to time; but one should be scrupulously careful not to worry troops needlessly.[1]

My French landladies sometimes enquire 'Monsieur, when will this terrible war end?' 'Madame,' I always reply, 'you may bet your shirt on it, we shall win in two, five, seven or ten years if we all hold to it.' The higher figures often cause a wince on their faces. It is probable that our 50- to 80-year-old men are fitter physically than Germans of like ages – thanks to golf, sport and games in general . . .

IN DIVISIONAL RESERVE
(Oct. 23rd–26th)

OCTOBER 26TH: SAILLY

. . . On the 23rd the Battalion returned to divisional reserve in

[1] *It is interesting to note the identity of attitude of thoughtful professional soldiers. Thus Haig, in January 1915, finding some men in reserve in General Monro's I Corps not being allowed to remove their boots, wrote: 'Very strict discipline is necessary, but unnecessary fussiness and over-anxiety should be discouraged . . . I telegraphed to Monro . . .'*

order to prepare for another attack by the 8th Division, in which the 90th (2/Cameronians) is to be one of the leading actors.

Facsimiles of the hostile works to be attacked have been traced in this vicinity by sod or tape, and assaults practised on them. A hundred other preliminaries to action have also been overhauled. It seems that some hint of our preparations has come to the ears of the enemy – very likely by means of their aircraft – because they have been heard to shout across No Man's Land 'When is your attack to begin?' . . .

IN THE LINE
(Oct. 27th–Nov. 1st)

NOVEMBER 2ND: FLEURBAIX

. . . Our Battalion Headquarters are at Temple Farm. This sector is full of spectres for me; the 19th Brigade was sometimes hard pressed by the enemy at this very place just twelve months ago . . .

The weather has been foul and our shelters leaked like sieves. To my disgust I found a frog in my 'bed' (2 blankets and a coat) the other night and had a long job carrying it too far away to invade my sanctuary again before daylight. Then a cat gave me a start by dropping on to my body from a shelf. Another trench cat, a friend of mine, sleeps by my feet, preventing attacks on my person by the voracious mice, the permanent tenants of the lodging.

The Colonel visits all four companies daily attended by Colin Stirling, Cooke (Medical Officer), the Regimental-Sergeant-Major, and a couple of orderlies. I also am of the party when free from other work . . .

During last month Brigade Machine Gun Companies have been formed by withdrawing the four Vickers guns per infantry battalion . . .[1]

---

[1] *The Machine Gun Corps was raised by Royal Warrant on October 22nd 1915; by November 1918 its strength was 6,432 officers and 124,920 other ranks.*

IN DIVISIONAL RESERVE
(Nov. 5th–10th)

[On the 6th] 'Sandy', 'Mickie' Stirling and I refreshed ourselves by attending the Divisional Theatre in a barn. The artistes are soldiers, with some sort of flair for the stage, belonging to the divisional troupe of entertainers, who provide hearty, if not high-class, performances to keep things going.

We are enjoying good winter weather.

I am engaged in arranging a football cup tie for one team from every platoon.

Our bagpipes, sent Home some time ago, have just been returned to us, so I am having drums made by the battalion pioneers from biscuit tins painted with the regimental colours; we cannot manage to inscribe on them the Battle Honours. The value of music to enliven the spirits of troops on the march as well as in quarters appears to have been overlooked by High Command.

Leave is good at present . . . About 30 of all ranks travel weekly to the United Kingdom on seven days leave. I have again declined my turn, which was originally due at the end of September. I do not want it; others do.

We have been continuing . . . to practise for the attack which had been planned. It has now been put off – the longer the better . . .

IN THE LINE
(Nov. 11th–16th)

. . . The nights are cold. I manage, however, to sustain a little heat in my body by means of an open coke stove in the shelter. The fumes partially asphyxiate callers with less sound lungs than mine.

Muddy as the line is, it is dry indeed compared with its knee-deep state all last winter when the infantry were not nearly so often out of it . . .

IN BRIGADE SUPPORT
(Nov. 17th–18th)

NOVEMBER 18TH: FLEURBAIX

After sunset on the 16th the 2/West Yorkshire relieved the Battalion, which marched here in brigade support. On the way out of the line a salvo of shells burst right among 'D' Company without hurting anyone.

The Battalion had only one casualty last tour, Rifleman Hannah killed . . .

IN THE LINE
(Nov. 19th–23rd)

NOVEMBER 23RD: CORDONNERIE FARM

[On the 20th] our artillery and trench mortars, with machine gun fire added, bombarded the enemy's line at intervals to destroy his mine shafts, besides inflicting other damage. The German reply was insignificant . . .

The Medical Officer has raised two more blankets for me to assist in circumventing the infernal cold which prevents one from sleeping . . .

THE MOVE TO ARMY RESERVE
(Nov. 24th–26th)

NOVEMBER 28TH: MORBECQUE

[The 25th] was spent in resting and cleaning up. At 11 p.m., however, we were roused to receive a message from High Command saying that our machine gunners were to parade with their companies, and not as machine gun crews, at the Commander-in-Chief's inspection on the 26th. What is the sense of waking one up for a trivial order of this kind which could well have waited till the morning – as it did in the case of our companies?

On the 26th the Battalion marched at 7.30 o'c on a raw morning . . . to Morbecque, the day's journey being about nine miles with few falling out.

Soon after reaching our destination at 11 a.m. we learned

that the inspection by the C.-in-C., Sir John French, due almost immediately, had been cancelled on account of the infernal snow storms. The Chief, however, issued a Special Order – read out to the troops – in which he expressed his entire satisfaction with the performances of the 8th Division during the September operations, and said how useful they had been to the main attacks.

This, of course, was intended to raise morale, and 'pour l'histoire'. But it should be remembered that the men of 1915 were not as sceptical as later 'generations' of the P.B.I. became, mainly during 1917.

IN FIRST ARMY RESERVE
(Nov. 27th 1915–Jan. 10th 1916)

(*The Eighth Division in the War, 1914–1918* tells that this period in reserve was the first on which the Division had been out of the line for a rest for more than twelve months. This may have been so as regards Divisional Headquarters, the artillery and other units. But to my mind the infantry had been frequently out of the line – the Front Line – although not, perhaps for more 'rest' than they enjoyed at Morbecque.–J.L.J.)

DECEMBER 5TH: MORBECQUE

. . . Our residence is officially described as a 'Hut Camp'. There are, no doubt, several canvas huts – unfinished when we arrived – but, in fact, we are all in bell tents in perishing weather alternating between severe frost, snow and rain, the last making a quagmire of the soil . . .

On November 24th there arrived without notice three officers to join the Battalion. One of these, Captain Braithwaite Wallis . . . being seven years older than I, and none too sound physically, has been asked to assume the duties of Second-in-Command and I have willingly returned to 'B' Company . . .

On November 29th the Corps Commander[1] called, and the Divisional Commander[2] motored over . . . The latter expressed

---

[1] *Lieut.-Gen. Sir W. P. Pulteney.*   [2] *Maj-Gen. H. Hudson.*

his dissatisfaction that the morning's parades had been cancelled because of the vile weather. I wonder if such small matters might not be left to the discretion of battalion commanders? A few days later the D.C. came again to visit us; this time he was 'satisfied' . . .

Company training, including a weekly route march, is in full swing. Besides this, half our officers together with some N.C.O.s are attending a three-day course of instruction under the Royal Engineers, the elementary programme being well known to all ranks through constant practice in the Line. It is not lack of knowledge that causes mediocre work there, but mud, darkness, shells and exhaustion, and the want of supervision and discipline on the part of half-trained junior leaders. The standards of leadership are nothing like so high as they were in the experienced 1914 British Expeditionary Force.

We have raised a Battalion Rugby football team, to which I have given a ball. Three days ago . . . I played full back, my second Rugby game in the last twelve years!! . . .

DECEMBER 12TH

. . . Poor Wallis fainted at a lecture the other day. He has been far too long in tropical Africa to stand the rain and cold here. I ran to my tent to fetch him my flask of precious brandy, filled at Thornhill and not touched – only sniffed – since then. Our friend recovered as soon as the spirit touched his lips; but, to my horror, he seemed about to collapse again and I imagined the tiny flask would soon be emptied, little as I grudged it to save a comrade. This dire disaster did not, however, take place . . .

DECEMBER 19TH

. . . Our Rugby and Association football teams have been practising hard. The former won its match against the 2/Middlesex on the 16th by 14 points to nil. Two days afterwards we drew our game with a much heavier team of the 2/Devonshire. Our star performer, Ferguson, a great big strong active subaltern plays Association football for his company side three days a week and for my Rugby team on most other days . . .

*Association Football was the favoured pastime of the rank-and-file;
Rugby was mainly for officers. Ian Hay in 'The First Hundred Thousand' has described the reaction of the soldiery on first witnessing this
sport: '. . . in five minutes their mouths were agape with scandalized
astonishment; in ten, the heavens were rent with their protesting cries.
Accustomed to see football played with the feet, and to demand the instant
execution of any player (on the other side) who laid so much as a finger
upon the ball or the man who was playing it, the exhibition of savage
and promiscuous brutality to which their superiors now treated them
shocked the assembled spectators to the roots of their sensitive souls.
Howls of virtuous indignation burst forth upon all sides.'*

ON DIVISIONAL MANOEUVRES
(Dec. 20th–23rd)

DECEMBER 24TH

. . . On the 20th the Brigade marched 14 miles, its units getting
into billets about 8 p.m.

The following day we set off at 8 a.m.; practised advanced
guard duties in the morning; made an attack in the afternoon;
and at 9 p.m. – after an hour's rest – took up an outpost line
for the night.

On the 23rd the Brigade, again on the move early, was engaged on rear-guard exercises during the day, the last battalion
reaching its quarters at 9 that night . . .

Personally, I thought it a deadly four days. The preparations
for the use of land and accommodation were not thorough
enough, and I had not time to become properly acquainted
with them.[1] The weather was foul and our billets – sometimes
châteaux – were cold as the tomb. We were up nearly all night
with orders, reports and so on. During the day landowners had
to be argued with; and there was great difficulty in arranging
night quarters to suit tactical dispositions as well as to meet the
objections of householders. Some of my billeting dispositions
were not of the best tactically, as I thought it wiser to avoid
worrying the troops too much; besides, the enemy was represented only by very few men with flags.

As 'Sam' Darling, an exceptionally fine soldier, told me after

[1] *Jack was temporarily standing in as Staff Captain, 23rd Brigade.*

the battle of Loos, 'We are now an amateur army taking on professionals' – thanks largely to our government's neglecting the Military Security of our Country . . .

Sir Douglas Haig, the commander of our First Army, has lately succeeded Sir John French as C.-in-C. of the British armies in France.[1] Sir Douglas, then Inspector-General of Cavalry in India, often joined us at games of polo in Meerut about 1907 . . .

JANUARY 2ND 1916

On the 25th of December, in vile weather, all the officers went round the company dinners, according to well-established custom, to wish their men 'A Happy Christmas'. A good plateful of plum-pudding concluded a substantial repast . . .

Next day at church I could not help smiling at the thought of all the Christian peoples at war beseeching the Almighty at this season of goodwill to see to the triumph of their cause – the cause of Right, of course – and to deliver up to them their bloodguilty enemies.

Two battalion concerts brought an end to the year's festivities . . .

Last winter we had neither a man nor a shell to spare, the 18-pounders being often down to a paltry allowance of a few rounds a day, except during emergencies. This winter we have been able to bombard the enemy quite freely. The launching, too, of raids by 20 or 30 men to capture prisoners and to harry the Germans has been a feature of our operations. The taking of prisoners is always important . . . The bayonet and hand-bomb are the weapons mostly used for trench-raids . . .

I have not heard of any repetition of the 'unofficial truces' that took place between our men and the Germans on parts of the Front at Christmas 1914. While these lasted friend and foe met amicably in No Man's Land for a chat – for games, too, I was told. The frowns of High Command and increased bitterness must have stopped them.

I used to wonder as to the result of sending into No Man's Land on these occasions trays laden with wine and cakes for the entertainment of the Germans, and of our offering five

[1] *Haig became C.-in-C. on December 19th, in his 56th year.*

pounds on the spot, as well as a free passage to any port, to all who surrendered – a cheaper way of reducing the number of enemies than fighting.

We brought in the New Year in fine style. There was an excellent dinner at which the divisional band, lent for the occasion, reinforced our pipe music. Many guests, too, helped to 'light up' the proceedings . . . R.-S.-M. Chalmers arrived with the compliments of the Sergeants' mess and was invited inside. Standing very erect, he spoke of the great traditions of the Regiment in tones that thrilled the last-joined subalterns especially. Into this scene of boundless enthusiasm there came an Army Service Corps friend of ours, who was heard to exclaim fervently, 'Gad! how grand it must be to belong to an infantry regiment!' (This 'grand' feeling is apt to evaporate a little in a muddy trench, on wearisome night duties, sometimes in action.) Finally, after seeing the camp quiet I lay down at midnight. But a couple of revellers on the road outside wakened me, and I had to get a picket to assist them to their tent . . .

JANUARY 9TH

. . . We are packing up tomorrow to return to the Line . . .

At 35 years of age I have been lame from football kicks during most of our stay here; but they have not interfered with duties. Our Rugby team has put up a very good performance considering that nearly all its members were 'soccer' players.

All ranks are in good form following their long 'rest', in spite of the discomforts due to foul weather and tents in a morass.

IN DIVISIONAL RESERVE
(Jan. 11th–17th)

JANUARY 17TH: SAILLY

. . . Two days ago poor Wallis was sent to hospital en route for England, intensely disappointed that his health has broken down without his having had the chance of getting into the Line with his regiment. We are all sorry at his departure.

I am, therefore, again Second-in-Command of the Battalion;

124

but 'Sandy', with his usual consideration, asked me to stay with my company for a day or two since battalion head-quarters are so cold and my bad circulation notorious . . .

IN BRIGADE SUPPORT
(Jan. 18th–22nd)

JANUARY 22ND: FLEURBAIX

. . . Among the mails which I found on arriving here was a bill for thirty-seven boxes of chocolates, Christmas presents to my friends and their children, twenty of them for the wives of fellow-officers in the Regiment, several of them widowed in the War . . .

IN THE LINE
(Jan. 22nd–26th)

JANUARY 26TH: LA BOUTILLERIE

After dusk on the 22nd, following a march of 2½ miles, we took over from the 2/West Yorkshire the identical line held by the 1/Cameronians when trench warfare first began in October 1914. Conditions are, however, not nearly so bad as they were then . . .

Many German aeroplanes – many more than formerly – are appearing over our lines without much hindrance. On the 24th I saw a very fast Fokker flash right between five of our aircraft and escape . . .

IN BRIGADE SUPPORT
(Jan. 26th–30th)

JANUARY 30TH: FLEURBAIX

. . . A battalion of the Tyneside Scottish from the 34th (New Army) Division is attached to the 23rd Brigade to gain ex-perience of trench warfare. They are a tough-looking lot.[1]

[1] *The 102nd (Tyneside Scottish) Brigade consisted of 20/, 21/, 22/ and 23/Northumberland Fusiliers.*

IN THE LINE
(Jan. 31st–Feb. 3rd)

FEBRUARY 3RD: LA BOUTILLERIE

... On my usual afternoon walk today a shrapnel shell scattered a shower of bullets around me in an unpleasant manner.

IN DIVISIONAL RESERVE
(Feb. 4th–13th)

FEBRUARY 13TH: SAILLY

... A French interpreter attached to the Brigade comes daily to brush up my indifferent knowledge of his language. In answer to his question as to how long I think the War will last, I gave my habitual reply: 'Monsieur, you may bet your life on our winning in two, five, seven or ten years, provided we do not falter.' He answered most earnestly: 'Do you know, mon capitaine, that the French cannot last two years longer?'[1] We sometimes forget that the entire French nation has been engaged up to the hilt ever since August 1914, its armies losing thousands to our hundreds; while our manhood and resources, almost negligible in numbers and quantity (not in quality) for the whole of the first war year, are not even yet fully deployed.

The other evening an army chaplain, who had been present at the battle of Loos, dined with us and mentioned an incident that I think *highly disgusting*. He related that a British private soldier whose unit had suffered terrible casualties in the battle was told to escort twenty Germans back to the prisoners' cages. Passing one of our machine guns immediately afterwards, the 'escort' prevailed on a member of its crew to open fire on his charges. There may, of course, have been extenuating circum-

[1] *This was becoming an increasingly material consideration for responsible British commanders. As early as June 14th 1915, Haig recorded; 'Captain de Couvreville (from General Joffre's H.Q.) came to see me ... One serious statement he made. This was to the effect that "the French people are getting tired of the war".' On January 14th 1916 Haig wrote: 'There is no doubt to my mind but that the war must be won by the forces of the British Empire.' By December 31st 1915 French casualties amounted to 1,961,687, compared with British losses of 512,420. It was this comparison which brought about the sombre experiences of the British Army in 1916.*

stances unknown to me; and the Germans have 'played very rough' at times too.

(I heard of only one other similar British case throughout the War. It seems quite clear to me that soldiers in action are not bound to accept the surrender of their enemies, although it is the custom of civilised armies to do so. But when this has been done – amounting to a broad guarantee of safety – the lives of foemen must be respected whatever the temptation to individuals to 'get their own back' . . .–J.L.T.)

IN BRIGADE SUPPORT
(Feb. 15th–19th)

FEBRUARY 19TH: LAVENTIE

. . . At dinner a few nights ago a New Army officer made scathing remarks about the waste of officers' lives in my battalion at Neuve Chapelle.[1] The best defence to the charge that I could think of at the moment was to suggest that it is an officer's duty to 'go down with the ship' if necessary. This he countered by saying that the taxpayers expected better value for their money.

I consider that in this and similar assaults our casualties in officers of irreplaceable value were far too high. Too many of them were sent charging across open, bullet-swept ground when experience and training were largely at a discount and little more was required than bulldog courage. At the same time one must weigh the effect on the morale of the men if their officers do not share their dangers. The mistake was in having so many valuable officers present with battalions at all . . .[2]

The appointment of second-in-command to 'Sandy' is a poor one. He sees to everything himself. I have no real responsibility beyond keeping my skin whole, but do what I can to help, and read much.

The Medical Officer . . . says he has never seen such small battalion 'sick parades' as ours. Our daily average of men reporting sick is about 6, and he has been acustomed to 20

---

[1] See p. 101.
[2] German battalions would go into the line with 8 or 9 officers compared with about 25 in a British unit.

or 30. The size of the sick parade is one of the guides in assessing the value and morale of troops.

IN THE LINE
(Feb. 19th–23rd)

FEBRUARY 23RD: FAUQUISSART

. . . The weather is vile following a few sunny days. Snowfalls have replaced incessant rain. The lines are in a terrible state of mud, and pumps are kept going all the time to persuade the water to flow along – not down – to the Layes stream . . .

IN BRIGADE SUPPORT
(Feb. 24th–27th)

FEBRUARY 27TH: LAVENTIE

. . . The Laventie sector is about the best in which we have been. The Guards left the defences and everything in perfect order; the billets are comfortable and seldom shelled . . .

'Sandy' was lucky enough to get away on the 24th just before the closing of leave for all ranks. I am, therefore, in temporary command during his absence, and as busy as one could wish to be . . .

On the 21st inst. the Germans opened a very heavy attack on the French fortress of Verdun. Their success is described as unimportant, and we hope they paid through the neck for it.

IN THE LINE
(Feb. 27th–Mar. 2nd)

MARCH 2ND: FAUQUISSART

. . . It takes me about 5 hours daily, generally in the mornings, to go round all the companies thoroughly; office work accounts for several more hours. I do not sleep well in the line – not that there is much time for it anyhow. Any unusual racket wakens me at once – old memories, I suppose. The doctor has given me some pills which help . . .

IN BRIGADE SUPPORT
(Mar. 3rd–6th)

MARCH 6TH: LAVENTIE

. . . When we were dressing this morning eight howitzer shells burst among our billets, one of them in the house just across the street from ours. Later in the day shells set alight 'B' Company's farm . . . These small affairs resulted in no more than one or two casualties.

IN THE LINE
(Mar. 6th–10th)

MARCH 10TH: FAUQUISSART

. . . The Colonel has returned from leave – and his marriage. He seems suitable for double-harness; I am not. His presence allows me to resume my unexciting occupations.

The weather continues to be foul . . .

IN BRIGADE SUPPORT
(Mar. 10th–14th)

MARCH 14TH: LAVENTIE

. . . The battle of Verdun continues to rage. Reports say that the Germans have made little progress in return for very severe losses inflicted by the stout-hearted Frenchmen defending the fortress.[1]

I have been suffering from a bad chill for some days.

IN HOSPITAL
(Mar. 14th–18th)

MARCH 19TH: ESTAIRES

On the 14th I was admitted to the hospital of the 24th Field Ambulance . . . for a patch-up – and a rest following my 14 days' work (!) while the Colonel was away for his wedding.

[1] *In fact, during the German offensive phase at Verdun, French casualties greatly exceeded those of the enemy; Fort Douaumont was lost on February 25th, Fort de Vaux on June 9th.*

The hospital is in a large modern villa, with ceilings and indoor walls profusely 'ornamented' with mouldings and such-like in horrible taste.

I have been enjoying a lazy four days in great comfort, the luxury of hot – not merely warm – baths, and excellent food . . . A glass of 'bubbly' (Champagne) is offered at dinner and a glass of fair port at the end of the meal. I notice that the medical orderlies also appear to enjoy the wines . . .

IN BRIGADE SUPPORT
(Mar. 19th–22nd)

MARCH 22ND: LAVENTIE

. . . on discharge from hospital perfectly restored to health by four days' rest and good fare, I walked back the three miles to rejoin my battalion here . . .

IN THE LINE

MARCH 26TH: FAUQUISSART

. . . Two companies of very good quality from a New Army battalion are attached to us to gain experience in the line. One often hears the New Army improperly described as 'Kitchener's Army' or even as 'K's Army'. One Army is enough, the 'King's Army'; and His Majesty's illustrious subject, the Minister for War, ought not to be credited with the possession of soldiers of his own.

The weather is infamously wet, cold and snowy; the pumps are on the go all the time trying to reduce the floods at the breastworks. We get back from inspections of companies plastered with mud from head to heel . . .

I have thought of a plan to suit various parties; it is based on the following ideas: (*a*) There is undoubtedly too much water here and too little in, say, Egypt. (*b*) Judging by the amount of official correspondence we receive there must be enough waste blotting-paper in our military offices to absorb the excess of water. (*c*) By using some of our vast shipping the saturated blotting-paper could easily be transported to the desert sands and there pressed out, a boon both to us here and to our Egyptian friends. (High Command did not accept this view.) . . .

IN DIVISIONAL RESERVE
(Mar. 27th)

MARCH 27TH: SAILLY

. . . The Battalion is packing up today for a move somewhere by train; we do not know for which part of the Front the 8th Division is bound . . .

The London Gazette just received announces my promotion to the rank of temporary major . . . A month's probation in a higher rank, without the extra pay of that rank, has to be completed and a satisfactory report obtained before an officer's new rank is confirmed. I have always disliked the title 'major'; it has suggested to me, for no adequate reasons, corpulence, port and soft living. 'A captain, a colonel or a corpse' has been my text in this connection. Still, my majority is only temporary and perhaps I shall live down the sinister ring of the name.

Cf. Siegfried Sassoon:
> *'If I were fierce and bald and short of breath,*
> *I'd live with scarlet Majors at the Base,*
> *And speed glum heroes up the line to death . . .'*

ON THE SOMME FRONT
(Mar. 28th–July 7th)

APRIL 1ST: ST VAAST

. . . Following a very cold, uncomfortable night journey we detrained outside Amiens at 9 o'c [on the 28th] and proceeded ten miles northwestwards through that town to billets in this village. Seventeen men fell out of the company ranks on the way but managed to struggle into quarters hanging on to the transport vehicles . . .

131

We are in good billets; the weather is bright, though infernally cold with occasional snow showers . . .

. . . we have lightened our valises by sending home some extra kit . . . The extra weights did not affect the transport when battalions seldom moved far by road in winter; but that stationary life is likely to cease this summer.

APRIL 3RD: DERNANCOURT

. . . This morning I have been arranging billets for my battalion. In the afternoon I visited the line about La Boisselle, a dreadful area, shelled, bombed and trench-mortared, with many of the posts in mine craters; some posts only about 30 yards from the Germans cannot be entered during daylight . . .

The 8th Division is taking over the La Boisselle–Thiepval sector from the 32nd Division.

IN BRIGADE SUPPORT
(Apr. 4th–9th)

. . . 'Sandy' and I spent most of . . . two days in making ourselves acquainted with the front . . .

The village of La Boisselle is no more than a mound of rubbish; its buildings and trees have all been pulverised by shell fire. Our posts in the mine craters there exist in an inferno of rifle-grenade and trench mortar fire. The rest of the line is not quite so bad, but sniping is active throughout the sector. Almost everywhere, however, the trenches, cut out of the chalk sub-soil, have been blasted by shells, in some cases blotted out.

I have gained the impression that the troops formerly here have allowed the Germans to get the upper hand too easily. One must always hit back as hard and as often as one can; to do less is to invite the bullying to continue . . .

This area differs widely from the flat, industrial, 'over-watered' plain of Flanders. The country here is agricultural, very open and rolling, resembling the English Downs. Streams are scarce; a number of large woods stand a mile or two eastwards; trees generally border the main highways which, like the lesser roads, are unfenced. Many villages with their orchards are scattered over the land, those on the actual front having been blown to pieces in contests for this or that position. It is a fair land to look upon, not greatly scarred by war a mile or so behind the front; one can ride freely across it . . .

My bed-chamber is a solitary dug-out hewed eight foot deep in the chalk near the point of Chapes Spur, an eerie residence, like a sepulchre, dark as the grave save for the flicker from a candle whose beams dimly light up the ghostly white walls. A rough bedframe, a small table and chair from Becourt Château make up the furniture . . .

The 8th Division now forms part of . . . the Fourth Army under (Sir Henry Rawlinson).[1]

The fury of the German assaults at Verdun remains unabated . . .

IN DIVISIONAL RESERVE
(Apr. 9th–16th)

APRIL 16TH: HENENCOURT

. . . Home leave has been stopped. I do not care about this personally, but the Colonel desires me to have a short change when it reopens . . .

On the night of the 11th/12th the Germans, covered by a bombardment with gas shells, raided the trenches of the 1/Royal Irish Rifles (8th Division) and inflicted many casualties on them including a number missing. We were ordered to stand to arms in case of further developments.

Steel helmets have been issued to all ranks; formerly only the company snipers wore them. It is said that while they save some heads they cause more serious wounds to others . . .

IN THE LINE
(Apr. 17th–23rd)

APRIL 23RD: AUTHUILLE WOOD

. . . Battalion Headquarters are in good but rat-ridden shelters

[1] *The Fourth Army was formed on March 1st 1916.*

built into banks near the Ancre and some 1,100 yards from the front line. This is too far back so we have shifted them about 700 yards forward into the Wood . . .

The Brigade Commander and his staff call on us occasionally as well as officers from Divisional Headquarters. They are all qualified soldiers – and welcome visitors.

The maze of German trenches lies on rather higher ground than ours for the most part, and the protecting wire entanglements are strong. The distance between the opposing front trenches here is some 300 – 500 yards instead of approximately 150 yards as in Flanders. There is a curious, sharp little salient called 'The Nab' in the left of our line, at the head of a gully.

These trenches are much drier than were the breastworks on the Armentières front; the dug-outs, too, are deep and plentiful as well as quite substantial.

There is at times a trifling amount of hostile shelling . . . since it comes mainly from field guns no one takes much notice of it . . .

Last night parties from the battalions on either flank of ours raided the hostile trenches under cover of a bombardment by our artillery. We were not due to perform, I am happy to say. Reports allege that the raid by the 17/Highland Light Infantry . . . was most successful, from which I suppose that some prisoners were taken and casualties inflicted on the enemy. There was a considerable hostile reply which, together with our cannonade, made a devil of a row for the greater part of the night . . .

IN BRIGADE SUPPORT
(Apr. 24th–29th)

APRIL 29TH: ALBERT

. . . The accommodation for troops on the Somme front is generally very good, better than in Flanders; the bright days having, perhaps, something to do with the preference.

This red brick, or colourwashed, town, considerably mutilated by bombardments, is occasionally under long-range fire. One shell has caught the church spire, bending the figure of the Virgin Mary as if it might topple down at any minute.

Many of the streets are, however, little the worse for the War and there are quite a number of inhabitants still in the place.

In the mornings the few men available for parades carry out a short close-order drill, under Regimental Sergeant-Major Chalmers, which I always attend . . .

The Battalion finds large working parties under the Royal Engineers near the line nightly. Their tasks chiefly comprise the digging of communication and reserve trenches, constructing dug-outs, carrying stores forward, bridging ditches for artillery, and repairing roads. Beside the Aveluy road we see brand-new emplacements for heavy howitzers, dumps of shells and other stores, all carefully camouflaged beneath netting or roofs; while signallers are laying telephone cables on the ground everywhere. All this work, besides the receipt of voluminous instructions for training and organisation, points to a coming battle. These preparations cannot all be hidden from the enemy; his airmen must discover some of them; only the date of the attack is really secret . . .

. . . the remark of my friend George Boyd rather nettled me. He said 'I suppose you Regulars like this sort of life?' Hating it, and dreading the approaching battle, I replied 'As much as you do, I suppose.' . . .

IN THE LINE
(Apr. 29th–May 3rd)

MAY 2ND: AUTHUILLE WOOD

. . . 2 a.m., 30th, a furious cannonade broke out just clear of our right company; then we heard that a German raid on the adjoining battalion had failed.

Visiting our trenches a couple of hours later I found our men naturally very much on the *qui vive* and our special flank posts at their stations in case of the enemy penetrating round our sector – one can find out so little of what is happening during actions at night . . .

The same evening there was another devil of a row. Although this was further away than that of the morning, troops so close to the enemy as we are must never relax vigilance for an instant, during the hours of darkness at any rate. Late at night the disturbance was repeated. We are facing a much more active enemy than the easy-going Bavarians in the Sailly sector . . .

IN BRIGADE SUPPORT
(May 3rd–4th)

MAY 5TH: MILLENCOURT

. . . 'Sandy' . . . informed me that my leave to the United Kingdom has been signed for today. I have not been . . . Home for nine months, having declined my turns for leave because of over four months' absence from the Army in France early last year and on account of low spirits. It is now, however, imperatively necessary to get freshened up for the battle.

ON HOME LEAVE
(May 6th–17th)

Jack spent this leave partly in Scotland, partly in London.

. . . Our eighty-year-old spinster [Aunt Margaret], spry and neat, continues to rise at seven in the morning and takes a walk before breakfast. In the course of conversation she said how glad she is at my having missed 'those terrible battles in France'. It has been my custom to write her as if I were always in safety in the rear areas, and I have not yet enlightened the dear old lady whose socks, cardigans and other gifts have come to me so regularly . . .

I notice that men in London are less particular than formerly about their evening dress. The black dinner jacket and black tie have largely ousted the long black tailcoat with white tie, even at restaurant and theatre . . .

IN DIVISIONAL RESERVE
(May 19th – June 3rd)

MAY 28TH: HENENCOURT WOOD

. . . Training Programmes, submitted to a zealous High Command even before we left the line, are scheduled to cover $6\frac{1}{2}$

hours daily, commencing on our first day in reserve. Sunday the 21st was, however, granted as a day of rest . . . But the fine-looking programmes, all neatly typed, have been pretty well ruined. Since the 26th half our dutymen have been required to spend the whole of most nights on fatigues near the line, and although they proceed there and back in motor transport the men are too tired on their return after dawn for more exercise that morning. Besides, they are often very wet from heavy showers of rain.

High Command appear unable to understand that troops in the front line get practically no rest during their tour of four to six days there, and that they must have a little rest on coming out if they are to be physically and mentally fit for the intense strain of battles. These very detailed Training Programmes seem to regimental officers as little more than eyewash to alleviate the suspicions of Superior Authority that without them troops will perform no training, or the wrong kind of training. The programmes are, however, generally cut down to meet day-to-day conditions, experienced commanding officers using some discretion in the matter . . .

This entry and the next are most revealing (and see p. 53). The rapidly expanding British Army was now in a cruel dilemma: on the one hand there was a vast amount of manual work to be done; on the other, the new recruits and formations badly needed training. Haig told the C.I.G.S. (Sir William Robertson) on February 3rd 1916: 'I regard the Labour Battalions as quite essential . . .' But Robertson was finding it hard enough to obtain reinforcements of soldiers, let alone such 'extras' as these. So the infantry, already destined for the greatest enterprise yet undertaken by the B.E.F., had to go on exhausting itself with fatigues.

Then, on May 17th, Fourth Army Headquarters issued a 31-page pamphlet of 'Tactical Notes', for issue down to captains. This became the training 'bible' of all units concerned in the coming attack, and this was the reason for the 'High Command' preoccupation to which Jack refers.

No doubt there were instances of unreasonable demands; no doubt some intermediate commanders could have deployed their resources better, and avoided some harassment of the troops. But fundamentally, the contradiction between elaborate training and constant work was insoluble. The result was that Haig's statement to Kitchener in March remained true for most of the year: 'I have not got an Army in France really, but a collection of divisions untrained for the Field. The actual fighting Army will be evolved from them.'

In the face of the German Army, this evolution proved appallingly costly. The reason for it lies in the reluctance of the Government to rally the nation fully behind the fighting men.

JUNE 4TH

We have been having a hard task to find the nightly quota of labourers to help with preparations for the battle.

At 4.30 a.m. on the 1st all the officers, with skeleton companies, left camp to take part in a large-scale Divisional Practice Attack . . . Flags represented the enemy's redoubts and strong points while his trenches had been traced partially with sods of earth. At the end of the exercise conferences were held on the spot to discuss errors and improvements. The men are pretty fit; the fourteen-mile march there and back did us good. But the practice was not complete and thorough enough to provide real lessons for the small number of troops engaged in it . . .

The Battalion is moving forward this afternoon, following our fortnight's 'training' here. We have done our level best to instruct all ranks and tune them up for the battle ahead. But the very heavy all-nightly and daily fatigues – carrying stores to the front and other manual labour, in the forward area, often under shell fire, often in the rain – have swallowed up almost all the officers and men who should have been putting the finishing touches to practice for operations, and who in my opinion are still not PROPERLY TRAINED, although full of courage . . .

We have just heard that the British and German Fleets met in a great battle off Jutland on May 31st and that the enemy's ships, turning tail, evaded total destruction. The news is, however, not too reassuring; many of our vessels have been sunk.

IN BRIGADE SUPPORT
(June 4th–7th)

... Yesterday I took company commanders and others to reconnoitre the line just south of Authuille Wood, the Ovillers–La Boisselle sub-sector, an evil neighbourhood. The day was wet and we all got soaked.

Last night Sergeant T. Stewart, one of our best non-commissioned officers, was killed after having served with the Battalion ever since its arrival in France in 1914 ... I commenced to read the burial service myself; but the loss of my friend was too much for me and I could not carry it through ...

H.M.S. *Hampshire* has been lost off the Orkney Islands with all hands, including Lord Kitchener, Secretary of State for War, together with his staff ... I have twice spoken with this tall, impressive, reserved war-lord – just a word or two – when he was Commander-in-Chief in India about 1908.

IN THE LINE
(June 8th–12th)

JUNE 12TH: AUTHUILLE WOOD

... Constant heavy showers keep everything damp; many shelters are leaking like sieves ...

While the battle storm blows up in front we have to ride out a gale of paper at our backs. There are sheaves of orders, amendments, counter-orders, returns and reports to be dealt with. But, by the Grace of God, we may be able to overcome all our enemies, the Germans in front, the Staff in rear. If writing can win a campaign our foes may soon be at our mercy. (This reference to the Staff is perhaps less than just to a gallant, able and painstaking body of men. Nevertheless, their paper barrage was blinding at times.—J.L.J.)

IN DIVISIONAL RESERVE

JUNE 18TH: HENENCOURT WOOD

... Our companies, robbed by nightly fatigues near the front of most of their men have been carrying out the customary scale of parades and training ...

On rides round the country for many weeks past one has seen the battle omens thickening. Banks beside once quiet lanes are lined with heavy guns and howitzers in their emplacements. Villages, leafy woods and farmyards have become crammed with soldiers and stores. Camouflaged tarpaulins on the open ground hide great mounds of shells. Field telephone poles and cables mark fresh lines of communication connecting all units with their headquarters. Throughout every night is heard the clatter of trucks along the new narrow-gauge railways, the rumble of artillery and transport on the roads, the tramp of infantry on relief or with pick and shovel – as well as arms – proceeding patiently, and often under fire, like the others, to their tasks on light bridges, more trenches and dug-outs. The whole area bears signs of battle and I detest the prospect of another murderous assault . . .

JUNE 21ST: HENENCOURT WOOD

A draft of four young officers and thirty other ranks joined us yesterday. But for the operations ahead the former would shortly be going off on courses to learn their job – which should have been taught them before they left England – while some of the men seem to be rather 'crocks', likely to become hospital patients before long . . .

Constant German attacks [at Verdun] ever since February have not succeeded in gaining the French main positions although important forts have fallen . . .

IN BRIGADE SUPPORT
(June 22nd–24th)

JUNE 25TH: LONG VALLEY

. . . Before dawn yesterday all officers visited the front near Ovillers to refresh our memories about the divisional sector for the assault.

Heavy rain-storms, some of them torrential, have soaked everything . . .

Yesterday our intense, ceaseless artillery bombardment of the German positions by pieces of all calibres commenced to pave the way for the approaching assault. In the afternoon I rode to a small crest to watch it. At times the village of Pozières, two miles beyond our front trenches, to the northeast, was being completely smothered with shells, while in their turn Thiepval, Contalmaison and Fricourt were subjected to the hurricane.

Today, following church parade, I again rode a short way forward to watch our cannonade which, delivered in bursts, continues day and night, sometimes drawing a severe reply from the enemy's guns which have not yet, however, found our bivouac lying in a fold of the ground.

Overhead large squadrons of our aeroplanes are constantly in view and appear to have driven practically all hostile air-craft out of the skies, including three captive observation balloons which I have just seen sink to the ground wrapped in orange-coloured flames.

IN THE LINE
(June 25th–28th)

JUNE 28TH: OPPOSITE OVILLERS–LA BOISSELLE

... I have been writing my orders for the two companies acting under my command when the battle opens ...

Colonel Sandilands and his headquarters officers, including myself, have visited all our posts soon after dawn daily, proceeding thither by way of Hodder, Argyll and Ryecroft 'Streets' (communication trenches) which, together with many portions of the front trenches, have been severely knocked about by shell fire ...

Before us No Man's Land is some 750 yards wide – exceptionally wide – the long, rank, yellow grass plentifully sprinkled with bright scarlet wild poppies. The country ahead is perfectly open, treeless and devoid of buildings save for those lying in broken heaps in the shell-blasted villages.

One thousand yards in front of the battalion left flank, and on rather higher ground, lie the pulverised ruins of Ovillers amid a maze of trenches and posts half a mile in depth, heavily wired and reported to be full of machine guns. This 'fortress' is the First Objective of the 23rd Infantry Brigade.

Slightly below us and 1,200 yards to our right front are the ashes of La Boisselle, similarly fortified, the First Objective of the 34th Division.

These two villages form the horns of a re-entrant in the hostile line with the shallow Mash valley, to be crossed by our battalions, leading into it . . .

About two miles northwards, on still higher ground, the entrenched ruins of Thiepval face the 32nd Division.

A complete system of German trenches, elaborately wired and apparently fully manned, links up every inch of their front.

Just over a mile beyond Ovillers, further up the ridge, is the Second Objective of the 23rd Brigade, a strongly wired and entrenched line immediately in front of the village of Pozières. The Third Objective is a good half-mile in advance of the Second, on the crest of Pozières Ridge.

During the night of the 25th/26th the 2/Royal Berkshires (8th Divn.) successfully executed a surprise raid on the Germans and found those of the enemy not accounted for in their trench singing happily in dug-outs 30 to 40 feet below earth notwithstanding our bombardment – singing, that is, till our hand-bombs crashed down the dug-out stairs among them.

Since the 25th smoke shells have been added to our H.E. bombardment; on the 27th, gas was set free as well, by special Royal Engineer personnel, from cylinders placed in recesses made for them in the front parapet, the discharge being from a nozzle at the end of a long pipe.

All the time there is a buzz of work in our headquarters office in a tiny dug-out as orders and amendments from Higher Command, besides reports from companies, arrive.

Practically all the time, too, the air reverberates to the drum of our cannonade, the shells from which we hope are blasting the enemy and his positions into powder. The concussion from one of our 18-pounder batteries close behind our headquarters is stunning; we get scarcely any sleep.

The German counter-bombardment is often heavy. We have suffered considerable casualties, and many parts of the trenches have been blown in; the field telephone lines also have been constantly cut. Repairs to parapets, communication trenches and cables; the removal of wounded and the nightly porterage forward of stores for three-quarters of a mile, entail constant very hard work for almost all the men. There are for them besides these duties the finding of sentries, and patrols in No Man's Land to keep touch with the enemy and with his doings as well as may be . . .

I confess to feeling the strain of the preparation and waiting.

IN BRIGADE SUPPORT
(June 29th–30th)

. . . The bombardment of the enemy's positions continues with unabated fury.

Our lads are in grand form, quite carefree, itching to cross the parapet to meet the Hun, and sure of victory. I wonder how much of this admirable spirit will survive the German fusillade?

A few days ago I met a staff acquaintance from the division which is to follow the 8th, and must have said goodbye to him in rather a final manner. He assured me, however, that the enemy have no chance of holding up our assault, covered as it will be by such a terrific cannonade following that of the last seven days; and that his division is due to take over Pozières from our brigade tomorrow evening. Having known such staff optimisms to be unwarranted before, now we remain sceptical . . .

The German retaliation to our artillery fire has been less, even little, for the past two days . . .

THE BATTLE OF THE SOMME
(July 1st 1916)

Leaving Millencourt after sunset on June 30th, the headquarters and the four companies of the 2/Cameronians, some 20 officers and 650 other ranks, filed with intervals by road to Albert . . . The River Ancre was next crossed by a temporary wooden bridge and we followed along the marshy valley to Aveluy. The track then mounted the slopes eastwards until we entered Preston communication trench for the last part of the 5-mile march to our Assembly Positions in Ribble Street, with

Battalion Headquarters at Ovillers Post close by. The assembly was completed shortly after midnight without incident.

Reports were to hand that our bombardment had well cut the German wire; that exit lanes had been made in our wire entanglements and temporarily blocked with chevaux de frise; and that the new assembly trenches close to our front line had been completed after hard digging in the chalk. All fresh work, visible to the enemy, was naturally done at night . . .

About 4.30 a.m. on July 1st, following an almost sleepless night of work and tension, with the deafening cannonade, too, still ringing in our ears, I rose, shaved – there was not enough water for washing – slipped on tunic, boots, accoutrements and silver spurs in order to be 'properly dressed' for, likely enough, the last time. Holden, who had cleaned my uniform and belts as well as possible, gave me a final brush before a breakfast of tea, bread and butter only, the more solid of our mess rations having been lost during shelling on the way up the previous night. The meal over, I proceeded to Ribble Street to see that 'D' and 'B' Companies (from right to left), which I was to lead forward behind the 2/West Yorkshire, were 'present and correct'.

At 6.25 on a still, fine, hazy morning our artillery reopened the bombardment after a lull. This immediately drew from the German guns a heavy reply.

Thirty-five minutes later the intensity of our barrage increased to drum fire and I led my two companies up Hodder Street to the rear of the West Yorkshire in Houghton Street, as well as in new assembly trenches off it, which had been for some time, and still were, under the terrible blast from the enemy's howitzers.

At 7.22 a.m. our mortars joined in the tumult. Simultaneously the 2/Middlesex and the 2/Devonshire, climbing out of their trenches by short ladders placed on the fire-steps, crept through the lanes in our wire. Each battalion then extended in four waves to cover about 300 yards of frontage and crawled forward to begin crossing the six to eight hundred yards of No Man's Land.

Eight minutes afterwards, on the tick of Zero Hour, and following the explosion of mines under the La Boisselle salient, our field gun barrage, till then falling on the first German trench line, lifted to a further line. Both battalions, rising to their feet, now advanced in quick time through the rank, knee-deep grass, the four waves at one hundred paces interval, to close on the foe with the bayonet.

A hail of bullets from shell holes clear of the blasted German trenches in front, as well as from either flank at La Boisselle and Ovillers, presently mowed down the three leading waves now breaking into a charge. In spite of this, about 200 of the Middlesex pressed into the enemy's front line, and a few even into the support line in rear. Scarcely any of the Devonshire, which had also suffered terribly, were able to enter the hostile trenches at all. Those of both battalions who succeeded in gaining an entry fought hand-to-hand with bayonet and bomb till they had either become casualties or were forced to retire some two hours later to the scanty cover afforded by the grass and weeds in No Man's Land, there to await the friendly mantle of night before withdrawing to their lines of that morning . . .

To the right (34th Division) and left (25th and 70th Brigades) of the 23rd Brigade, the attack fared just as badly. The 8th Division was stopped in its tracks. Its opponents were the 180th Regiment of the 26th Reserve Division.

About 7 o'c . . . I reached the junction of Hodder and Houghton Streets at the head of 'D' and 'B' Companies which, in single file and with intervals between platoons, extended some distance back inside the trench first-named.

For over an hour my men, crouching at the less exposed side of the trench, were subjected – as were also the West Yorkshire – to an infernal pounding from the enemy's howitzers. I could see nothing of what was going on in front . . . Time and again we were covered with soil and débris thrown up by the shells. The strain on the waiting men was very great, so I took to joking about the dirt scattered over my well-cut uniform, while dusting it off with a handkerchief.

We knew at 7.30 that the assault had started through hearing the murderous rattle of German machine guns, served without a break, notwithstanding our intense bombardment which had been expected to silence them. The fire from these guns periodically sprayed the crest just above our heads.

Towards 7.45 the West Yorkshire began moving forward down the gentle slope into the furnace. Apparently they advanced across the open – I saw those near me climb out of their trench. The enemy's machine guns, some 1,400 yards from my position, now swept the crest like a hurricane and with such accuracy that many of the poor fellows were shot at once. This battalion had 280 casualties in traversing the 600 yards to our front line.

For the past hour, or thereabouts, groups of wounded had been dribbling back along Hodder Street, among them, latterly, several who were unhurt, or only slightly so, but who had given way to terror. One of these, a fine-looking sergeant, ran past me; he had lost his self-control; it would have been useless to stop him. Presently an unwounded private nearly collided with me. Him I seized by the shoulder and asked what train he intended catching, saying he need not hurry as there were plenty of them. We then posted a sergeant in the trench to steady down any more who might be travelling back so fast, as I feared their example might unsettle my own men.

A little after 8 o'c it became our turn to go forward. I had decided that we had better do so by the shell-blasted communication trenches rather than across the open ground . . . Our progress was hindered by having to crush past orderlies and walking wounded proceeding along the trench to the medical aid post, as well as those who could not be removed at once and others past remedy. Round one traverse I came on three Yorkshiremen, two of them shattered, the third sitting quite naturally, but dead . . .

Presently we arrived at the 'Russian tunnel' leading into the front line. It had been blown in in places, and was full of dead, wounded and stretcher-bearers. At the end I met a badly-hurt fine young Devonshire subaltern who faintly enquired how things were going. I lied 'Splendidly, my boy', before turning away to hide my feelings.

During this unpleasant journey my companies suffered relatively few casualties.

146

About 8.30 a.m. I reached the front trench, then occupied by various parties belonging to the battalions preceding us, and by one company of the West Yorkshire, together with wounded who had been able to return from the hellish arena ahead.

From the first news that I could glean it appeared to be highly improbable that any of the Middlesex, Devons or West Yorks were then in action beyond No Man's Land; no communication with them, however, was possible. All was quiet on our front.

The sun had now dispersed the morning haze and the day promised to be warm. On the upward slope behind us lay many bodies of the West Yorkshire . . . No Man's Land was strewn with prone forms; up against the hostile wire they showed thickly, the regimental helmet badge being easily recognised on some. Not all of these were casualties, however; among them were men driven out of the German trenches and taking what cover they could in shell holes amid the long grass decked with sunlit scarlet poppies on our side of the enemy's wire entanglements. These men remained still as the dead to avoid drawing fire till darkness should screen their escape; others not so close to danger would make a dash singly or crawl patiently towards our trenches, sniped at on the way.

About this time our 18-pounder barrage was brought back to the Ovillers line from its expedition further afield.

On arriving at the forward end of St Vincent Street tunnel, I had to make up my mind forthwith what was to be done. The situation was that 'D' and 'B' Companies were shortly due in the front trench; they presently reported being so. This continuous trench held also men of other units, and in the jumble I could not for a time find the West Yorkshire commander, although he was said to be somewhere at hand. It was reported that three of his companies had gone 'over the top' and my orders were to follow this battalion and to consolidate the First Objective. But what had become of these companies, or indeed of any companies that had gone forward? And had any Objectives been gained to consolidate? It seemed obvious that in our sector the attack had failed completely although occasional shots were heard in the German lines from points very hard to locate.

One or two returned wounded furnished me with vague items of information (the only word received till now) to the effect that parties of Middlesex and Devons were holding out in some trench and at some hour, neither of which could be specified. With evidence pointing in opposite directions the strain of deciding where one's duty lay was very great. On the one hand, was it pure madness to take my companies forward? On the other, what would be said of the 90th (2/Cameronians, Scottish Rifles) were they in any manner to desert comrades on the battlefield or evade making an effort to carry out at least part of their orders?

At this moment a message from Major Savile, 2/Middlesex, in the enemy's second trench, asked for help. Although the time on the message was rather old when I got the appeal, some definite information was given on which I could act. Feeling that we must honourably try to reinforce him, I stepped back several paces to take a running jump on the parapet, sound my hunting horn and wave my waiting men on, when a signaller thrust into my hand a message, timed 9.45, from the adjutant and sent by orderly (the telephone lines being broken), saying that no further advance was to take place without fresh orders. What a relief to be rid of such a grim responsibility!

During the day . . . both companies, assisted by sections of the 15th Field Company, Royal Engineers, were engaged in repairing the inside of the trenches under continuous shell fire which, although mainly from field guns, caused considerable casualties . . . Save for occasional short bursts of firing silence reigned on the other side of No Man's Land.

The Medical Officers – to whom I had given my 'ration' of morphia – together with the stretcher-bearers, had their hands full. Only wounded able to walk, however, could withdraw before nightfall, and they ran heavy risks in their passage. Stretcher cases had mostly to wait till dark, when they were carried back in the open . . .

In the afternoon the telephone line to Battalion Headquarters at Ovillers Post was again working, following frequent breakage by shells. This repair simplified the sending of reports on the situation and on casualties besides saving orderlies and time . . .

In the afternoon I was ordered to prepare to lead 'A' and 'C'
Companies – still behind in Ribble Street – in a fresh attack,
covered by artillery, to be delivered on the Divisional front on a
limited scale at 5 p.m. The few unused infantry in the Division
and the 56th Infantry Brigade, 19th Division, were to be
employed as well . . .

At 3.30 o'c I again reported the presence of hostile machine
guns about La Boisselle and Ovillers. But in consequence of the
proposed new offensive I was instructed urgently to send out a
patrol to discover if the German line opposite our right company was held, and by whom. Accordingly, as soon as arrangements could be made, 2/Lieut Fraser with one sergeant and
five privates from 'D' Company stole forward. This was
the smallest number of men we could employ, compatible with
carrying out the order; they were told to go very carefully,
returning at once if seriously fired on.

We were thrilled to watch, about 5 p.m., British infantry
groups swarming ahead south of La Boisselle, and hoped that
their advance would make Fraser's mission less dangerous. But
later the patrol reported back in our trenches having been
heavily fired at; Fraser was missing, believed killed, to my pro-
found sorrow.

Shortly before the hour of the meditated attack we were informed of its cancellation owing to the possibility that some
of our troops might still be holding out in the German trenches.
Although this could not be verified owing to the breakdown of
all communication across No Man's Land, the risk of shelling
any such was too great to be taken. In any case another assault,
hastily prepared, covered by a barrage inferior to that of the
morning, against a resolute enemy in position and on the alert,
and with few really fresh troops, seemed to me bound to fail.
By now, however, I was almost past caring, personally,
whether we attacked or not . . .

At 7 p.m. a message arrived to say that we were being relieved
that night . . .

Two hours later Preliminary Orders came for our relief by
a battalion of the 12th Division which subsequently took over
from us without much interruption. Thereafter 'B and 'D'
Companies, stolid as in the morning, in spite of their battering,

filed back . . . to join the remainder of the Battalion . . . The reaction from this dreadful day, one of the worst I have ever experienced, was so great that, having seen to the relief of my companies, I was forced to ask the Colonel's permission to withdraw ahead of him. Accompanied, therefore, by an orderly kindly sent by 'Sandy', I quitted the field on which such brilliant success had been expected that fine summer morning, leaving behind, dead or maimed, in that vast garden of scarlet wild poppies, some 90% of the officers and about 60% of the other ranks of the twelve infantry battalions of my division.

Exhausted and depressed, I stumbled into our bivouac at Millencourt at 6 o'c on the morning of the 2nd . . .

July 1st 1916 was a freak catastrophe in the British Army's history. Only on the extreme right of the Fourth Army, beside the French (whose attack came as a surprise to the enemy), were any significant gains made and held. The total British casualties for the day were 57,470 officers and men, of whom over 20,000 were killed and missing.

The losses of the 8th Division are given in the Official History as 5,121; its neighbour in III Corps, the 34th Division, lost 6,380.

There are slight discrepancies between the figures given for the 23rd Infantry Brigade by the Official History, and those of the History of the Division ('The Eighth Division in the War, 1914–1918'):

Unit	Off. History		Div. History	
	Off.	*O.R.*	*Off.*	*O.R.*
2/Middlesex	22	601	22	600
2/Devonshire	17	433	16	415
2/West Yorkshire	8	421	16	490
2/Cameronians	—	—	6	65
Total	*Incomplete*		60	1570

Jack tells us that in 2/Cameronians the losses (almost all in 'B' and 'D' Companies, which he commanded) were:

	Killed	Wounded	Missing
Officers	1	5	—
Other ranks	1	60	4

150

There is little doubt that these low figures were mainly due to his own discretion and initiative in keeping his men under cover, and avoiding rash enterprises as far as possible. It was laid down in G.H.Q. Instructions that '. . . the assaulting columns must go right through above ground *(my stress) to the objective in successive waves or lines . . .' We have seen from Jack's narrative what the cost of this dictum was to the 2/West Yorkshires, advancing in Brigade support. Untrained New Army officers naturally felt more inhibited at setting aside the regulations of High Command than Old Army men, working together in such harmony as that between Jack and Colonel Sandilands.*

The relative immunity of the Cameronians was small consolation, however, for the massacre of the Division. By early afternoon, says the Official History, 'the Germans were again in complete possession of their defences opposite the 8th Division . . .' La Boisselle was not taken until July 4th (by the 19th Division) and Ovillers not until July 16th (28th Division).

In all, the Battle of the Somme, after this disastrous opening, lasted for 140 more days: a staggering feat of courage and endurance. The final cost of it, as stated in the British Official History (1916, vol. ii, p. xvi; published 1938), was:

British	*419,654*
French	*204,253*
	623,907
German	*680,000 (approximate).*

'The Somme,' wrote a German General Staff Officer, 'was the muddy grave of the German field army, and of the faith in the infallibility of German leadership . . .'

What this meant, in simple terms, was that after this battle the Germans no longer enjoyed the marked superiority over the improvised British armies which was the motif of 1915 and 1916, and the refrain of so much of Jack's diary up to this point.

Much bitter fighting was required to produce this result; none of it, fortunately, ever quite so barren as that of July 1st. Of that occasion, the Official History says: 'The prime causes of the general failure were the strength and depth of the German position and its stout defence by our opponents . . .'

Jack says much the same thing in different words: 'We relied far too much on our artillery fire not only pulverising the hostile works – which it did – but also on its maiming or cowing into inertia practically all the defenders of each trench line in succession – which it did NOT. Indeed the enemy, with great acumen, generally vacated their blasted works effectively to man shell holes clear of our barrage, from which they were able to maintain very heavy small-arm fire during our assault.

'On 1st July twelve imperfectly trained battalions of the 8th Division were opposed by two fully trained German battalions (180th Infantry Regiment). These lost 7 officers and 273 other ranks only on that day . . .'

A remarkable German eye-witness account of the 8th Division's attack may be found in the British Official History (1916, vol. i, pp. 392–3). It makes harrowing reading from any point of view, and ends with the very fair statement: 'It was an amazing spectacle of unexampled gallantry, courage and bulldog determination on both sides.'

It must never be forgotten that the German Army of that period really was very good indeed.

THE MOVE TO THE LOOS SALIENT
(July 2nd–7th)

JULY 7TH: BARLIN

We all did justice to a late breakfast in bivouac at Millencourt on Sunday the 2nd, as only snatches of food had been available since the evening of June 30th.

I have been feeling the effects of the terrible strain on the 1st, wondering if my decisions on that day were right, until a mountain of doubt was lifted through being told that I could have done no more.

Comrades, however, were soon back again in their usual good spirits. For one thing, the Battalion has been extremely lucky in escaping severe loss; for another, healthy young soldiers recover with remarkable rapidity from the most gruelling experiences when they have a good sleep and a square meal.

That evening, the 2nd, we marched 5 miles and entrained . . .

IN THE LOOS SALIENT
(July 7th–Aug. 22nd)

. . . In fine weather, we have been cleaning up; all ranks had a much-needed wash at the divisional baths after church parade on the 9th. Besides reorganising, the usual parades are held, including a short close-order drill under the Regimental-Sergeant-Major. On the 19th, General Hudson, the Divisional Commander, came to see companies on parade and extend his congratulations to the Battalion for, its conduct on the Somme . . .

This village stands in the grubby, industrial area of Lens, with mines and slag-heaps all around, so different from the clean countryside behind the Somme, where the village walls are festooned with roses.

To my deep sorrow, death has been busy among my friends these last few days . . .

The 8th Division has been transferred from the III Corps, Fourth Army, to the I Corps, First Army . . .

IN THE FRONT TRENCHES
(July 14th–26th)

. . . Our front and support trench lines are in very good order, well protected by wire entanglements and furnished adequately with strong dug-outs some 15 to 20 feet deep. The German front trenches are generally 100 to 150 yards from ours, across a jungle of long rank grass, weeds and poppies . . .

Each side mines assiduously to blow up the enemy, to wreck his defensive works and to destroy his mine shafts; sometimes the greater part of a company becomes casualties from the explosion of one mine. These mines have thrown up great cratered mounds of chalky soil, many of them touching one another; the near lips of the craters, usually the scene of severe encounters immediately after the explosion, are held respectively by British and German posts, often no more than 20–30 yards apart – within hand-bombing distance. Besides mines, there are shell, trench mortar, machine gun and grenade fire to contend with, in addition to sniping.

The sanguinary battles staged here and the mix-up of trenches have turned the salient into a huge cemetery, some seven miles wide and three deep in the middle . . . Frequently the stench is horrible . . .

JULY 26TH: CAMBRIN

. . . At daybreak on the 17th the Royal Engineers exploded one of our defensive mines considered to be a greater danger to us than to the enemy. We watched the blade tips of the German spades throwing the earth over the far lip of the crater to form a post. That night a bombing party of ours, under Lieut McLellan secured the near lip with little loss; but the sappers digging a trench out to it suffered a number of casualties. Two nights later the consolidation of the near lip of the crater in our line was completed. The staff appear to become unduly excited about a minor matter like this; I was kept up during most of the night reporting progress on the telephone . . .

On the night of the 18th/19th German bombing parties attempted to rush two of our sapheads. In one case our post improperly 'withdrew', sustaining casualties in so doing. In the other post of four men, two, Privates Thompson and Brown, were severely wounded by bombs; nevertheless, the former at once leapt out of his trench and charged the three Germans, capturing one while the others bolted . . .

IN BRIGADE SUPPORT
(July 26th–30th)

JULY 30TH: GINCHY

. . . During the 13-day tour in the line the companies, constantly under trench mortar, rifle grenade and sniping fire, and liable to be blown up by mines at any moment, have had 48 casualties, including one subaltern . . .

With a good supply of shells nowadays – in spite of the demands on the Somme – we can afford to answer the Germans effectively and 'soft-pedal' any aggressiveness. Standing up to an adversary is almost always the safest course to pursue in the field – in any walk of life – besides being the course to maintain one's self-respect. Troops tamely submitting to the enemy's fire without retaliating are likely to be victimised still more; those hitting back hard and swiftly have at least the satisfaction of making the enemy pay in full for any damage inflicted on themselves. I have told our men that they should consider any molestation by the Germans as a personal impertinence ...

One bother is ... having to master a new set of Routine and Standing Orders on joining each different Corps. Much Army routine could surely be standardised, thus saving the inconvenience and work involved through differences in various units ...

It is cheering to see our aeroplanes chasing those of the enemy every other day, and to hear that they are doing him a lot of damage. The Royal Flying Corps have been perfectly splendid throughout the War ...

The reference to Corps routine is significant; Corps commanders exercised a special form of authority which is often overlooked. Divisions came and went, but Corps sectors remained largely static (except for the Canadian and Anzac Corps, which usually entered and left the line in a body). A corps commander would rarely have less than 50,000 men under his orders; often he would command more men than the Duke of Wellington ever disposed of in battle. Yet most of these generals remained semi-anonymous figures, with little opportunity of winning distinction, despite their imposing commands. The frustrations are obvious; equally, the temptation to 'put on a show', to plan and carry out 'minor' operations which would indicate keenness and ability – unless, of course, something went wrong, which was always liable to happen in the face of the German Army. It was then that costly tragedies occurred; an example of such was the action at Fromelles on July 19th/20th 1916, in which the 8th Division's artillery took part, and which cost over 7,000 casualties without procuring any useful result whatever. Not all Corps commanders were guilty of such dangerous ambitions; but they were always a factor to reckon with. Enemy and Allied armies were similarly afflicted.

IN DIVISIONAL RESERVE
(July 31st–Aug. 7th)

AUGUST 6TH: LA BOURSE

. . . The commander of the First Army inspected the Battalion on the 2nd, the pipers playing companies on to parade to the 'Gathering of the Grahams'. Making no remarks in our presence he afterwards complained about the turn-out of the companies. He is, no doubt, unaware that the spare clothing which we were ordered to hand to other units on the Somme has not been replaced, and that the men have just been in trenches for seventeen days, the first thirteen pretty strenuous.

(The criticism of Sir Charles Monro may have been justified. First-class troops ought always to be smart, and clean when possible. We have not nowadays, however, got properly trained officers and other ranks who know the standards required of good soldiers. Moreover, much trench life, where personal tidiness is out of the question, is apt to lead to carelessness in the matter of dress.—J.L.J.) . . .

IN THE LINE
(Aug. 7th–11th)

AUGUST 11TH: HOHENZOLLERN SECTOR

. . . Part of our lines are in the famous Hohenzollern Redoubt . . . It is a disgusting sector with the parapets full of bodies, débris and rats.

In addition to other missiles the Germans keep delivering into our line a good many 'oilcans'. These large trench mortar bombs burst with a tremendous explosion. One may see them coming high in the air if one uses one's eyes, and dodge them by a display of agility if there is time to run round a traverse. On rounds yesterday, however, I came on four of our men killed in a bay of the support trench by one 'can' . . .

The Germans facing us at present are bold and active. Although the Army Commander may not like the look of our clothes I doubt whether any of his battalions strikes at the enemy harder than we do . . .

IN BRIGADE SUPPORT
(Aug. 11th–14th)

AUGUST 14TH

... At 8 p.m. on the 12th the Germans opened a most severe barrage on a sector of the trenches held by the 2/West Yorkshire and then raided them. My Battalion stood to arms in case it was wanted; but the affair presently blew over without our having to do more than send a lot of reports to Brigade Headquarters.

Yesterday, Sunday, I was president of a Court of Inquiry in connection with the raid. The West Yorks had a good many casualties, including several men missing, took four Bavarian prisoners and gave the enemy a hot reception. I cannot say who was to blame for our losses and the damage done to our works; the Germans appear to have been the principal offenders ...

On recent visits to Battalion Headquarters the Divisional Commander has remarked that I shall have to be going off soon to command another battalion. I have replied that I prefer to stay with the 90th ...

Reports describe British and French progress on the Somme from time to time, or the defeat of German counter-attacks – the first at fearful cost, we believe ...

IN THE LINE
(Aug. 15th–19th)

AUGUST 19TH

... Yesterday our sappers blew a mine on our front, an event calling for a mass of reports: its exact position; damage done to the enemy's parapet; damage to ours; the German reaction; a description of our action; together with other details, casualties among them. I left 'Sandy' to concoct his version of the affair and went to perform the morning rounds on his behalf ...
... the trenches are very wet ...

*   *   *

EXTRACT FROM GENERAL JACK'S
EPILOGUE TO PART III

. . For me, personally, the period covered by this chapter was far less eventful than those described in the other chapters of the Diary. As second-in-command for most of the time I generally enjoyed a calm life at Battalion Headquarters, the good fare provided there by Mess-Corporal Goodall, the attention of my servants in turn, Riflemen Poole, Holden, and others for shorter periods . . .

I was in poor spirits during most of this time. The War – especially the Somme – the loss of friends and other matters, rudely shook one's Faith, and not enough responsible occupation as second-in-command gave too much time to think about it. It did not seem possible that a gentleman could abandon, so fully as Providence appeared to have done, his servants to the cruelties of the world on the specious grounds that human agency must have a free hand.

'Except ye *believe in* (not *serve*) Me, ye shall in no wise enter My Kingdom' – a harsh threat, I thought, that no gentleman would utter to any servitor who, not in this world of his own accord, nevertheless carried out his duties to the best of his ability, maybe giving his life for them.

Well, I laughed, if this is to be the reward of Service, however lacking the Faith, many will have scored over Providence by giving All, free, gratis and for little or nothing, for the honour, perhaps, of a grave on a battlefield.

As is told in Chapter IV of my diaries, I went my way in Pride and Temper until in the course of years mental balance on this subject, temporarily upset by strain, had been restored.

Ingratitude is a bad fault. In the chapter just mentioned the large slices of good fortune meted out to me have been thankfully acknowledged. My military successes have been, I believe, due mainly to 'luck' sent from Above.

IV

Commanding 2/West Yorkshire
Regiment, France and Belgium

THE WEST YORKSHIRE REGIMENT

The West Yorkshire Regiment, which Jack now joined, was an older corps than the Cameronians. It was raised in 1685, and its first Battle Honour is the siege and assault of Namur in 1695, when the Regiment lost 10 officers and 129 other ranks. As the 14th Foot it won further Honours in the siege of Gibraltar, at Corunna, at Waterloo, at Sebastopol, in New Zealand, and in India on various occasions. As the West Yorkshires, it took part in the relief of Ladysmith. There is strong evidence that the originals of Rudyard Kipling's 'Soldiers Three', Privates Learoyd, Mulvaney and Ortheris, were in fact men of the West Yorkshires whom Kipling met and chatted with on hot sleepless nights when he was a young journalist on 'The Pioneer' at Allahabad. The Regiment was serving there at that time, and its pre-war components always included a proportion of Irishmen and Cockneys.

It is now amalgamated with the East Yorkshire Regiment to form The Prince of Wales's Own Regiment of Yorkshire. This amalgamation is less unhappy than some, since the East Yorkshires were its immediate followers in the old Army List, the 15th Foot.

IN DIVISIONAL RESERVE

AUGUST 27TH: BEUVRY

On the 22nd I was suddenly ordered to assume command of the 2/West Yorkshire Regiment ... vice Lieut-Colonel Hume-Spry, D.S.O., who has left for another appointment. So, an hour later, I reluctantly quitted my old battalion, and followed by my trusty soldier servant, Holden, carrying my kit, walked along a few hundred yards of trench in the Hohenzollern Support Line to take up my new duties. On the way one of our aeroplanes, hit by an anti-aircraft shell, comes swirling down a short distance away like a piece of tin, with no hope for its crew. A sickening sight!

My new battalion has a fine reputation, and after I have

'taken over' the officers welcome me most kindly, although no regiment likes being commanded by a stranger. Their friendship with the 90th is, however, a help to me.

The West Yorks have had a bad time lately, being twice raided by the Germans in the past few weeks, suffering many casualties and a severe shaking. My first business is to gain their confidence . . .

Our first day out of the line is spent resting, cleaning, inspecting arms and equipment. Thereafter, except on Sundays when we hold church parade, companies carry out the Standing Scale of Parades which I have drawn up.[1] A regular daily routine covering in due proportion all the training necessary saves time, prevents misunderstandings, and reduces the repetition of orders . . . On the conclusion of the morning's exercises, companies, having adjusted their equipment, march past me in column of route with bayonets fixed . . . Tactical training is equally carefully carried out, and where the whole battalion cannot act together companies adhere to the programme individually . . .

On the afternoon of the 25th the Divisional Horse Show took place nearby. The transport men and grooms are so keen and hardworking that the vehicles, horses and harness were fit to appear in London or anywhere. The British Army has an incurable habit of polishing up for all functions, to the amused delight of our French friends, for whom there is no topic but the War, and who regard us as being rather mad in this respect. Nevertheless, polish, when it does not interfere with efficiency, is of great value in assisting to maintain esprit de corps . . .

AUGUST 31ST

Welcome news; Roumania has joined the Allies and the Italians have scored a success. The help of anyone, be he Jew or Gentile, is gratefully received by either side in this 'dogfight'.

The weather is very bad; it rains in torrents.

Brig.-General Tuson . . . has left for England to the regret of all . . . His only son went down with his ship at the Battle of Jutland three months ago.

[1] *See Appendix II.*

Last night after a short walk up the street, I dined with our new brigadier, General E. Fagan of Jacob's Horse, Indian Army. He is a very attractive type of cavalryman, lean and active, with penetrating yet kindly eyes. We had a good dinner, a glass of excellent wine, 'and so, comfortably to bed', as Mr Pepys would have put it . . .

We are due for the trenches presently. Yesterday I rode as far forward as possible, and walked the remainder of the way to visit our new sector. On my path lay the grave, marked by a small wooden cross, of Austin Deprez (Captain, Royal Artillery) who was killed at the Battle of Loos eleven months ago. There is scarcely a cemetery on the whole British Front lacking the names of some of my friends . . .

Drafts of 70 men, mostly West Yorks, of good quality, have joined in the last few days.

IN THE FRONT TRENCHES
(Sept. 1st–12th)

SEPTEMBER 3RD: QUARRIES SECTOR

2/West Yorks relieved 2/Rifle Brigade in the Vermelles area on September 1st, by daylight and without incident.

. . . The Rifle Brigade had just lost heavily in a full battalion raid on the German line, the operation being covered by a powerful artillery barrage – perhaps rather short of howitzers. I think that the attack should have been cancelled or the infantry numbers reduced, because on the preceding night an R.B. patrol had become missing, and it was fair to assume that the enemy had captured it and had possibly obtained some hint of the plan from the men, unintentionally, or from notebooks with them. The Germans withdrew from their trenches beforehand, and on arriving in them the raiders were met by very severe shell fire while machine guns swept No Man's Land, thus blocking the retirement. The operation was a failure, the R.B. casualties being 11 out of 22 officers together with a large proportion of other ranks . . .

My daily trench routine is: Dawn: – Holden wakens me and

produces a cup of tea and a biscuit. 6 a.m.:– Breakfast; receive the companies' written reports and send my battalion report by orderly to Brigade Headquarters in dug-outs near Vermelles. 8–1 o'c:–Walk round the companies' trenches accompanied by the adjutant, medical officer, our three orderlies and one bugler. 1 p.m.: – Lunch and two hours' rest. 3 o'c: – Write and despatch to Brigade Headquarters the Situation Report for the day. 4 p.m.: – Tea, after which, except for dinner, there are papers, organisation and other matters to be dealt with till midnight – often later – when I lie down on my bed, a wooden frame covered with wire mesh, constructed by Sergeant Gardner's pioneers, with blanket and greatcoat on top . . .

SEPTEMBER 10TH

. . . Fifty yards of our front parapet were blown in by trench mortars on the 4th, entailing a great deal of repair work. The shell fire is disagreeable now and again, falling on one occasion during our luncheon, a discourtesy not to be readily forgotten . . .

The Rifle Brigade dead lie all over No Man's Land, some hanging on the German wire which they were trying to cut or surmount when killed; among them one whom I knew is easily recognisable.

The stench from the older corpses in our parapets is sickening in places; it has been reduced somewhat by sprinkings of Hinchcliffe's (Quartermaster) chloride of lime, and for me by a smelling salts bottle given years ago by an old aunt without any thought of this purpose.

On the 6th a British aeroplane, hit by a shell, came down on fire in No Man's Land near us. Its crew of two jumped out too late for their parachutes to open properly and dropped like stones before our eyes, to my horror. At night our patrols tried to find the bodies lying in the long grass, but did not succeed.

Although ballon observers were equipped with parachutes, they were not issued to Royal Flying Corps pilots and air crews. Marshal of the Royal Air Force Lord Douglas of Kirtleside relates: 'On my very last operational flight in France, two days before the end of the war, I saw a German pilot escape from his aircraft with the help of one. It was the only time upon which I ever saw such a thing happen.' Lord Douglas also states that the reason why British pilots were not so equipped was because some higher authority believed that they 'would be encouraged to abandon their machines'. He comments: 'When I learnt about that, and I thought about what we had had to endure and I recalled how so many men had died in such agony – all because somebody thought so little of us that they believed that providing us with parachutes would encourage us to abandon our aircraft – my anger was roused in a way that is unusual for me.' The two men whom Jack saw on this occasion had clearly jumped out of their aircraft, preferring to die in that way, rather than burn to death.

Our own and the hostile sniping is very active. The other day when looking carefully through binoculars over the front sandbags on the parapet, I saw the keen, hard face of a German, capless and with iron-grey hair, staring in my direction from a cleft in their sandbags 150 yards away. Quickly taking cover I picked up a periscope to try to see him with less risk, but he also had vanished.

Yesterday Fenton (Lieut, Cameronians) was killed. He twice looked over the top of his parapet from the same spot, and the second time received two bullets through the head from different snipers. One should really not look over the top at all, and never twice from the same place. Telescopic rifles make it almost certain death to be seen first by the enemy's marksmen at such close range . . .

Commenting on a similar incident later, Jack says: 'So the horrid man-hunt goes on.'

SEPTEMBER 13TH

. . . During the night of the 11th two Germans, revolvers in hands, with wonderful coolness and audacity, crawled through our wire on to the parapet and shot two sentries at their stations in the trench. After this very fine performance the daredevils disappeared. The incident has rather 'put the wind up' our posts.

Some of the trenches have again been badly mauled by minenwerfer fire, three men being blown to bits by one bomb.

These heavy trench mortar shells, with their terrific explosion, are intensely disagreeable . . .

On the afternoon of the 11th we received orders to prepare to carry out a raid in a few days' time . . . Since then we have been busy with preparations for the raid, whose main purpose is to secure prisoners for examination by the Intelligence Officers at Divisional Headquarters, and so to identify the German divisions opposite with a view to finding out how fast they are being used up in the battle of the Somme, as well as the state of their morale.

The personnel forming the raiding party were withdrawn yesterday to Battalion Headquarters for rest under more comfortable conditions than with their companies, and for training . . .

IN BRIGADE SUPPORT
(Sept. 13th–17th)

SEPTEMBER 17TH

. . . Raids are just miniature attacks, both requiring most careful preparation.[1] Successful operations raise the morale of troops, while costly failures lower it temporarily, perhaps considerably.

On the 13th, 14th and 15th our party (volunteers) to be employed were fully engaged in rehearsing their duties on an exact replica, marked by tapes on the ground, of the works to be entered; the practice ceasing and the tapes being covered if the enemy's aeroplanes appeared, lest their photographs should disclose the design.

As few men as possible ought to be engaged in a raid, because if the enemy are surprised small numbers will suffice for the purpose, while if surprise is absent the enterprise is hopeless and large parties risk greater casualties.

Every man must know his role intimately. The precise points to be attacked must be carefully settled, and minutely examined through binoculars as well as by small patrols (unobtrusively,

---

[1] *This is somewhat misleading: there was one vast difference between a raid and an attack. The first was designed to* enter *enemy trenches, which was done constantly by all armies; the second was meant to* hold *them, and advance further.*

to avoid rousing the enemy's suspicions). One must also consider: the best line of approach; the cutting of exit gaps in our wire after dark on the night of the venture; the time to be spent in the hostile trench; the signal to withdraw and the method; artillery and machine gun support; the commander's post; together with many other details.

AN ATTEMPTED RAID ON THE GERMAN TRENCHES

At 9.30 p.m. on the 15th the Raiding Party of 24 under 2/Lieutenants G. Smailes and Fisher assembles in the front trench, where I take post.

The night is suitably cloudy. Our artillery, trench mortars and machine guns are ready to fire at prearranged targets on my call for it by code word on the telephone or by rocket signal.

At 9.45 the group proceeds noiselessly in single file through a gap cut in our wire and then among some mine craters till its head is about 30 yards from the German gap to be entered.

Unfortunately new belts of wire are discovered; Smailes, therefore, leaving his men under cover, crawls back to report the fact to me, and I bid the party to return so that the changed situation may be considered.

Telephoning to Brigade Headquarters 'in clear' for instructions is forbidden so close to the enemy lest he 'taps' the message, and there is not time for other communication.

It is intensely difficult to decide what to do next. The operation has been specially ordered by High Command, and prepared. If we make no attempt we shall likely have to carry it out on another night, perhaps under peremptory orders and less favourable conditions. The enemy has apparently not been put on the alert by the first movement. The officers therefore agree with me that we ought to try at a fresh place that has been previously noted.[1]

A little later the party, reduced to 15 men with both officers,

[1] *N.B. 'previously noted'; often the very essence of a military operation is an agreed alternative plan; sometimes, however, this is not possible.*

silently crawling through the long grass and shell holes when the moon is obscured, and lying still when it is bright, reach the wire 20 yards in front of the German parapet and silently push the Bangalore torpedo[1] underneath to blow it up. At this point, however, the wire belt is too wide to be cut properly by the explosion.

All remaining quiet, the party, on Smailes's responsibility, move along a short distance to try at yet another place, and is shoving the torpedo under the wire when a German sentry gives the alarm. Rifle fire at once breaks out from the hostile trenches, and the raiders are forced to withdraw immediately by way of the craters after discharging some bombs at the enemy.

Just as all have nearly reached our lines in safety, Private Standish is killed and Sergeant Mellor wounded in assisting him.

Smailes, Fisher and Fayle (Captain, Medical Officer), although driven several times to take cover from the bullets, at last succeed in bringing in the two casualties.

This wretched affair concludes at 2 a.m. (16th), and the men engaged return to the comforts of a hot meal and warmth in the reserve trench dug-outs. I do not finish my reports on the operation till 3 o'c and am exhausted by the strain of the night, yet thankful that our loss is not greater, holding myself, as I always do, responsible for the lives and welfare of all under my command.

However disappointing the material failure, the cool, determined courage of the officers and men concerned in persistently attempting to carry out the spirit of their instructions has been admirable, as is admitted by High Command . . .

IN DIVISIONAL RESERVE
(Sept. 17th–20th)

SEPTEMBER 20TH: BILLETS: LA BOURSE

On the 18th the Battalion was dragged out to witness in pouring

[1] *A 2-inch sheet iron cylinder in 10-foot lengths, filled with gun-cotton, to be pushed under an entanglement, fired by a primer in the trailing end, so clearing a narrow path. Still used in World War II.*

rain a demonstration on the handling of flamenwerfer four miles away. This weapon has not been used in action for about 18 months, does not appear to be suitable for battle, and I think that a day's rest and clean-up would have profited more . . .

The British first encountered flame-throwers at Hooge in July 1915. There is evidence that they were a French invention, first used in the Argonne in the autumn of 1914. Jack's views reflect a common British attitude, but in fact flame-projectors were used by all armies to the end of the War. At Verdun in 1916 they produced some useful results, largely through their terror value. They were also used freely in World War II.

. . . This morning orders arrive for the Battalion to proceed to the trenches tomorrow. My company commanders, Kerr (Adjutant) and I therefore . . . reconnoitre the line, ascertain the manner of holding it, and arrange for the relief.

The 'Nth' Battalion, of another division, know nothing and do nothing, to which we are unaccustomed in the 8th . . .

IN THE FRONT TRENCHES
(Sept. 21st–29th)

SEPTEMBER 24TH: HULLUCH SECTOR

2/West Yorkshires relieved the 'Nth' (New Army) Battalion near Vermelles on September 21st.

. . . It is the worst unit I ever relieved. Their guides to lead us through the final maze of trenches were late; the wire, trenches and men's dug-outs were in a shocking state while the officers' dug-outs were pretty good – a bad sign. They handed over to us none of the usual maps, defence orders, or store inventories, and gave no help of any kind . . .

Accurate, rapid musketry, a special feature of pre-War British training, has been sadly neglected through undue reliance on the hand-bomb for nearly two years. Although the bomb is the more suitable infantry weapon for trench actions I am certain that first-class rifle marksmanship must prove of high value at times, particularly when troops are in the open during phases of major battles. Besides that, trench warfare may yet give place to mobile operations, like those of 1914. I have therefore ordered that every man in the front trench is to fire daily, at dawn or dusk, under supervision, two rounds at tins hung on our wire. My text 'Shoot and charge' has also been given out as brief advice for emergencies at close quarters; one must neglect no means of acquiring sound habits . . .

We have orders to patrol actively (at night, of course) . . . There is also the disagreeable prospect of our having to carry out a raid . . .

My patrol leaders understand that I trust them to do their best, but nothing stupidly rash. When they are going in front with their men on important missions I take post in the advanced trench to cancel the duty if conditions are unsuitable, and to be responsible if Higher Command are dissatisfied with the endeavour.

Our patrols are always accompanied by one or two Lewis guns on the principle impressed on all ranks, 'Always engage the enemy when he is close at hand'. In order, however, not to lose the guns should they be dropped in the dark owing to casualties, we tie a long rope to each – the loose end fastened near our wire – so that they may be dragged back or otherwise found and recovered . . .

McConville (Lieut, better known as 'Mac') with a few men carried out an excellent patrol two nights ago, hoping to capture a prisoner from a German patrol or working party in No Man's Land. Failing to meet an enemy in the open, his party crawled right up to their wire and 'beat up' one of their posts with hand-bombs, a feat requiring the stoutest nerves. This, of course, drew heavy fire, but happily 'Mac', Sergeant Chamberlain and his men all returned safely.

SEPTEMBER 27TH

. . . To the indignation of our support company a heavy trench mortar has just been placed in a pit made for it close behind their dug-outs; its fire is sure to invite retaliation in which they are likely to suffer.

Another grievance: Higher Command have altered our carefully drawn-up system of trench routine, and hours of work in arranging it are wasted . . .

The Brigade Commander calls during my two-hour afternoon rest, and, not wishing to disturb us, considerately visits our lines without me or my adjutant. On awaking I am handed his note remarking on a number of serious faults he says he has discovered, which faults were not observable in the morning. I therefore proceed forthwith on a second 4-hour tour of my companies to investigate; and, considering many of the complaints to be without due foundation, write politely – but perhaps rather curtly – to give my explanation, as well as to request permission to relinquish my command and return to my own regiment.

I am well aware that discipline required tightening up. My officers and men, however, insufficiently trained nowadays, are doing their best to carry out orders to this end; while I myself work to the limits of my strength every day to increase efficiency all round, so far as that can be done in the trenches.

I must, however, admit that General Fagan takes the greatest personal trouble to find out the state of his command, and is always willing to help; we are very fond of him. Nevertheless I lie down at midnight tired and in ill humour with this added worry.

SEPTEMBER 29TH

. . . This afternoon the Battalion is relieved in the rain by the 2/Middlesex, and files back three-quarters of a mile to the support trench.

On my arrival there a telephone message bids me report at Brigade Headquarters; so thither I proceed forthwith on a pedal bicycle expecting a reprimand from the Brigadier for my letter of the 27th. General Fagan, however, received me most kindly, shakes my hand, says that I must have a cup of tea or a whisky and soda as he is sure I am tired, and scarcely mentions the incident. After tea and apologising for any discourtesy I depart feeling very touched at his tact and understanding. One's nerves sometimes get terribly frayed with too much, and too anxious work . . .

IN BRIGADE SUPPORT
(Sept. 29th–Oct. 6th)

... We hear the constant 'drum' of guns on the Somme about 25 miles southwards. It is reported that our G.H.Q. are 'very pleased' with the results of the battle. I understand that German G.H.Q. are also 'very pleased'. How satisfactory that pleasure pervades both sides of the line! ...

The amount of office work is inconceivable. One can now comprehend the significance of the dictum, 'the pen is mightier than the sword', as the swords are dying or becoming worn out while the pens keep driving on with increasing rapidity.

I draft all important orders and reports myself. Finch (Lieut-Col, 2/Middlesex) discovering this peculiarity, laughingly asked me, 'Why keep a dog (the adjutant) and bark oneself?' The reason is that I know precisely what I want written, and find it easier and quicker to express it personally than to correct the manuscript of another.

As to the pen, known as the Colonel's 'battle pen': it once was an 18-inch sprey scarlet quill holding a metal nib, but many packings in my despatch case have reduced its stature ...

OCTOBER 6TH

... We can carry out practically no training here other than attend to discipline ... The men are busy repairing the earthworks and improving the dug-outs, by day; porter duties besides mending roads claim most of them at night ... Hinchcliffe, a valuable asset to any unit, sends up beer when he can, to the delight of the men ...

On the night of October 5th/6th, the 2/Devons carried out a raid in strength on the German lines; a few prisoners were taken, but the Devons lost 30 men.

Perhaps there is not sufficient 'surprise' about a number of our operations; but if too much is sacrificed to surprise, thorough (possibly vital) preparations for an attack may have to be curtailed. The proper balance between the advantages of 'surprise' and 'preparation' is almost beyond the power of human decision. In war 'luck' holds the trump cards.

During the past several days I have been fully engaged in considering and writing up the half-yearly Honours List; there are many genuine cases to assess – I dismiss all others. Specially distinguished services may, of course, be reported immediately.

No work is less grudged than that of trying to get just acknowledgment for the services of the heroes under my command.

. . . Recent additions to our luxuries, when in support, are a gramophone and some records for it, my favourite pieces being Rubinstein's 'Melody in F', Schubert's 'Unfinished Symphony' and a charming air called 'Penitence', by Jones. My comrades, however, mostly prefer music which they describe as 'brighter', while the men's taste cannot be broken from 'Take me back to England',[1] 'Hullo London', 'Pack up your troubles', besides songs about mothers and best girls . . .

IN THE FRONT TRENCHES
(Oct. 7th–12th)

OCTOBER 12TH

. . . On the night of the 9th, McConville, our star patrol leader, a lank, good-natured Irish lad, set off with Sergeant Chamberlain and 8 men with the intention of capturing a German from his post in their trenches. Crawling through the long grass of No Man's Land when the moon was obscured, the party reached the hostile wire belt where the men were left in shell holes while 'Mac' and the sergeant hand-cut their way through the wire – a slow job and interrupted by passing sentries. When they were almost through the obstacle and just under the parapet a German raised the alarm and fire broke out, 'Mac' and Chamberlain replying to it on the spot with their bombs; then, waiting in shell holes till all was quiet, the complete patrol regained our trenches, after a notable performance, with three of their men slightly wounded.

On the 10th two patrols of 6 men each, under Ernest Fox and

[1] '. . . *dear Old Blighty*'?

Drake (2/Lieuts), both capable officers, attempted at different hours to take a prisoner by entering the German line through gaps previously made in the wire by our mortars, and noted. Fox's group had nearly reached their gap when an enemy sentry in front of the parapet fired and ran back shouting to his trench. Some men of this patrol, retiring too hurriedly under the ensuing fire, were mistaken for Germans by one of our posts which, not hearing the answer to their challenge, rather witlessly opened fire, killing one and wounding two of the patrol.

Troops rushing back to their lines at night or in misty weather do so at their own risk.

Drake's party, at another place, was discovered before proceeding far and withdrew without casualties.

Two other patrols under non-commissioned officers, going out later to engage hostile working parties in No Man's Land, carried out their mission apparently with some effect and returned safely, to my relief.

Last night two small company patrols went forward; but the night was too bright and one of them under Littlejohn (Lieut) had difficulty in withdrawing, covered by its own fire, from a strong body of the enemy which tried to cut it off, without, however, inflicting any loss . . .

A large raid by the 14/Argyll and Sutherland Highlanders, on our immediate right, failed with severe casualties on the 10th.

IN CORPS RESERVE

OCTOBER 14TH: BILLETS: LA BOUVERIE

. . . Out of 90 days spent 'recuperating' in the Loos Salient after their fearful losses on July 1st, the 2/West Yorkshire has been in trenches for 70; it is nevertheless in a good state. Discipline and morale are satisfactory; we have kept frightening the Germans by every available means; and our patrols (one of which gained my £10 reward for capturing a prisoner) have got the upper hand in No Man's Land, a matter of supreme importance to morale, since troops who habitually allow themselves to be pinned by the enemy behind cover admit their inferiority to him. The companies have been quick to seize opportunities . . .

All duties mentioned have been performed for trifling casualties in action . . .

The 8th Division, now in Corps reserve, is returning to the Battle of the Somme, a hated prospect for those who have been there already . . .

SOMME FRONT
(Oct. 17th–Nov. 19th)

OCTOBER 19TH: MEAULTE

. . . Yesterday morning companies held kit inspections, completed their battle stores, and paraded for one hour each of tactical training and lectures on forthcoming operations. Following lunch all officers of the 23rd Brigade appeared before Lord Cavan, Commander XIV Corps,[1] who gave us the comforting assurance that he will not send us into any ill-judged attack. As he has a fine reputation with his troops we are inclined to believe him.

The Prince of Wales is on his staff. H.R.H. called on the mess of the 90th, who found him pleasant, unaffected, well-informed, and looking as smart as a pin; another splendid Royal Edward, I have heard . . .

Winter being now upon us, jerkins (loose leather jackets) are issued to all ranks . . .

Jack and his company commanders now went up to inspect the front near Montauban.

Bits of walls mark the spot where stood Montauban, but Guillemont has been so entirely obliterated by shells that we can scarcely identify the site in the mud. As far as the eye can see in every direction, the rolling, open, blood-soaked landscape, resembling Salisbury Plain, has been completely devastated by tornadoes of shells. The once pretty villages and

---

[1] *Lieut-General the Earl of Cavan's XIV Corps Headquarters began to relieve XIII Corps (Lieut-Gen. W. N. Congreve) on August 10th.*

farms are now represented by piles of rubble, the woods by bare, shredded stumps of trees. Around localities which were the scenes of assault or defence the shell holes touch one another. Derelict trenches, barbed wired entanglements, light-railway lines, equipment, rifles, wrecked field guns and howitzers, two abandoned tanks,[1] and a number of bodies not yet buried, litter the face of the ground . . .

OCTOBER 21ST: BIVOUAC, BERNAFAY WOOD

. . . At the north-eastern edge of the skeleton of Bernafay Wood our bivouac – officially described as 'Camp D' – is situated. The 'camp', however, consists of nothing more than shell holes and a few bits of derelict trenches which the men have covered with their waterproof sheets, a couple of tarpaulins and several sheets of corrugated iron. Battalion Headquarters are in a smelly German trench which is made more habitable by the discovery of an old door and a piece of metal sheeting for a roof; later, a small disused shed and a stove are found to add to the amenities of our lodgings.

At a short conference of battalion commanders on the march, General Fagan announced, to my horror, that the 8th Division is to assault presently. ('Horror' is not too strong a word to describe my feelings. – J.L.J.) . . .

All the afternoon our bivouac hums with the sounds of preparations; with pencil, order-book and map we are busy in our rude candle-lit shelter till late at night with a multitude of details. In accordance with Army Orders, the second-in-command, 2 captains, 5 subalterns, Regimental-Sergeant-Major, 2 Company-Sergeants-Major, and 10 others per company are to be left at the transport lines as a reserve in case of too serious casualties. This practice has resulted from the crippling losses generally sustained in trench attacks on the Somme; losses which have left battalions with insufficient personnel to reorganise them on coming out of action . . .

OCTOBER 22ND

. . . The West Yorks are to act in close support to our brigade

[1] *Tanks made their first appearance on the Somme at Flers-Courcelette, on September 15th.*

176

1. Captain J. L. Jack,
November 1914, in full-dress
uniform of the Scottish Rifles.

2. 'The French public are very
anxious to examine . . . '
Scottish Rifles and French
civilians at Le Havre, August
16th, 1914.

3. ' . . . we detrain at Busigny
. . . ' Train passing through
Busigny station, August 20th,
1914: each train carried a
whole regiment with baggage.

4. H.Q. 1/Cameronians before Le Cateau, August 25th, 1914:
a consultation between Sam Darling, Hamilton, Colonel Robertson,
Ronnie MacAllan.

5. The retreat from Le Cateau: breakfast and toilet at Pontoise, August 29th,
'The men urgently required rest . . .'

'The B.E.F. ceased attacking after the 15th . . .' Front-line trench of 1/Cameronians
the Aisne, September 24th, 1914. A primitive affair; note absence of parapet,
·ados or traverses.

'In a few moments the "soixante-quinze" field guns are blazing away . . .' French
mm. field gun, October 21st, 1914. Davidson and Churchill behind limber.

8. 'The weather is raw and cold.' H.Q. 1/Cameronians, November 18th, 1914. Ja
by now, was on sick leave; left to right, Oakley, Col. Robertson, Davidson, Darli

9. '. . . one sees the enemy's rust-brown wire . . .' View from the front trench
1/Cameronians, December 5th, 1914. The German trenches were 150–200 yards awa
the wrecked houses concealed their snipers. Chimney-stacks and other tall pla
offered vantage points for observation.

10. ' . . . the ordinary round of duties . . . is carried out . . . ' Original sketch by Lieut. J. D. Hill, 'C' Company, showing Capt. Jack on observation and Lieut. Money in bed. Jack comments – 'The parapets, traverses, sandbags, and sides of the trench are drawn trim and exact as it was hoped they would be, not as they really existed.'

. '...the company is in a good state ...' 'Company, 1/Cameronians, December th, 1914. Note the steel loop-hole.

12. '... the trenches are in an indescrib-able state ...' Col. Robertson returning from 'rounds', January 5th, 1915.

13. '. . . cool-headed, cheery young officers . . .' Lieut. Becher and Capt. Ja[
January 5th, 1915.

14. '... our battalion ... stood to arms ...' A new weapon of early 1915 – the rifle-grenade, fired from a fixed wooden holder.

15. '. . . infantry requirements of kinds . . .' Trench periscope, used 1/Cameronians, February, 1915.

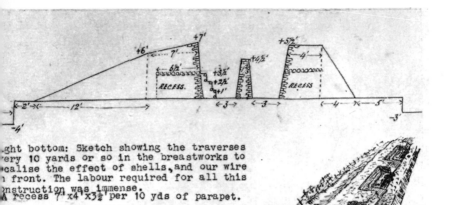

ght bottom: Sketch showing the traverses
ery 10 yards or so in the breastworks to
calise the effect of shells, and our wire
n front. The labour required for all this
nstruction was immense.
A recess 7' x4' x3½' per 10 yds of parapet.

'. . . we hold a line of breastworks . . .' Section of the Flanders breastworks,
pleted mid-1915, from Jack's original notebook.

17. '. . . only partial
success . . .' Page
from Jack's miniature
diary, September 27th
and 28th, 1915,
Bois Grenier sector.

18. '. . . our intense, ceaseless artillery bombardment commenced . . .' Br
artillery fire on the German positions at La Boisselle, July 1st, 1916.

19. '. . . the intensity of our barrage increased . . .' At zero hour, mines were explc
at certain points along the British front. The mine at La Boisselle made a h
crater, but in no way helped the attack.

). '. . . First Objective of the 34th Division . . .' La Boisselle, July 1st, 1916.

. '. . . soon back again in their usual good spirits.' Soldiers cooking on a 'scroung-
' stove near Ovillers, July 1916.

22. 'It was like walking through caramel . . .' Mud at Lesboeufs, November 191

23. 'It is high time these railways were laid. . .' Shells being transported; Somme, 191

'. . . unspeakably thankful to be quitting the Somme . . .' These remains of a
wn-up ammunition dump near La Boisselle in late 1916 give some idea of the
er destructiveness of the Somme battle.

'. . . a much needed rest . . .' Soldiers at a coffee-stall near Ovillers, late 1916.

26. '. . . a shell-swept, stinking heap of ruins . . .' Ypres in 1917.

27. '. . . on an unforgettable morning . . .' Battle of Pilckem Ridge, July 31st, 191
troops digging trenches, stretcher-bearers bringing out the wounded, a fatigue par
with coils of wire and water in petrol tins going up with 'Yukon' packs.

'. . . nearly all my dear West Yorkshire friends were swept away . . .' Men of the t Yorkshire Regiment waiting to go into action at Gravenstafel, September 1917.

29. 8th Division Christmas Card, 1917, designed by Captain Sidney Rogerson.

30. (*above*) 'The desolation . . . is beyond belief . . .' Ypres in September 1918.

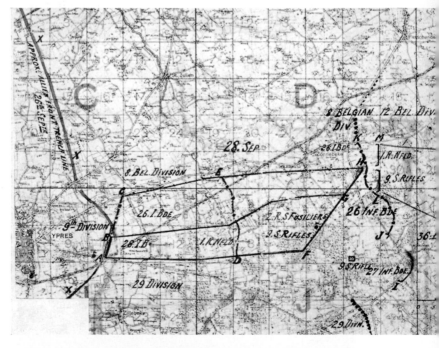

31. (*above*) 'This is to be a big battle . . .' French cavalry and men of the British 29th Division examine trophies outside Ypres, September 29th, 1918.

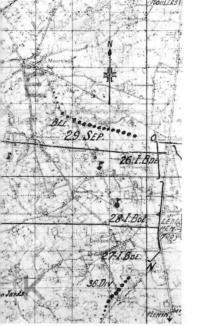

32. (*left*) Map showing the 28th Brigade (9th Division) sector of attack in September 1918, one of Jack's original documents, reproduced from his diary. 'All the land from Ypres', he comments, 'as far as the top of the Passchendaele-Gheluvelt Ridge was honeycombed with trenches and barbed wire, British and German.'

33. Brigadier-General Jack on 'Oudenarde', Cologne, 1918.

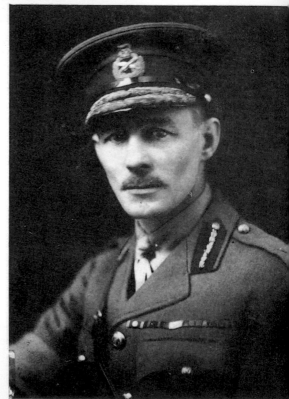

34. James Jack, January 1919. See Plate 1; only 4½ years had passed.

tomorrow. So, in the afternoon, McLaren,[1] Hawley and some orderlies accompany me on foot into the valley beyond the Ginchy—Flers Ridge to select the best position for the Battalion, which is to march at dusk . . .

By midnight there is no sign of the Battalion, now two hours overdue. McLaren, Hawley and the orderlies set off in different directions to search for it on their way back to the transport lines. I and my bugler suffer a miserable night's anxiety . . .

LE TRANSLOY

OCTOBER 23RD

About 5 a.m. the 2/West Yorks . . . reached Windmill and Shine trenches, our station in support . . . The late arrival of my battalion was due to its having been required by the staff, after I had gone ahead on the previous afternoon, to carry stores and ammunition, of which duty I had no notice.

Although the men were exhausted by working and marching all night under considerable shell fire, which to my sorrow killed 2/Lieut Smailes and 6 men, I was forced to order them to dig hard till daylight as their incomplete trenches would then be in view of the Germans . . . So breakfast had to wait. By daylight the trenches were deep enough; tea was then brewed on tiny smokeless fires, a portion of the field rations consumed, and all ranks got a much needed rest in quiet . . .

While realising the difficulties of High Command and their staffs, all formerly gallant and capable regimental officers, one feels that in many cases they are out of touch with the fighting troops, with the effects of mud, shells and exhaustion.

It seems to me that commanders have few duties more important than the ensuring, if possible, that their men go into attacks fresh. Wearied soldiers are well able to defend positions, but in that state they are neither physically nor mentally at their best to attack, particularly in the terrible conditions here.

I think that any other unit ought to have been used for the fatigues on the night of the 22nd – even one resting out of the

---

[1] *Major R. J. McLaren, second-in-command.*

line – rather than my battalion, due to take an immediate part in important operations.

Fortunately the West Yorks were not called upon for major exertions on the 23rd. The attack on Le Transloy was carried out by the extreme right of the Fourth Army in conjunction with the French Sixth Army. The 23rd Brigade was on the right of the 8th Division front, with 4th Division on its right, 25th Brigade on its left, and 24th Brigade to the left of that. 2/Cameronians and 2/Middlesex carried out the 23rd Brigade attack, capturing Zenith Trench in front of them, and pushing on into Orion Trench. The inability of neighbouring units to keep abreast, however, prevented further advances, and when the inevitable German counter-attacks came in, parts of these gains were lost. Characteristic ding-dong fighting then ensued.

OCTOBER 24TH

After a night of rain another assault by the 25th Brigade at 3.50 a.m. fails in the mud with severe casualties, and further attacks are put off till later . . .

At night my battalion relieves the Cameronians in persistent rain, deep mud, shell fire and bullets . . .

Our casualties for the day are 20.

OCTOBER 25TH

The weather has become worse . . .

The Middlesex and my battalion hold a pronounced salient; with a foe like the Germans one can afford to take no chances. Their bombers in the road cutting and earthworks on our right flank are a continual menace, but our trench blocks are complete and Lewis guns are aligned on all approaches . . .

At night our patrols search all dead ground in the immediate vicinity of our lines to ensure that hostile bodies are not collecting there for minor attacks. One patrol, under 2/Lieut Peters, captures 16 prisoners, who say they would have surrendered earlier but their sergeant – evidently a hard-hearted man – would not allow it.

We have lost today 3 officers and 41 other ranks . . . nearly all from shell fire . . .

In the evening as we sit dead-beat with work and worry on

a bundle of foul straw in the dim candlelight, dealing with orders and reports, an orderly comes down the dug-out steps and reports 'Captain Fayle (R.A.M.C.) has just been killed, sir, on the road outside.' What a shock to lose this brave, lovable little doctor, and without being able to thank him for his last 48 hours of ceaseless work . . . Captain Elkington, R.A.M.C., arrives in a few hours to take Fayle's place . . .

OCTOBER 26TH

General Fagan arrives on foot at our headquarters about dawn, and we proceed to the line together in the rain . . .

'B' Company (Capt. Gordon-Alexander) and 'D' Company (Lieut Sankey) get a merciless shelling daily and are digging short trenches off the main trench in an effort to escape it. Since all their slope of the ridge is bombarded at uncertain hours no other remedy can be suggested; we cannot take these companies out of the line and leave those in front isolated.

There are no dug-outs in the forward area . . . officers and men have no cover from the fearful weather except their waterproof sheets rigged up in the trenches to form roofs . . .

The Brigade Commander notes several points for correction but is satisfied with his inspection . . .

The Battalion casualties today number 30, chiefly to carrying parties and to support companies. I am quite sick with wondering how to obviate further losses.

OCTOBER 27TH

This morning I . . . am ordered to prepare a bombing attack to clear the enemy out of that portion of Zenith Trench still in his hands . . .

After dusk daily . . . all stores are carried by hand to the companies; their delivery in the dark, through deep mud and usually under fire, occupies one-third of the men for the greater part of these very trying nights.

The food is ample, arrives regularly, and consists of tea, cocoa or soup, bully beef or stew, beans, butter and jam – all in tins – besides bread or biscuits, and cheese. The men, however, can scarcely get a hot drink since smoky or bright fires are forbidden . . .

Our dug-out is crammed with the headquarters officers of two battalions . . . sleep being out of the question except in brief snatches . . .

OCTOBER 28TH

. . . In the communication trench . . . the knee of a German partially buried by the shell that killed him forms a stile over which we step daily; further on the head of another . . . protrudes from the trench bottom.

The dead of the action on the 23rd lie on the open ground, a daily sickening sight. But we cannot bury them all; my men can do no more work; they have done well enough; besides, their own safety and comfort come first.

There is no more word of our bombing operation, but another attack by the brigades on our flanks . . . only awaits better weather. At present to assault through the quagmire would cause extravagant losses.

The Battalion area is again heavily shelled; insistent claims for more artillery retaliation have, however, borne fruit at last and the frequent terrific bombardments must be giving the Germans hell.

At night company patrols take two prisoners; the enemy's morale seems to have dipped a little although it remains unpleasantly high . . .

By this time the Battle of the Somme had fully evolved into what some German writers have called 'die Material-Schlacht', in other words, the long-awaited application of British productive capacity to battle needs. The effect of this was best observed in the development of artillery; hence the statement in the Official History that 'The Somme was an artillery battle.' This may seem curious, in the light of the immense infantry casualties sustained, until it is remembered that a high proportion of these were inflicted by the German guns. On the British side the expansion of artillery was particularly marked: in mid-November the Fourth and Fifth Armies, on the Somme, possessed over 800 more guns than in mid-July, despite battle losses. Not only that, but British ammunition, very defective (30 per cent, according to some authorities) in the early stages, was now much improved. The Germans began to sense the pressure of apparently limitless material resources against which skill and courage availed little. Their sentiments are well expressed by a soldier of the 66th Infantry Regiment, writing at the end of September:

'I send you greeting from my grave in the earth. We shall soon become mad in this awful artillery fire. Day and night it goes on without ceasing. Never has it been so bad as this before . . .'

Two world wars have revealed the extraordinary tenacity of German morale under appalling conditions; yet by the end of 1916 it was definitely taking a 'dip', as Jack notes. This was recognised by General Ludendorff in his decision (early September) to begin the construction of the Hindenburg Line, far in rear of the Somme front. In January he told the Reichskanzler 'we must spare the troops a second Somme battle'; in February, retirement to the (still incomplete) Hindenburg Line began under the renewed pressure of the British forces. Thus this retirement, despite the unlooked-for tactical advantages which it produced in the frustration of French offensive plans, must be seen as an acknowledgement of defeat on the Somme, mainly at the hands of the still largely 'amateur' British Army.

OCTOBER 29TH

. . . We are being relieved tonight . . .

Our headquarters always move back as soon as they are relieved, but I, my adjutant and our orderlies never leave the line till all the companies have reported on passing. We sit up all night waiting with some concern – and annoyance – for these reports . . .

OCTOBER 30TH

Towards 7 a.m. our last company, after stumbling about on handing-over duties all night in the rain, mud, shell fire and bullets, reports 'Relief complete'. It is the worst relief I have experienced during more than two years in France, and the fault lies only with the appalling conditions. Thankfully quitting this cursed place my small staff and I follow the company . . .

Following a five-mile march . . . we visit the companies at [breakfast], but the reaction and weariness of these eight dreadful days are so great that I can scarcely keep sufficiently composed to say a few words to the gaunt, exhausted, patient lads who have come through the ordeal . . .

IN DIVISIONAL RESERVE
(Oct. 30th–Nov. 6th)

OCTOBER 31ST: MAXWELL CAMP

Reveille today is disgracefully late as I think that all ranks had better have a good rest . . .

On the 22nd the Battalion (less reserve and transport) went into action 437 strong, losing in the following eight days 6 officers and 214 other ranks, the chief sufferers being 'B' and 'D' Companies, the carrying parties and stretcher-bearers. These casualties, practically all from constant shelling, have been incurred merely in holding the line; assaults cost far more, as a rule . . .

Having discovered today that several Lewis guns and much equipment are deficient after our tour in the line, I reluctantly send those responsible, under the orderly officer, back towards Bernafay Wood to search for the equivalent, though damaged, items from the wreckage littered about derelict trenches. The party returns in the evening bearing a miscellaneous collection of gear, which is handed to a smiling Hinchcliffe to exchange for serviceable articles from the Ordnance Department. No doubt, many of the deficiencies could not have been avoided, but unless one is firm with regard to them they increase; besides, it is unsoldierly to lose arms and equipment . . .

NOVEMBER 2ND

. . . A draft of 200 men had joined us. Circumstances permitting, reinforcements from the Base are sent to their own regiments; but the battles of the Somme have imposed an exceptional drain on personnel, and this draft consists largely of Northumbrian and Durham miners, with a sprinkling of Midland lads and cavalry, besides some of our own corps. We hope that the strangers will soon settle down, as I have done, to be West Yorkshiremen while with the Regiment.

As soon as possible after coming out of the line, or when otherwise necessary, I hold a conference with all officers and senior non-commissioned ranks to discuss errors – carefully written in my notebook – that we have committed. This list is often long, but softened by references to work well done. These informal talks help greatly to improve leadership . . .

On the 3rd the Battalion, leaving its Méaulte billets thoroughly clean, marched four miles to this camp . . .

First-class troops never hand over dirty quarters and we are particular in this respect, McLaren or I invariably making an inspection half an hour before the Battalion moves off to another place. This old Regular Army custom is often indifferently attended to nowadays, without sufficient excuse.

This camp, improved since our arrival, comprises some half dozen bell tents and tarpaulin sheets pitched in a quagmire on the side of a bare hill; the cold is perishing and the discomforts great.

The companies can carry out practically no training here as there are so many fatigues . . .

When in the line the West Yorks have few cases of sickness despite the conditions; in reserve we have more, the numbers in the different companies varying too much for no apparent reason. By taking the company with the smallest medical list as a standard, one usually finds that the higher figures of the others are due to inferior discipline or administration, which we keep watching assiduously . . .

IN BRIGADE SUPPORT

NOVEMBER 8TH: TRONES WOOD

On the 7th 2/West Yorks advanced 5 miles to bivouac at Trônes Wood, relieving the 19th Brigade.

. . . Owing to perhaps unavoidable leisureliness in laying light railways to near the front, our road, over the ankles in mud and full of large holes from Montauban onwards, was crammed with a stream of horse and motor transport. Through this medley of traffic my own laden men filed as best they could, dragging their cursed Lewis gun carts and being sometimes jostled into the ditch by waggons.

The Lewis gun cart resembles a coffin (suitable for containing the body of their designer) mounted on two strong bicycle wheels with solid rubber tyres. It is so low-set that the men hauling and pushing it must crouch. Each of our carts used to

183

be towed by a pack mule, and it was then sufficient for a couple of soldiers to merely balance the vehicle. But this labour-saving practice has recently been disallowed; why, I cannot conceive.

At Trônes Wood we found the nearly officerless remnant of the 5/Cameronians, who had just suffered heavily, still in possession of our bivouac; they obstinately refused to budge from this wretched spot to billets in rear before the appointed time. We were, therefore, forced to sit in the rain for an hour until these perverse Scots had vacated their scraps of shelter and several bell tents.

Battalion Headquarters are well housed in an old German trench blocked at one end by a door, roofed with some sheets of corrugated iron, and with sandbags filling the cracks . . . To my joy there is also a stove, rescued in the nick of time from the clutch of Rogerson's enterprising servant Purkiss, who was purloining it for his master . . .

That evening Jack dined at the H.Q. of the 17th Division, commanded by Major-General P. R. Robertson, his old 1/Cameronian colonel of 1914.

As we drink a whisky and soda at 10 o'c, just before my departure, the chief Staff Officer, immaculate and confident, re-enters the mess from his office. Our talk turns on the large number of men demanded from the infantry for multitudinous duties away from their units, which can ill afford the loss. Being irritated by today's requests for more of these, I remark mischievously that when we absolutely cannot spare the personnel I initial the demand 'A.O.R.', which my adjutant understands to mean 'Any Old Rubbish'. This solution of the difficulty nettles the G.S.O.1, who says that I will only cut my own throat by following it. I reply that we shall more surely fall into disgrace by failures in action, and that *he* would not accept as excuse for such failures the excellence of our grave-diggers 25 miles away, or that of the West York cook at Boulogne.

We willingly release to other spheres of duty officers unsuitable for the infantry, as well as war-worn other ranks, and nominate for courses of instruction the best we possess. But after all, the Battle Efficiency of his unit must be a commander's first concern. Arrangements, other than bleeding battalions, should be made to provide men for non-combatant duties . . .

(My practice in this matter has been impugned. I may say, first, the 2/West Yorkshire had no 'rubbish'; all were soldierly and we heard no complaints about any transferred elsewhere. Secondly, I know the importance of allowing to leave a unit for other employment only those who will maintain the reputation of their corps although away from it. This was my custom when possible. In these days, however, first-class officers, N.C.O.s and privates were irreplaceable. Moreover, inefficient battalions penalise others in action with them. – J.L.J.) . . .

IN THE FRONT LINE
(Nov. 9th–13th)

LESBOEUFS

It is not proposed to follow Jack's description of the short spell of front line duty now performed by 2/West Yorks. For their colonel it was, as ever, a time of strain and anxiety, but by comparison with the preceding tour, uneventful. On the earlier occasion, he says, 'I was completely exhausted and dreaded my journeys to the line and back; a commander must, however, suppress the least sign of weakness. If this was the bodily and mental state of the lieut-colonel in his relatively sheltered position, what must have been that of his much more exposed and overworked young officers and men? The trials of the second, 5-day tour were many degrees less acute as far as I was concerned.'

A full account of this period may, however, be found in Sidney Rogerson's 'Twelve Days' (Arthur Barker, 1933) with its most interesting Foreword by Captain Liddell-Hart. The dominating feature of trench life at this time, Rogerson makes clear, was Mud – 'mud which was unique even for the Somme. It was like walking through caramel . . . No one could struggle through that mud for even a few yards without rest. Terrible in its clinging consistency, it was the arbiter of destiny, the supreme enemy, paralysing and mocking English and German alike. Distances were measured not in yards but in mud.'

In this glutinous morass Rogerson, inspecting the short front of the two forward companies which he commanded, found 'that the round of a few hundred yards had taken over two hours of strenuous walking'. Jack, as was his custom, visited the front line every day, each visit, says

185

Rogerson, taking him not less than four hours. On one occasion he was accompanied by Brigadier-General Fagan: 'How long it took the Brigadier to come up from still farther in rear can only be conjectured, but the very fact that he would thereby be absent from his headquarters for many hours should be some answer to those who demand to know why general officers did not put in more frequent appearances in the front line.'

Lieutenant Matthew McConville, M.C., D.F.C., of Rogerson's 'B' Company, has given an impression of Jack as he saw him on the night that the West Yorks entered the line, at Battalion Headquarters in a sunken road:

'It was characteristic of the man that even in that low filthy dug-out, crowded to twice its capacity by two sets of occupants, he still preserved an atmosphere of dignity and ordered control. I have met Colonel Jack in many situations in and out of trenches, but never once when my hand has not instinctively come to the salute. And yet he was no soulless martinet. Without ever suggesting familiarity, he had the knack of lifting now and again the barrier of rank and of striking just that personal note of man-to-man encouragement which, after his entirely unaffected contempt for his own safety and comfort, was the secret of his place in the spontaneous respect of every man in his command. That night, he outlined with the least delay the general situation, and handed to each Company neatly and concisely written Orders for the night's work.'

McConville adds that (also right in character) Jack had caused the Royal Engineers to lay a guide-tape for his battalion beside the sunken road, considering it a dangerous approach to the front line. They all had reason to bless his foresight in avoiding the road when 'the Hun dropped along it sudden vicious salvoes of heavy High-Explosive'.

NOVEMBER 15TH: BRIQUETERIE CAMP

. . . The Battalion casualties for the last 5-day tour are two officers[1] and 16 other ranks. On this occasion we have next to no deficiencies of arms or equipment, our practice of sending those losing them back towards the line to retrieve the equivalent items having proved effective.

Yesterday we rested and cleaned up. All ranks are expected to shave daily, even in the trenches, but this order is relaxed when conditions are extremely bad . . .

This rainy morning the Battalion marches four miles to

[1] *Both under remarkable circumstances; see 'Twelve Days' or 'The Eighth Division in the War'.*

186

Citadel Camp, near Fricourt. The road is in its chronic winter state of mud and crammed with military traffic. On the way we meet a Guards battalion, clean, equipment properly fitted, erect and with ranks 'dressed', proceeding to the trenches. The West Yorks, however, have straightened themselves up quite marvellously in the past twenty-four hours under wretched conditions. I am proud of their appearance as well as of their performance . . .

At Bernafay cross-roads a particularly smart young officer is conducting traffic duties in a most businesslike manner, and I am delighted to recognise him as one I recommended for staff duty because he lacked decision in action . . .

NOVEMBER 18TH: CITADEL CAMP

Dry and perishing cold. The Battalion is officially described as 'resting', but at 6 a.m. on the 16th it found 6 officers and 300 other ranks who, proceeding in motor lorries to the Trones Wood area, were engaged till after 3 o'c in levelling a track for a light railway. Yesterday 4 officers and 200 other ranks on the same duty sustained two casualties from shell fire . . . It is high time these railways were laid as the wastage of time and the exhaustion of men and animals is very great . . .

The 8th Division has been relieved by the 29th Division and is being withdrawn from the Front for a much needed rest . . . We are unspeakably thankful to be quitting the Somme again . . .

NOVEMBER 19TH

At 2 a.m. on another perishing night, full, final orders for our move to the Amiens area arrive. How often the staff wake us up with instructions which should normally be despatched in time to reach troops about dusk. Perhaps they do not realise that late orders rob soldiers of rest vital to efficiency . . .

After this unpleasant beginning, the day continued on similar lines, including waiting for a train for some four hours in the rain at 'a military siding devoid of any shelter on the bleak uplands above Meaulte'.

At 4.30 p.m. the train arrives; but the West Yorks have by no means wasted the day. A 'dump' of equipment salvaged from the battlefields early catches their eyes and, in the absence of any referee, some New Army leather equipment in our possession is exchanged for the lighter Regular Army web, while other suitable stores are also selected . . .

IN XV CORPS REST AREA NEAR AMIENS
(Nov. 20th–Dec. 27th)

. . . These five weeks at Le Fay were spent in heavenly peace and comfort although the weather was raw and wet. The pleasant little brick village lay in an undulating, farming, well-timbered countryside; the French inhabitants being, as usual, kind and accommodating.

The Battalion polished and drilled daily besides carrying out battle training and a 4-hour route march once a week. Guard duties and the evening mounting of all company guards together received unremitting attention, as did musketry exercises against the day when open warfare might replace trench assaults.

With the approval of my Regular West Yorkshire officers I had the Battalion drums – sent Home before I assumed command – returned to us. These now arrived with pipeclayed cords and inscribed Battle Honours. Drum-Major Cole soon produced a particularly smart little drum and fife band which played at guard-mounting, on all battalion parades, and at the more important mess dinners.

The afternoons were devoted to specialist training and games . . .

In November drafts amounting to 451 other ranks joined the Battalion, one of 76 consisting mainly of fine Northumberland Fusiliers. One subaltern was invalided Home. The reinforcements received in December numbered 4 officers and 166 other ranks, while one officer and 13 men left to join the railway service. . . Regimental-Sergeant-Major Kenyon, M.C., having served with the Battalion in France since November 1914, was by now exhausted with work and strain. I therefore reported him to Higher Command as worn out, and requested that he be sent Home for a change from battles. The curious reply came that there was no such thing as a soldier being 'worn out', and my application was refused. As, however, Kenyon was in the state described, I sent him on leave to England with a note to his doctor saying that he needed a good rest. This settled the matter. To have kept him under the circumstances, brave, capable and uncomplaining as he was, would have been unfair to the Battalion, to the warrant-officer, and to myself . . .

Well-run messes have a great influence on the tone of a unit, and exacting as I was about duties, I aimed at maintaining the friendliness and manners of a good family when off duty. The officers' mess is their home, and I believe that ours was a very happy one . . .

The warrant-officers and sergeants, and the corporals also had good messes. The men were as comfortable as we could make them, and enjoyed occasional concerts besides other entertainments at some of which the Divisional band and troupe of artistes assisted . . .

Soon after arriving at Le Fay I was highly flattered by being offered a month's leave; only those thought worth preserving were recommended for so long a term. Although I had not been away from duty for over seven months I at first declined the offer since many matters with my battalion required attention; moreover, one had become hardened to the War and did not care to break the sequence. But, urgently requiring a rest, I later accepted the leave . . .

ON LEAVE IN THE UNITED KINGDOM
(Dec. 7th 1916–Jan. 8th 1917)

At Home the country was steadily pursuing its war work, but no particular bustle was noticeable in the ordinary life of the community . . .

As it seemed unlikely that I would be deprived of my command – unless by the enemy – I got my London tailors, Messrs Johnson, to fit me out as a West Yorkshire man . . . my view was that the Cameronians, having ample credit apart from me, would not wish one to be discourteous to another unit . . . by not wearing its uniform . . .

Thoroughly rested, I left London 7th January to resume duty in France.

BACK TO THE SOMME FRONT

The Official History speaks of the Battles of the Somme 'ending' on November 18th 1916, following the capture of Beaumont Hamel by the 51st Highland Division on November 13th. The winter of 1916–17 proved to be exceptional: icy cold and snow began to arrive in October, and snow continued into April. Nevertheless, the British forces on the Somme, particularly General Gough's Fifth Army in the Ancre sector, continued to press the enemy as far as the unspeakable weather and ground conditions permitted. This was in accordance with Inter-Allied policy, desiring not to give the Germans time to recuperate from their heavy losses, and to strike another united blow as early as possible, in order to end the War before the already visible cracks in French and Russian national morale widened disastrously. The aim was laudable; the effect on the British troops concerned, however, was another series of ghastly experiences, though not on the scale of the great 1916 battle. The change in French command at the end of that year, and consequent change of plan, rendered much of the effort valueless; but it had an undoubted effect in accelerating the withdrawal of the Germans to the Hindenburg Line, contrary to all their previous doctrine of war.

JANUARY 8TH: CAMP 'X', MAUREPAS

. . . This sector had only recently been taken over from the French, who apparently held the line with isolated posts, the trenches being flooded. Very little protective wire existed, no dug-outs, and the line was in a dreadful mess; our sick list, mainly from trench feet, was therefore considerable . . .

IN CORPS AND DIVISIONAL RESERVE
(Jan. 9th–Feb. 20th)

JANUARY 11TH: CAMP III, NEAR BRAY-SUR-SOMME

. . . On returning yesterday from a ride to visit 'D' Company I find our new Divisional Commander inspecting the lines. (Major-General W. G. Heneker succeeded Major-General

190

Hudson on December 8th 1916.) He looks very soldierly and is well dressed but has a cold manner. After searching me up and down with his eyes, General Heneker asks, 'Pray, who are you?' I introduce myself and we proceed. Although we are just back from the trenches and providing strong working parties daily he is dissatisfied that the men are not looking cleaner and smarter; a bit hard! To my sorrow Palmes[1] cannot tell him the position of his company latrines, which it is, of course, his business to know despite his having been away on duty all day. I tell the General that Peter is a splendid officer in every way, but he remains annoyed and the inspection concludes rather frostily. During the interview I glean word that our Intelligence Staff still maintain, as they have done for months past, that the German morale is 'definitely on the decline', a decline not observable to those meeting them in action . . .

JANUARY 12TH

At 10 a.m. a message from General Fagan orders me to accompany him . . . to Divisional Headquarters . . . Wondering 'What's the matter now?' (under General Heneker a commander's saddle is a slippery one), I hastily don my best tunic, cap, belt and gloves, and we set out on our $2\frac{1}{2}$-hours journey . . .

The Divisional Commander is exceptionally thorough, and the conference of brigadiers is convened for the purpose of sifting every detail of organisation with a view to improvements. My lowly attendance at so august – and so chilly – an assemblage is due to my being required to command the brigade for a few days . . .

JANUARY 18TH

Jack returned to the 2/West Yorks on the 16th.
. . . There a bombshell greeted me; a note saying that I have been selected to attend a course of instruction for higher leaders at the Senior Officers' School in France. A complete change from the present life may sound attractive but I consider it to be an infernal nuisance. I have just been away from my battalion for a month's leave, and this period out of the Line is providing one with the only good opportunity for

[1] *Captain J. P. Palmes*, M.C., *commanding 'A' Company.*

thoroughly overhauling organisation, together with training officers and men for the actions sure to be staged for Spring . . .

I have told General Fagan that I really cannot spare the time to go away again so soon . . .

JANUARY 21ST

At 10 a.m. on the 19th, a couple of hours late, an ancient motor bus arrived to convey me and three other officers of the Battalion . . . to witness a 'demonstration' by specially trained troops of the manner in which attacks should really be delivered – not as we have imperfectly carried them out under fire for the past year or two . . .

One must not be unfairly critical about 'demonstrations'. They are very carefully arranged by the Staff and are a valuable means of training troops. But were our soldiers sent to France properly trained as they ought to be, or even if they had the same practice here as the demonstrators, under good conditions and with the best coaching, they also would likely put up as fine a performance in the absence of shells, bullets, mud and exhaustion . . .

A week ago 2 officers and 41 other ranks left for courses at Schools of Instruction in the rear areas . . .

I have heard no more about my own attendance at the Senior Officers' School, and surmise with relief that it has been cancelled.

Masses of orders and instructions have arrived from High Command. Sometimes they come like a flood . . .

JANUARY 23RD

. . . Yesterday I had to proceed in a staff car to Divisional Headquarters . . . At the conclusion of the conference all save senior officers leave the room and the doors are shut. The Divisional General then announces 'Gentlemen, you will be glad to hear secretly that the 8th Division has been selected to carry out an attack in the near future.' It is on the tip of my tongue to reply that this is the worst news I have had for a long time.

JANUARY 28TH

. . . A recent High Command order directs that troops are not to wear leather jerkins or greatcoats on the march – lest they get overheated? I scarcely possess sufficient clothes to keep out the 'purple' cold; we are all blue from it. Surely senior regimental officers are fit to decide on the apparel to be worn! . . .

. . . the Battalion has been practising the latest methods of attack. Although principles do not alter, the manner of applying them may. The state and formation of the ground, new weapons and better ways of using the old, besides other constantly changing conditions, impose variations in tactics which are quickly mastered by first-class troops. Others with inferior training require more coaching as well as more stereotyped plans for operations . . .

I learned that Divisional Headquarters have rather given way about not wearing jerkins on the march. Some men have caught chills, and all have suffered extreme discomfort from the intense cold, amounting on some nights to over 20° of frost . . . More snow storms have added to the unpleasantness of things . . .

FEBRUARY 9TH

The weather continues icy. Our regular attack exercises are handicapped by it and by orders to find large working parties.

On the 6th General Heneker was good enough to motor me to see French troops carry out a practice attack near Aumale – a 3-hour drive. Their infantry, in Roman helmet and baggy horizon-blue overcoat, are not so smart as ours but seem most efficient. Our Allies do not hesitate to use live ammunition in their exercises, and take risks that we consider too great for training. Their object is to make lessons as real as possible, and an occasional casualty is disregarded.

They also appear to have different ideas to us about preparing troops for battle. I am told that for a recent attack the French brigade concerned was thoroughly trained and rested far behind the Front till just before the action; it was then conveyed in motor buses near to the trenches; carried out the assault and, having been relieved by other troops, promptly returned to its cosy billets and canteens.

Our infantry, on the other hand, are often given too few

facilities for rehearsing their role in detail, and their energy is squandered on labouring tasks till shortly before attacking. 'On paper', no doubt, they are both trained and rested.

If overdone, however, the first system leads to the formation of corps d'élite, and the quality of those troops outside this group deteriorates. Our infantry remain of pretty equal value . . .

This is a thorny controversy. The conscript armies of France and Germany had, from the beginning, certain differences of quality within them. In France there existed Active Divisions, Reserve Divisions and Territorial Divisions. The last of these categories consisted of elderly men, quite unsuitable for attack; they could, however, take their place in the Line for holding purposes, thus allowing Active troops to rest. (We have seen that they also relieved Active troops of much tiring labour.) The system has its obvious advantages; Jack points out an important drawback, which was well illustrated in 1940.

On the other hand, the pressure of circumstances in war, such as heavy casualties, leading to 'scraping the barrel' of man-power, tend towards the evolution of corps d'élite, as the general level declines, and the need for really dependable units grows. Thus, by 1918, lacking proper reinforcements, diluted with the too-young and the unfit, over-hastily reorganised and weakened in numbers, the British Line Infantry Divisions revealed a distinct drop in quality. The Army then leaned heavily on those divisions which retained their value: the Guards, the five Australian divisions, the four Canadian and the New Zealanders. This is not to say that British Line Divisions did not perform some fine exploits; it merely stresses that these were more difficult for them. The weakness of corps d'élite was seen in the German Army in late 1918, when the 'Storm Troops' were destroyed.

FEBRUARY 12TH

. . . Yesterday morning the Battalion marches five miles to Corbie, entering that old-world town in good style, at the slope, with drums playing the 'Prince of Wales' March' and 'Ça Ira'.[1] The men are fit, so we again arrive in billets in good order and complete . . .

We detest 'straggling on the march' . . . anyone quitting the

[1] *Regimental March of the West Yorkshires.*

ranks, except at the regular halts, parades on the next morning for medical treatment if he is ill, and for more practice in marching if he is not. We practically never have any stragglers . . .

. . . The very night battalions quit the Line, they must render to Higher Command a 'programme of training' in triplicate for their 'rest' period. This programme is, however, almost always wrecked through orders to find working parties, detachments and other duties. Nevertheless, our companies, each about 50 strong, have contrived to carry out much useful battle training here, including lectures to officers and N.C.O.s.

Every month battalions must submit the names of five non-commissioned officers or privates for commissions. We normally render the names of our best Warrant Officers to fill our own vacancies, and others of high quality for promotion to any unit after tuition at an Army school. In this war battalions require leaders and fighters at once, rather than scholars later.

A strong Officer Corps, the troops on service being given a proportion of the vacancies, should have been formed on the birth of the New Armies.

Orders amending details in organisation arrived three days ago. It is a pity they were not produced at the beginning of our training period instead of at the end . . .

FEBRUARY 20TH: CAMP 117, SUZANNE

. . . The 8th Division is in the Line again after six weeks of varying duties and discomforts in camps. Our Fifth Army, which has been slowly driving back the enemy on the Ancre, has opened a successful attack there . . .

IN THE TRENCHES
(Feb. 21st–25th)

FEBRUARY 25TH: FRONT TRENCHES: BOUCHAVESNES

The companies spend the morning of the 21st rubbing their feet with the new French preparation just issued. This oil is said to ward off 'trench feet', as the malady caused by constant exposure to wet mud is called. Soft thigh-high rubber gumboots are drawn at the same time by all ranks.

At dawn on that day Cropper (Intelligence Officer) accompanies me on a second visit to the front. We reach the support trench safely and there find Wallace Cunningham, Life Guards . . . He describes the position in frank – but unprintable – terms . . .

The trenches are thigh-deep in liquid mud; the sentry posts, standing on little raised islands, are for that reason isolated by day; the two communication trenches, Alpha and Agile Avenues, are in the same state as the other trenches. The enemy have good observation from their higher positions, so sniping is sharp. There are no dug-outs in the Line . . .

Yesterday, after a long, concentrated watch through binoculars from a front post, I believe I located four German posts behind their thick barbed wire 150 yards off; anyhow, the position of one of them was certain, since a German sentry, shifting his weight from one leg to another, caused a ray of light on his helmet to sway for a second.

A few of the enemy are to be seen outside their parapet when the light is dull, a sign that their trenches are also waterlogged. Our marksmen are keeping the hostile snipers quieter and better concealed.

It is tricky work moving close to the front line by day as little cover is to be had there; but officers must take risks to get through their work. Experience, care, activity, and wearing the minimum of equipment reduce the danger. A private, however, has incurred my displeasure through getting hit by a bullet when crossing the open, against any express orders that no man is to be above ground by day unless absolutely necessary.

Tonight patrols under McConville and Drake go forward to dispute, if needful, the ownership of No Man's Land; none of the enemy is met and our lads return unharmed . . .

ON THE SICK LIST
(Feb. 27th–Mar. 7th)

Having been the victim of a feverish chill for almost two weeks, I was forced to 'report sick' . . .

One hated leaving one's men just as they were going into action, even as supports, but it could not be helped ...

In my absence Dick McLaren commanded the West Yorks with ability.

At 5.45 on 28th February we were roused by a tremendous bombardment caused by the artillery of the 8th Division, augmented by other batteries, reopening the Battle of the Somme in its southern sector ...

The 8th Division attack took place on March 4th, as part of a series of operations designed to hasten the now apparent German withdrawal to the Hindenburg Line. The 24th and 25th Brigades carried their objectives on a front of 1,200 yards. The enemy reacted sharply, making no less than five counter-attacks on March 4th and another on March 5th. The Division's casualties during this operation amounted to over 1,000, but, says Jack, 'the men themselves, as well as High Command of course, considered it a success ... 217 prisoners, of less than the normal good German physique, had been brought in. On the 4th many hostile parties and guns were seen retiring within easy range, but the unaccustomed sight surprised our troops, untrained to act quickly under novel conditions, and the fleeting opportunities of annihilating them passed by.'

This was to be a recurring feature of the 'pursuit' to the Hindenburg Line, and of important phases of the great attacks of the year 1917.

Casualties in 2/West Yorks (supporting the main attack) between March 3rd and 7th, when they were relieved, were 3 officers and 80 other ranks.

MARCH 11TH: HOSPITAL WOOD, NEAR COMBLES

... Sad news greets me on returning to the Battalion; General Fagan, our popular brigade commander, has left owing to a difference with the divisional general, a fine but exacting chief. General Fagan is the third brigadier to quit the Division within a few months; other commanders and staff officers have also felt the blast ...

Lieut-Colonel George Grogan, 1/Worcestershire, 8th Div., is the new commander of the 23rd Infantry Brigade; he has a first-class reputation.

A frigid letter from High Command complains of the large

number of 'trench feet' in the battalion at the end of last month. We are charged with:

1. Working our men too hard.
2. Wearing rubber boots too long.
3. Not putting on dry socks sufficiently often. (One senior medical officer actually suggests changing wet socks for dry two or three times a day, but does not say how this may be done.)
4. Failure to use the anti-trench-feet preparation fully. Our unpublished replies are:

1. We greatly resent the extra work added by High Command to our normal duties.
2. Gumboots are worn only when necessary; they cannot be exchanged for ankle boots during marches at night under present conditions, and must therefore be worn for the whole journey; they keep legs dry even if the feet get wet.
3. The Quartermaster sends up dry socks nightly, but they become wet when being changed in the mud; we cannot ensure relays of dry socks unless a laundry is installed in the trenches.
4. We use all the trench-feet preparation issued to us and think the old whale oil more effective . . .

Lack of care may have been partly responsible for so many trench-feet; nevertheless, the difficulties of infantry companies do not appear to be fully realised in High Circles, few of whom come to see for themselves the appalling conditions in the trenches, especially during reliefs in glue-like mud and under shell fire. Too often impracticable orders are issued . . .

IN THE TRENCHES
(Mar. 12th–13th)

MARCH 13TH: RANCOURT

Yesterday afternoon, following a 4-mile march, the Battalion took over without incident 1,000 yards of line from the 2/Middlesex . . .

The weather is vile. The posts and trenches are water-logged . . .

Peter Palmes and I have been especially busy arranging to raid the Germans tomorrow night . . . Our raid volunteers, under Lieuts Ben Clayton and Ernest Fox, have been resting and training at the transport lines for the past three days. I allow raid leaders to go into No Man's Land, as spectators only, with one or two reconnaissance patrols beforehand. Much tense employment ruins the nerve.

Tonight Peter and I see the usual number of Very rockets rising from the German trenches, and heads moving in an advanced sap. Later, a message says that a raid by the Guards, on our immediate left, has just been repulsed. The enemy, therefore, seems to be holding his positions here; this is confirmed by our patrols . . .

It is announced that we have taken Bagdad, and that there is a revolution in Russia.

MARCH 14TH

A busy day. It is reported that the German line appears to be held in the usual strength.

After lunch Peter and I make a final reconnaissance for the raid tonight. The ordinary desultory sniping and shelling are in evidence. Until dusk no change in the enemy's usual procedure leads us to expect his withdrawal. At that time, however, we notice a strange absence of Very rockets from the hostile trenches, and a couple of shells, apparently German, burst in them – highly significant omens.

I hurry back to instruct 'B' and 'D' Companies to send patrols into the enemy's trenches at once, as well as to inform Brigade Headquarters of these happenings. On the way Cropper comes running up with a message from Rogerson saying that the Guards have just occupied the German lines facing them without opposition. This is astounding news, and we order all companies to make ready to advance forthwith, issuing two web bandoliers of extra ammunition (50 rounds in each) and two bombs to every man, while serving out rations, water, entrenching tools and other stores. At the same time Hinchcliffe proceeds to send up our ankle boots to replace the trench gumboots.

The German Drossen Trench having been reported clear by prompt patrols under 2/Lieuts May and Hall, 'C' Company (Lieut Myers) moves across No Man's Land about 8 o'c and occupies the trench on a front of half a mile, sending patrols to gain touch with the Devons on our right, the Guards on our left, and with the enemy.

Soon afterwards 'B' Company (Lieut Clayton) advances into line with 'C' . . .

The lines of our two leading companies, in small, widely separated groups with patrols ahead, now form a sharp salient 1,500 yards long. The night passes quietly, busily and rather tensely.

MARCH 15TH: ST PIERRE VAAST WOOD

From a captured German order it appears that our patrols entered the hostile trenches only one hour after they had been vacated; pretty sharp work, particularly on May's part. The Guards, too, must have been awake indeed.

About 10.30 this morning 'A' Company . . . advances in widely extended order one mile through the undergrowth of St Pierre Wood, drives back a few Germans, and occupies Bacchus Trench on the eastern edge. Its patrols, pressing on another half-mile, are stopped by fire from Vaux Wood and Government Farm. At the same time 'C' Company moves forward to Larch Trench, in the middle of the wood, to protect the left of 'A'.

The German trenches we have 'taken over' are deep, well-constructed, and surprisingly dry; but we are in a most insanitary state, with a poor field of fire. The numerous dug-outs are good; most of the entrances, however, have been blown in by the late tenants. Masses of beer bottles (unfortunately empty) are strewn about, and guncotton, attached to shell cases and grenades, has been left ready to explode when picked up or accidentally kicked. We have had five casualties in this way, and the men have orders not to enter dug-outs, or handle ammunition until it has been properly inspected.

Late in the afternoon a message says that Divisional Headquarters are apprehensive about the situation of the Battalion because aeroplane reports say that the flares lit by the leading companies to show their position are far in advance of the rest of the line. We are therefore ordered to withdraw somewhat. The order is, however, rescinded on my assurance that our position is perfectly secure and all is quiet; that our arrangements have been completed and alterations will cause unnecessary confusion besides fatigue.

At dusk the Battalion holds a very long front of 4,000 yards[1] . . . Throughout the day long-range patrol actions occur with no loss to us.

Messages from the Division and Brigade express great satisfaction with the prompt initiative and handling of the 2/West Yorks' companies and patrols.

Last night passed quietly, with all ranks 'keyed up' since even a moderate German attack might pierce our attenuated lines.

Much as we should like to get along we have orders to 'stand fast'; active patrolling is, however, in progress. It is thought that there are no more than weak rearguards before us . . .

At 5 p.m. the 2/Middlesex companies arrive at 15-minute intervals to relieve the Battalion . . .

The events of the past few days have put us all in wonderful fettle.

MARCH 18TH: HOSPITAL WOOD

. . . We have been cleaning up, refitting, and doing a little drill . . . The prospect of mobile operations has introduced a new crop of lessons, since scarcely any in the Battalion has had proper training in mobile warfare . . .

Our armies have taken Bapaume and Péronne.

THE ATTACK ON NURLU RIDGE

MARCH 19TH

. . . At two o'clock this morning orders arrive that we are to be ready at 9 a.m. to cross the Canal du Nord at Moislains

---

[1] *Average ration strength: 400; actual front-line strength often less.*

(just occupied by the 2/Cameronians) and are thereafter to seize, in conjunction with the Corps mounted troops, the Wiltshire Yeomanry, the low ridge running north and south through the village of Nurlu on the Péronne-Cambrai road. There is an immediate stir in our lines . . .

At 6.45, preceded by scouts, the five[1] companies, 17 officers and 280 other ranks altogether, in full marching order of dress which we have not worn in action for years, plus additional ammunition, file forward at a hundred paces interval.

Followed by our chargers with buff browbands, rosettes, headropes and girths, the pack animals with ammunition, tools and half water ration, we cross our old trench line and the shell field of No Man's Land where until a few days ago none could show his nose and keep his skin whole.

After living like moles for two and a half years with no view beyond the trench ahead, the effect of advancing in the open acts like a tonic on all ranks; there is a cheer as we file through the pickets of another regiment in the late German lines.

Passing the unburied French dead of 1916 in their faded horizon-blue uniforms, the hastily dug graves marked here and there by a muddy helmet mounted on a rusty bayonet or rifle stuck into the ground, a skull or a few bones, we skirt St Pierre Vaast Wood and reach Moislains after a three-mile march.

A letter places me in command of the divisional outpost line, and a field battery, whose commander says he has not had time to bring up many shells, reports for duty. The order also says that the 2/West Yorks are not to advance till the mounted troops have reached a certain line in front. Reports on the situation are conflicting; some allege that the enemy has retired, others that his posts are in fair strength . . .

At 2 p.m., as I have reported that the Yeomanry appear unlikely to be able to advance further, the 2/West Yorks are ordered to clear the ridge. Picks, shovels and other equipment are issued from our pack animals, two Brigade machine guns are attached to each company, and the men shed their heavy valises which are stacked under company guards.

[1] *Battalions had recently formed 'Headquarters Companies', composed of signallers, pioneers, medical staff, etc.*

Half an hour later, leaving 'A' Company at the canal in reserve, 'C', 'D' and 'B', in widely extended lines of sections fanning outwards, advance under negligible small-arms and shell fire. Riding with the centre company, 'D', I observe about 100 Germans in small parties retiring some 1,200 yards away.

Before dusk the opposition stiffens in spite of a little support from our artillery, and further progress is stopped. We have, however, gained most of the ridge in an advance of one and a half miles.

At nightfall, the Yeomanry having been withdrawn earlier, I order the three leading companies to dig posts on their 4,000 yards frontage . . . With so very long and unprotected a front, as well as with officers and men totally unused to these new conditions, we are a little anxious. Fox and I spend a large part of the night visiting the companies in perishing sleet showers, seeing from the higher ground the glare from villages burning in the German area . . .

This undulating countryside is open, unfenced, carpeted with long grass and weeds, treeless, save for those bordering main roads, besides some woods (mostly cut down) and orchards in the numerous rather dismantled villages, outside of which there are hardly any single houses. Maps show the land ahead to be similar.

MARCH 20TH: OUTPOST LINE

. . . Last night our patrols unsuccessfully attempted to press into Nurlu Wood and into the village of Nurlu. At dawn this morning, however, those of 'D' Company (Lieut T. Sankey) occupy the village with little opposition . . .

Immediately after this occupation our three advanced companies, moving 1,000 yards forward, establish a ring of posts from St Pierre Farm (on the Péronne road) round the enemy's side of Nurlu, thence back towards Manancourt, our left flank being rather exposed. These companies have orders to send strong patrols at once towards (into if possible) Liéramont Sorel and Equancourt, one and a half miles ahead. Although worrying the enemy's groups, none of these patrols is able to enter the villages . . .

Riding up on Warts[1] with my companies I am much annoyed with an advanced post for not seeing – and engaging – a group of Germans 100 yards away retiring on Fins. The matter is quickly rectified; we are not yet sharp enough in open warfare . . .

We have had scarcely any casualties in these minor operations.

MARCH 22ND: IN BRIGADE SUPPORT

Most of the Battalion have been on fatigue these two days entrenching on Nurlu Ridge under the Royal Engineers; otherwise we have been resting and 'tuning up'. Although I am delighted with the good leading and 'drive' of my companies, we have not neglected to overhaul lessons in detail. The more important are: engaging the enemy forthwith, whenever he is seen within range, with overwhelming fire; keeping touch with other units out of sight by means of patrols; placing company headquarters where they may easily be found; attacking or defending in small, mutually supporting lines or groups; insisting on a correct and soldierly bearing at all times, even to paying the usual compliments, when out of the enemy's view . . .

The advance is being retarded through unavoidable delays in bringing up artillery, shells and other stores, owing to the Germans having blown down or blocked by felled trees bridges and road culverts. Communications, too, have to be reconstructed across the many devasted miles of the old Somme battlefields. Military labour gangs in rear are hard at work on repairs . . .

When riding round the front area we are sometimes sniped at by field guns. The Germans must be firing off ammunition they cannot take back to account for so lavish a use of artillery on individuals . . .

'Hincher' has staged one of his miracles by sending up BEER for all ranks. No other neighbouring unit has beer; since its plunder on the way by thirsty spectators was possible, the bottles came under special escort.

MARCH 25TH: NURLU: OUTPOST LINE

On the afternoon of the 23rd, 'A', 'B' and 'C' Companies took

[1] *Jack's charger.*

over 2,000 yards of the outpost line in bitter weather from the 2/Middlesex with 10 men per company – few enough for so long a front, although Yeomanry vedettes are in advance by day. The remainder of the Battalion, armed of course, have been digging trenches daily on the ridge . . . It seems to me that so much digging constitutes an excessive amount of caution, and that we should rather try to forge ahead . . .

One sentry per half-company, with a Lewis gun, and two snipers per company are sufficient for observation duties in daylight; at night every post finds its sentry . . .

A platoon of the Divisional Cyclist Company is attached to us for scouting duties, and the Canadian Cavalry Brigade (Brig.-Gen. Hon. J. Seely, once Minister for War) is in the neighbourhood . . .

We keep coaching the companies for mobile operations as well as we can and lead a strenuous existence. Cropper, or Fox, and I rise at 4 a.m., and after a light breakfast visit all posts and men on other duties till 9 o'c. Then there is office work and preparation of various kinds, followed often by another tour in the dark.

Our sentries must sharpen up . . . in the safety of these open spaces and with the Germans further off, all sorts of soldiers come drifting about our posts and some may be spies. I have therefore instructed the sentries to fire at once on any not answering their challenge by night – and nearly fell a victim to my own order.

Sniping has become more active; this always happens when opposing forces get settled in positions. The enemy's field guns continue to squander ammunition on single men, and his heavy shells make excursions into Nurlu most unpleasant after dark . . .

MARCH 27TH: IN BRIGADE SUPPORT

. . . Yesterday morning the Canadian cavalry dashingly captured the village of Equancourt. Today, galloping over the open, whale-backed ridges so rapidly as to sustain few casualties, they seized Liéramont and Guyencourt, one to two miles beyond our outposts, the feat being possible by the almost entire absence of wire fences . . .

The 2/Lincolnshire have driven off a considerable counter-attack on Equancourt.

Last evening I was summoned to Brigade Headquarters to discuss future plans with General Grogan, a pleasant duty with one so sound and helpful. As I mounted at his billet door on departing in the dusk he quietly said that Higher Command are dissatisfied with the 'lack of push' of the infantry. What? After two recently expressed anxieties about the West Yorks being so far advanced, and then the daily placing of almost all my men on defence work! Furious at the suggestion, and snapping out 'I'll take my battalion into Heudicourt (the next German village) or go there alone, whichever is preferred' I dig my heels into Warts and splash out of the yard in the rain, to the kindly admonition of dear old 'Grogie' to do 'nothing rash'.

PRESSING ON AGAIN

At 4 p.m. today (27th) the 2/West Yorks, at a bayonet strength of about 16 officers and 240 other ranks, relieve the 2/Middlesex on Nurlu Ridge, where a strange sight – for this campaign of concealment – greets our eyes at dusk. The slopes eastwards are thick with mounted Canadians leisurely withdrawing to their night lines in rear after fine exploits.

Since the enemy's defence is likely to have been rather disorganised by the day's events, we take the chance of keeping up the pressure by pushing 'C', 'D' and 'B' Companies right through the Middlesex outpost line to a mile beyond it. By 9 o'c the posts of these companies, entrenched, are established on the low crest 1,000 yards from the hostile pickets in Heudicourt . . .

MARCH 28TH: OUTPOSTS IN FRONT OF HEUDICOURT

Before dawn this morning Sergeant Priestley, a particularly cool, determined N.C.O., with a patrol of 6, closely approaches the German pickets in Heudicourt with the object of locating their positions. On the way back at daybreak, hot fire is opened on the party, which is forced to take refuge in a shallow, disused enemy trench. There they spend an unpleasant day, 'potted at' by the Teutons, as well as by 'D' Company's sharpshooters who, stupidly perhaps, fail to identify them as friends. Happily the patrol returns at nightfall, unharmed but a trifle out of humour . . .

MARCH 29TH

At 2.45 o'c on this cold, showery morning, 2/Lieut May, with 15 men and two Lewis guns . . . sets out to harry the enemy as well as to locate his defences between Heudicourt and Sorel. Towards dawn they are fired on from a trench estimated to be holding 30 Germans, and promptly return the fire on a sound principle. Having completed its mission the patrol withdraws without loss . . .

At 8 a.m. I ride to 'B' Company's headquarters (some recesses dug in a bank) to watch the Corps mounted troops trying to capture Sorel, a good half mile northwards. We see single squadrons galloping forward, then back, in open order under small-arms fire, apparently suffering little loss. It seems a disjointed affair. Perhaps the horsemen met that bugbear, wire. Anyhow, the village is not taken . . .

At nightfall . . . two patrols, each of 15 men with two Lewis guns, under 2/Lieuts May and Yorke, attempt to occupy Heudicourt. The patrols have orders not to be stopped by snipers only, but are not to persist if the opposition is very severe . . .

Slipping carefully forward, Yorke's (south) patrol is met, about 10 o'c, by severe fire at a range of 100 yards or less. The officer and 7 of his men are wounded, 4 of whom (one killed) are, to our great distress, missing for some hours. Sergeant Priestley, whose gallantry has often been noticed, steadies his men in spite of the closeness of the fire, and then returns to collect the wounded.

May's (west) patrol enters Heudicourt at 8 p.m. without opposition, lights the flare signal arranged, and reports its position to company headquarters. An hour later, however, resolute German groups, firing hard, begin closing in on the patrol from different directions through orchards and yards. May's men reply vigorously; Corporal Pycock, shifting his guns

from one spot to another with great self-possession, keeps the
enemy at bay for a time. Finally, in order to avoid being cut
off, May skilfully withdraws his men without loss. At the headquarters of the forward company he suggests to me renewing
the endeavour with reinforcements, but this I forbid since the
Germans appear to be in strength, have been roused, and
appear determined to hold the village.

After midnight, on relief by the 2/Middlesex, our companies
march back independently 5 miles to Moislains, and reach
their cellars about 4 a.m. (30th), tired, ready for a hot meal,
blankets and a long sleep.

My adjutant, orderlies and I, following on foot the last
company, do not arrive till 5 o'c. Then, seeing all ranks settled
and writing accounts of the situation for Higher Command
occupy us for two hours longer. The reports include strong
recommendations for May, Priestley and Pycock for services
just rendered, besides others of the same high standard . . .

APRIL 1ST: NURLU: IN DIVISIONAL RESERVE

We had a good rest on the 30th (I slept till 3 p.m.) . . .

On the 31st we stayed in Nurlu till the afternoon.

Our successors in the Brickstacks dug-outs there discovered
a slab of guncotton cleverly inserted into the wall behind the
German stove that we had constantly used. Not wishing to enter
Paradise at short notice, our friends removed it quickly. Fortunately, the explosive raised no objection to the fires lit in the
stove during our residence.

Another device of the ingenious, industrious Teutons is the
attachment of an explosive to clocks, by means of which it is
timed to burst at certain hours. We begin to fancy we hear a
'ticking' in every dug-out we enter. There have, indeed, been
several accidents in these ways on other parts of the Front,
and all ranks have been warned about them . . .

Yesterday morning I rode alone to Heudicourt to reconnoitre
the most concealed route for the move of my battalion there
in the afternoon . . . On crossing a slope the loud 'drumming'
of a powerful aeroplane engine startles me, and on looking
round I am horrified to see a German 'Halberstadt' apparently

coming straight at Warts and me. It is flying so low that I can clearly distinguish the observer leaning over the cockpit. I draw my pistol on the principle 'Always engage', and prepare to return the expected fire. Mercifully, no engagement takes place; the machine is away in a second. Is it possible, I wonder, that the airmen are more afraid of the commander of the 2/West Yorkshire than he is of them? . . .

APRIL 8TH: NURLU

The United States of America have entered the War on our side.

The weather is perishing cold, with sleet showers and falls of snow. But in spite of it we have made ourselves comfortable . . .

When the companies are not on fatigues, mending roads and other navvies' work, claiming half the men for five hours daily, they carry out, in small bodies, a little strict drill, a valuable change from actions and marching. Tactical training, of which they have had plenty – against the enemy – since 14th March, consists mainly of lectures and short demonstrations. Instruction must not be overdone; one wants soldiers fresh, happy, 'on their toes', not stale . . .

The Official Battalion Diary, which I write up myself, relates an astounding change in the situation during the past fortnight; individual fighting, full of incident not too deadly, and over a wide expanse of country. The only blot on the record has been the vile weather . . .

The British Fifth Army reached the outer defences of the Hindenburg Line some days ago, while our (Fourth) Army is itself not far from the Line. The German resistance is stiffening and his counter-attacks multiply.

General Heneker recently visited our mess – cordially – and remarked on the soldierly appearance of our men besides their prowess in the field. He condoled with us on not having been required to carry out an attack lately. I detest attacks; they mean seeing friends lying about dead and mangled. In addition to this the personal attention to countless details before and during operations imposes a very severe mental and physical strain on one . . .

Two days ago (Easter Monday), when I am inspecting my companies in Nurlu, up canters the Army Commander, Sir Henry Rawlinson, full of life, riding a beautiful bay charger, also full of life. He is attended by an aide-de-camp and an orderly bearing an Army commander's pennon, both superbly mounted. Sir Henry leans down, shakes my hand, says my men appear to be in good form, and gives me the thrilling news that the British First and Third Armies have just broken the German defences at Arras on a 25-mile front, capturing 6,000 prisoners as well as no end of guns and stores.

The Battle of Arras (April 9th 1917) was undertaken by the British Army as the preliminary phase of a great Allied offensive, planned by the French Commander-in-Chief, General Nivelle, to break through the German positions and drive them out of France. The British effort opened with a striking success – the capture of the notorious Vimy Ridge by the Canadian Corps. For a time the possibilities of a deep rupture of the German front seemed very strong. Frightful weather conditions, however, plus the lack of experience of open warfare on the part of both commanders and troops, plus remarkable recuperative qualities displayed by the Germans, slowed the battle down into another trench-by-trench advance. The French attack in Champagne on April 16th, despite the immense resources behind it, entirely failed in its main purpose. The French sustained heavy casualties and a severe shock of disappointment which left its mark on their armies for the remainder of the War. The immediate result of their setback was that the British were obliged to continue what should only have been a large-scale 'diversionary operation' well into June, by which time it had cost them some 150,000 men, and – worse still – had consumed invaluable time and material which they would have preferred to devote to their own projected offensive in Flanders.

The 2/West Yorks are in grand spirits, rested, cleaned, soldierly, and having had the best coaching for action that we can provide under the circumstances . . .

APRIL 12TH

. . . Preparations for the General Attack keep us all hard at work. At periods throughout the day our artillery and machine guns fire on the nearer fringes of Villers-Guislain, not on the actual objectives, so as to avoid warning the enemy what they are to be. My company commanders and I also unobtrusively reconnoitre the ground from the outpost line and check compass bearings . . .

THE ATTACK ON BEET FACTORY AND MEUNIER HOUSE

. . . At 7.45 o'c,[1] at the end of an intense ten-minute bombardment of Beet Factory, Meunier House and the adjacent crests by our guns, 'C' and 'D' Companies advance in a blinding snow-storm – on their backs; a stroke of luck – in two extended lines 50 yards apart, followed by their mortars. One hundred yards behind (a reduced interval on account of the weather) 'A' and 'B', also in two ranks but less extended, lead on accompanied by their machine guns . . .

At 9.10 p.m., after advancing almost a mile up a gentle, open slope, 'C' Company occupies the factory and neighbouring ground against trifling opposition. 'D' is, however, seriously checked by machine guns and does not succeed in capturing its objectives till 11 o'c . . .

The seizure of the various points is signalled by rockets, the information being confirmed by messages sent by runners, or by telephone whose cables are laid during the operation . . .

These pleasing results are attained for few casualties . . .

APRIL 13TH

. . . A message to the 8th Division, circulated to all units, conveys the congratulations of the Commander-in-Chief and the XV Corps Commander on the results achieved . . .

At night a message from Higher Command says that the 2/Devonshire will attack Villers-Guislain at dawn tomorrow unless the West Yorks have occupied it before then . . .

We discuss the prospects for the Devon attack and conclude that it is impracticable unless the artillery can cut the wire belts seen by us, as well as shake the defenders, who appear

[1] p.m.; dusk was at 6.45 p.m.

to be in considerable numbers and fire heavily on our patrol, even bombing the closest of them.

Although my opinion had not been asked, I think it my duty to send an Express Confidential message stating these views to Higher Command at 11.30 p.m. At the same time another strong patrol is sent out further to test the strength of the German posts. This patrol confirms the previous findings at a cost of several casualties.

At 12.15 and 1.15 a.m. (14th) we despatch additional reports to Brigade Headquarters.[1] The Brigadier in acknowledging them says it is regretted that the attack must take place as it is to synchronise with others, and that he hopes our guns will have been able to cut the hostile wire before then. Needless to say, we breathe no hint of our apprehensions to the Devons . . .

APRIL 14TH

At dawn two Devon companies attack Villers-Guislain, are held up by wire and driven back with considerable losses. No blame whatever for the failure can be attributed to these gallant men . . .

APRIL 17TH: GUYENCOURT: IN BRIGADE SUPPORT

The weather is infamous, with continual showers of sleet; but all ranks have had a good rest and clean up. How quickly healthy men recover from exhaustion . . .

On the evening of the 15th I was summoned to Brigade Headquarters and heard with a shock that my battalion is to march to Villers-Guislain the next afternoon, dig assembly trenches for occupation that night, and assault the village at dawn on the 17th. These damned attacks seem to be endless . . .

Yesterday Generals Heneker and Grogan considerately come to our headquarters to discuss plans, instead of calling me back to Liéramont in the sleet. The former, after heartily complimenting the West Yorks on their efficiency, says that the attack has been postponed for a day, and that our plan of marching tonight to an assembly position in a hollow and attacking at dawn tomorrow without any delay has been accepted.

[1] *See Appendix III.*

This will give more time to make arrangements, and will save the men from the fatigue of digging trenches for one night's occupation, as well as much discomfort. After assuring me of adequate artillery support and that the wire will be properly cut, the generals have tea in the mess before departing. Thoughtful General Grogan has ridden over twice today to offer help, if necessary, and to leave his blessing.

The 'paper' strength of the Battalion is 35 officers and 717 other ranks, but the 'real' or 'ration' strength is only 22 and 505, the remainder being casualties, sick, absent on duties and courses of instruction, with a few on leave.

We must have no mishap. Every detail has been arranged to a hair-breadth, entailing concentrated thought and an immense amount of work. Fox (our Intelligence Officer), Richardson (Signals Officer) and their observers have spent these two days at the front, gleaning through telescopes and from the Middlesex all information possible. I have myself visited Colonel Hall to get the latest reports; he says that his battalion will render all the help it can, especially in preventing repairs to the gaps cut in the German wire by our guns. McLaren, who is to lead my battalion to its assembly positions, has reconnoitred the route with Cropper.

This morning our companies finally rehearse the exact procedure for tomorrow, after which they march past me for inspection, in fours, in battle dress, with sloped arms, like Guardsmen, to the drums.

Late in the afternoon Fox returns with favourable reports about the wire and other matters. Then he, Palmes and I walk forward to have a last look round, to get the latest news – which is satisfactory – and to see that the white tapes marking the forming-up position, laid after dusk in a shallow ground depression behind the Middlesex pickets, are exactly parallel to the line of advance. The tapes are out of alignment. We correct them by compass since the error may cause loss of direction in darkness or mist and hazard the chance of success . . .

The Battalion . . . is due at the starting tapes, 600 yards from Villers-Guislain, at 3.25 a.m. for the assault an hour later . . .

THE ATTACK ON VILLERS-GUISLAIN
ON 18TH APRIL

The Battalion is delayed – not McLaren's fault – by traffic blocks on the way. Its head does not reach the tapes till 4 o'c. Palmes, Fox and orderlies search for it, leaving me alone, sick with worry lest it be too late to get the support of our artillery barrage whose timing cannot be altered. Indeed, the last company appears just in time to draw the extra stores brought up on pack animals, fall in, throw off greatcoats worn over the equipment because of the sleet, and advance . . .

At 4.25 o'c, in a snowstorm, our artillery and machine gun barrage opens heavily on a section of the enemy's wire and on the nearer houses of Villers-Guislain. At this instant the four companies, with bayonets fixed, under Captain Palmes, advance in 'quick time' (walking) on a frontage of 400 yards up a gentle slope towards the village faintly outlined in the break of dawn.

Having loosed my lads off with a 'Tally-ho' on my hunting horn, I walk back to Battalion Headquarters at Vaucelette Farm just before a quite severe German barrage falls on the hollow, fortunately newly vacated by our companies. Battalion commanders are expected not to quit their headquarters during an attack, but one feels bound to see one's men set off in good order and give them a cheer.

Twenty minutes later (4.45) the leading companies, followed by those in support, rush through the well-cut wire gaps – kept open last night by the Middlesex – and enter the village against trifling opposition. The platoons told off to the various sectors immediately advance along the streets to clear the buildings, but the small enemy garrison (estimated at about 150 men) has dispersed, leaving in our hands 13 prisoners and 2 machine guns.

By 5.15 the whole of Villers-Guislain has been occupied . . .

Presently the West Yorks companies, which have completed re-forming, are debouching from the village to continue the attack . . . The leading companies are now pressing up the bare slopes with a good many Germans retiring in front of them. One body, about 50 strong, is seen streaming down the Petit

Burge Ravine, followed by another of smaller size, all of them under sharp fire.

By 6 a.m. the Battalion has, in one fine sweep, briefly interrupted only when re-forming in Villers-Guislain, gained all its objectives on the ridge half a mile beyond the village, and its patrols are attempting to work still further outwards. . . . The day's advance of nearly a mile has cost the Battalion only eleven casualties. We have taken 18 prisoners as well as 5 machine guns, and believe that the Germans have probably lost a further 30 or 40 men. The infamous weather helped many to escape.[1]

Although mindful of the valuable aid afforded by Higher Command, Duncan's trench mortars, the Brigade machine gunners, artillery and flanking units, the success of this operation may be attributed mainly to strict discipline, careful training, and minute preparation; to the dash, determination and quick, bold decision of all ranks, led by Palmes.

General Heneker telegraphed early in the day 'Well done, VAST' (our code name). General Grogan's appreciation is no less warm.

This is my thirty-seventh birthday, the best I have ever had.

APRIL 19TH: VILLERS-GUISLAIN

We are very tired – very happy, too – after my 'best birthday'.[2]

Before sunrise today several of our posts contrive to push nearer the crestline, and during the morning patrols go well forward to maintain touch with the enemy . . .

The line is being little shelled. The post trenches are small, widely separated, and all freshly turned earth has been concealed with sods. Moreover, I have promised punishment to anyone not on duty found exposed in daylight. The machine gunners with us drew some shells as they are too careless about exposure . . .

The situation is quiet, but the Battalion is occupying a pronounced salient . . .

---

[1] *The Divisional History states that 60 Germans were killed.*
[2] *See Appendix IV.*

At 4.30 a.m. Palmes accompanies me round the posts, practically all of which are by now established on the main crest line. We are, however, annoyed to find one important vantage point neglected, and take a Lewis gun section there to occupy it, since a hostile machine gun there would be most inconvenient for us. On the way we meet Corporal Robinson returning from a prowl with two men each carrying a German rifle. It seems that at dawn Robinson had discovered and rushed at two sleepy German snipers who, waking quickly enough, bolted without their arms . . .

Before returning to headquarters we hear the explosions of German mines demolishing bridges and buildings in front of the Hindenburg Line. Portions of the thick wire belts protecting the Line are visible two miles northwards, about Banteux; other portions are hidden by folds in the ground. The smoke from burning villages and farms is seen rising along the Escaut valley.

A much-needed sleep from 9 a.m. till 12 noon is followed by office work, and another three-hour tour of the companies at sunset . . .

APRIL 21ST

At dawn today the 25th Brigade takes Gonnelieu (one mile north of Villers-Guislain), 90 prisoners, machine guns and mortars . . .

APRIL 30TH: HEUDICOURT: IN DIVISIONAL RESERVE

The Battalion has been staying here happily since the 22nd in cold bright weather . . .

Since the 11th inst. we have lost in action only 2 officers and 25 other ranks, mostly wounded, a light list considering, too, that our patrols have constantly sought out and engaged the enemy. I am sure we could have harried the Germans more if an artillery officer had been with us, as we requested, connected to his battery by telephone. When troops have advanced at night there are nearly always targets to be seen at dawn next morning.

Leave to Paris for a few days is now open. We enjoin officers proceeding there to take a comrade as chaperon. To my sorrow I have had to stop the leave of one subaltern as his platoon is not quite in the state it ought to be. But he shall go as soon as he has made good . . .

A little drill, precise guard-mounting, and a march past by platoons to the drums at the end of the morning's parades, remain features of our daily exercises . . .

General Heneker has seen us training several times and has expressed his high satisfaction with the companies' work. His compliments are the more valued since he is very sparing of them. On one occasion he described a sentry as 'not up to West York standards'. I found the fellow to be a newcomer who should not have been posted on that duty until fit to represent the Battalion.

General Grogan and many others have also generously offered their congratulations on the gallantry, efficiency and smartness of all ranks; one going so far as to say that he cannot compete with it . . .

The British First and Third Armies on the Scarpe have advanced 4 miles up to date, capturing Vimy Ridge, 13,000 prisoners and 200 guns. But we understand that things have gone badly with the great French offensive in Champagne, which opened in so promising a fashion.

MAY 3RD: GOUZEAUCOURT: IN BRIGADE SUPPORT

. . . This afternoon companies parade behind cover for a presentation of medals by the Divisional Commander, Lieut May getting the Military Cross, Private O'Hara the Military Medal, and Private Buckingham an Italian medal for acts of valour in March.

The weather is excellent. I am glad to be able to say some good for it at last. But stay! The heat has burst the mess bottle for making soda water.

MAY 6TH: GONNELIEU: IN THE PICKET LINE

. . . Tonight the Battalion has relieved the 2/Middlesex on a frontage of 800 yards . . .

Nothing of importance is happening in this sector, nor is likely to happen at present, since we are up against the Hindenburg Line, reported to be a veritable fortress, and the bulk of our armaments are on the Arras Front . . .

The martial activities of the Battalion are confined to sharp-shooting, four men per company, in pairs, lying out all day ahead of the pickets, and to Lewis gun patrols which crawl forward nightly to fire on German working parties . . .

Some authorities consider such operations a waste of time and energy. I disagree with them when our casualty list is likely to be very small and the men are given sufficient rest, as with us. We must worry the enemy to death and maintain by every means our fine fighting spirit, so that all ranks may continue to realise that they are individually more than a match for the Germans . . .

IN XV CORPS RESERVE
(May 14th–28th)
CURLU WOOD

Our fortnight's peaceful stay here was enjoyed by all ranks after nearly three months continuously at the Front, during which the 8th Division and Corps cavalry, with very curtailed means, had advanced 15 miles, capturing some 21 villages and woods in constant skirmishes . . .

While the 'paper strength' of the Battalion yielded the attractively high figure of 37 officers and 680 other ranks, our 'real' or 'ration strength' was only 27 and 445 respectively, mostly of a fine self-reliant type, although my notes refer to the presence of 14 'cripples' whom we could not persuade High Command to accept for some sedentary occupation . . .

During this 15 days companies drilled a little daily and polished much, went for marches, carried out battle training, specialists' training and musketry . . .

For Battle Training we had several schemes carefully worked out and ready at short notice for display before any inspecting officer. These, with variations introduced during their execution, were soon performed at the double in grand style. The enemy were always represented by some men – a point that I consider vitally necessary to make soldiers use their eyes, and to prevent tactical training from becoming 'wooden'. Drums represented machine gun fire and umpires told units when they were being shelled. We practised a different limited phase of an operation daily and then discussed it; exercises dragging on make for slackness.

Before marching off for training the Battalion always fell in to the drum, and on returning to camp it marched past McLaren or me with sloped arms and fixed bayonets to the drums and fifes by companies, platoons, or even by sections to inculcate leadership. Those not up to standard were circled to the tail of the column to 'try again', a simple method for getting things done correctly . . .

The Corps and Divisional Commanders both expressed their great satisfaction with the Battalion in action, on parade and in its administration, as did our warm friend, General Grogan.

. . . Alterations in organisation had lately been decreed by Higher Command. Soon afterwards General Heneker, having found them neglected in some units, jokingly twitted me in public with similar errors. Although not sanguine about winning, I could do no less than bet him a 'fiver' that he would find no such omissions at his next inspection. Subsequently Colonel Hall (Middlesex) asked the General if he had yet 'caught Jack out', and was told 'not yet'.

In January 1917 'Superior Authority' (I forget how 'Superior') ordered all infantry battalions to form a Battle Patrol Platoon consisting of one subaltern and 53 other ranks who, leaving their companies, were to live and train at Battalion Headquarters. This honoured body was intended to exploit a success by pressing forward when the battalion had gained its objectives after an attack. Its members were to wear green distinguishing armbands and march at the head of the battalion when out of the Line. Although styled a platoon, it was nearly as large as a company of those days.

After faithfully trying the idea, we found that by the time this gallant band could reach the leading troops in action and decide on the best course to pursue companies on the spot had already taken all possible measures – as was their clear duty – to further their gains. Weak companies were therefore robbed of their best N.C.O.s and men, whom they could not afford to lose, without any advantage. At the same time, we had some 30 backward privates who might be improved under the eye of the Regimental-Sergeant-Major and Provost-Sergeant, and who would be useful for fatigues. These were accordingly attached to Battalion Headquarters vice the Battle Platoon; but on gala occasions 12 of the finest looking soldiers in each company were collected and formed up to head the march, after which they handed back their armbands and rejoined their platoons. I was forced into this hateful subterfuge in order to maintain the efficiency of my command, and confessed the misdeed to my immediate superior when Battle Platoons were shortly scrapped altogether . . .

Here we see yet another recrudescence of the 'corps d'élite' argument: in this case taking the form of a revival of the pernicious eighteenth- and early nineteenth-century system of 'flank companies'. These were the 'Grenadier' and 'Light' companies, which creamed off the boldest and most active soldiers in the regiments, and whose misuse (above all, their constant removal for indefinite periods on special duties) went far to ruin the Army for many decades. Fortunately the experiment did not long persist in the stress of 1917.

THE MOVE FROM THE SOMME
TO FLANDERS
(May 29th–June 3rd)

JUNE 4TH: OUTTERSTEENE, SIX MILES EAST OF HAZEBROUCK

. . . At 6.20 a.m. on the 1st of June, the 2/West Yorkshire marches from Curlu to quit the Somme for the third time with fresh laurels added to its illustrious name. A lovely morning, the early sun tinting the peaceful countryside, the long dry grass plentifully sprinkled with bright-scarlet wild poppies. The Divisional band passes first, playing a fascinating march 'The Long, Long Trail'; then comes the leading battalion of the brigade. We follow in our turn, preceded by two cyclists to give notice of any 'hostile' staff officers.

Thrilled, I watch my fine battalion march along, erect, clean, not a man, animal, vehicle, or piece of equipment out of the appointed place, the drums and fifes playing 'Colonel Bogey' and other airs; all this according to our habit when out of the Line. Thus we proceed to the coming battle in the north.

Presently our scouts warn me that the Divisional Commander and staff are standing beside the road a short way ahead to see the troops; a whistle sounds down the column, mounted officers get into the saddle, companies come to the 'slope' in succession, the band strikes up 'The Prince of Wales' March' and 'Ça Ira'.

On my reaching General Heneker and saluting, he rather coldly remarks 'Splendid battalion, Jack; it's a pity you are ten minutes late.' I cannot understand this, as Cropper has reconnoitred the 'starting point' beforehand, the time required to travel the distance from camp has been carefully calculated, and watches have been synchronised. I look at my watch and reply 'I beg your pardon, sir, we are fifteen seconds late.' After the transport (in rear of the last company) has gone by, the General repeats his two remarks. I salute, leave 'the presence', deny the accusation to Beddington (the pleasant and extremely capable G.S.O.1) standing behind, salute again and, considerably annoyed, ride to my place at the head of the column . . .

The 11-mile march continues through Méaulte to Buire-sur-Ancre, to our enjoyment of the first substantial roofs over our heads since February.

In the evening a polite Divisional message admits our punctuality in the morning, and says that the error was due to the preceding unit having been ten minutes too early.

We remain halted on the 2nd, during which I take some officers to visit the battlefield of Ovillers–La Boisselle, near Albert. What a ghastly 1st of July that was, almost a year ago! The concussion of the many previous days' terrific bombardments; the beautiful summer morning suddenly broken by the crash of our intense shell and machine gun covering fire, and the immediate German reply; the six assaulting 'waves' of the 8th Division practically all mown down before they could reach the hostile trenches; the ground littered with dead, dying and wounded; the Grand Attack on our divisional front crushed almost at once, a complete failure after such high hopes; the Division withdrawn from the battle that night, having suffered terribly . . .

JUNE 10TH: OUTTERSTEENE: IN ARMY RESERVE

The Battalion has spent the last week quietly here in fine weather. Our quarters are comfortable, though scattered; the beds are provided with sheets, a rare luxury . . .

Having remained out of the vortex of bombardment for some time, the area wears an aspect of normal prosperity. Throughout the 5th June, however, the air was rent by continual concussions due to a shell 'dump' near Bailleul having been hit by a bomb from a German aeroplane; this naturally caused a flitting of civilians in the vicinity . . .

At 3 a.m. on the 7th the explosion under the German trenches of many huge, long-prepared mines heralded to us the commencement of General Plumer's neat three-day battle, whose first assault caught the enemy unawares . . . Nearly the whole of the Messines–Wytschaete Ridge has been captured, together with 7,000 prisoners, 60 guns, many mortars and machine guns. Apart from prisoners the Germans lost heavily, while the casualties of the Second Army are only some 5,000. It has been a first-class performance, well planned and well executed . . .

The Battle of Messines marked the first stage in the 'Flanders Campaign' of 1917, whose primary strategic objective was the freeing of the Belgian coast (in particular the U-boat bases at Ostend and Zeebrugge) at the urgent insistence of the Admiralty. As Jack says, Messines was a triumph of planning and careful preparation: a preview of the 'Plumer method' which would again be employed with remarkable results later in the year. A limited operation, it finally cost the British Army some 17,000 casualties as German resistance recovered, but the cost to the enemy was about 25,000. This was a very good omen for the subsequent offensive; unfortunately, the long delay between Messines and the next stage went far to annul the advantages gained.

The battalion has received drafts amounting to 342 other ranks of good material – a battle omen; units are not made up to near their establishment to bask in idleness ...

HOME LEAVE
(June 12th–25th)

After work on the 12th I unexpectedly received a message offering me 14 days' leave. Since I had not had a single day's rest for five months, except for the brief period in hospital early in March, I accepted the offer so as to be fresh for our anticipated offensive in Flanders ...

In spite of disappointment with the results of the main Allied offensives in France, the serious activities of German submarines, and the expectation of further air-raids following that of May on Folkestone, there was no appearance of undue pessimism on the part of the British public regarding the general outlook. The War was just an accustomed unpleasant reality limiting amusements, and was faced with equanimity, even by those whose relatives and friends were reported as casualties in the daily lists. Work on armaments and industries was being prosecuted with full vigour. 'Labour' was, indeed, rather 'touchy', and small strikes of workers had sometimes occurred ...

Jack was somewhat astray here; no doubt his friends did not wish to worry a soldier on leave with the full story of what had been happening on the Home Front. In fact, there were 588 industrial disputes in 1917, the worst of them in April and May, affecting 860,727 workers, and causing a loss of 5,966,000 working days. The example of the Russian revolution in March created a wave of Labour unrest in every belligerent country, and Britain was not exempt from it.

Minor inconveniences arose through the 'Rationing Regulations', which put housewives to a little trouble in procuring their daily supplies of food in exchange for ration tickets, but there was no acute shortage of food, thanks to the Royal Navy and the Merchant Service ...

Here again, the full truth was somewhat different; rationing came as a great shock to many people, and its imperfect working produced the spectacle of long daily food queues as the year wore on. This also would be hidden as far as possible from a man due to return shortly to the Front.

JUNE 28TH: LILLE GATE, RAMPARTS, YPRES

This once beautiful old town, situated amid the sluggish brooks and ditches of Flanders (which I had the good fortune to see in all its charm in October 1914), is now a shell-swept stinking heap of ruins, under damnable daily bombardments. Almost all the gems of medieval architecture have been levelled by shells; scarcely one of the lovely old gabled houses is left standing . . . Vauban's 17th Century ramparts, encircling the old town, have defied the batterings of three years with astonishing success; on their eastern, southern and western sides a moat full of stagnant, smelly water has helped in saving them from obliteration . . . Joining the western part of the moat the Yser–Ypres–Comines Canal stretches northwards and southwards, its banks crammed with dug-outs for troops in reserve. Other accommodation exists in vaults in the ramparts and in cellars beneath buildings.

The Battalion area inside the ramparts near the Lille Gate is heavily shelled, less so on this wet day than previously. Two of our companies are in the ramparts, the other two in cellars nearby. The men are safe enough when underground, but the blast of howitzer shells outside is often terrific, especially at night when half the Battalion is on working parties and carrying stores . . .

Yesterday, after a full morning's office work and inspections, Palmes and I with a couple of orderlies and my bugler leave our rat-infested headquarters at the Lille Gate and cross the stinking moat to reconnoitre our sector for our Grand Assault next month. Battalion commanders have been told privately to expect it then; it is, however, 'secret' to the lower ranks – provided they are blind to the mass of obvious preparations for it . . .

Things are quiet, the afternoon being normally resting time for both sides. The light is dull and we can see little; the site of the village of Hooge and the wooded heights about Stirling Castle to the right front; the depression at Belle-waarde Lake, the tree-stumps on the crest, and the faint outline of Westhoek Ridge to the front. All else is a featureless blur of low ridges covered with long rank grass and weeds. Even with the aid of maps and binoculars, landmarks are hard to identify.

On our return walk the evening 'strafe' is commencing . . . the artillery of both sides has wakened up for the night.

When darkness has concealed the roads and tracks behind the Front (communications used only by small bodies of men in daylight) they will become crowded with troops till dawn. The tracks will bear infantry, Royal Engineer working parties, gunners, pack animals and companies carrying stores; the Pop-eringhe road (our main artery for supply) a continual procession of horse and motor transport, ambulances, troops marching forward and those relieved. All proceeding on the weary round of nightly routine are subject to shell fire, severe in places, for five or six miles in rear of the trench lines . . .

IN THE ST OMER AREA FOR BATTLE TRAINING
(July 1st–19th)

JULY 4TH: POLINCOVE

For the first few days here the companies rested, cleaned up, reorganised, and held short drill parades.

Yesterday Sir Claud Jacob, the II Corps Commander,[1] visited us without any fuss. He has a quiet, thoughtful, definite manner, and the reputation of being one of the soundest, most considerate High Commanders . . .

Today the Battalion commences battle training in earnest. Reveille being at 6.30, we march an hour and a half later five miles to the manoeuvre ground to practise an attack on a copy, to scale, of the German trenches we are to assault . . .

Our artillery 'creeping barrage' is denoted by parallel lines of men with flags, one hundred yards apart. Lines in succession, commencing with that next the infantry, raise their flags by signal from the officer checking the 'barrage table' to show

[1] *Later Field-Marshal.*

where our shells are falling, the flags of other lines being lowered. The barrage 'lifts' are calculated for an infantry advance of 100 yards every 3 minutes, and there are stated pauses on certain positions. This is the highest rate of advance found practicable for laden men across the rough, deep going of the shell-field, through the remains of wire entanglements and in face of the enemy.

The foremost infantry must, at all costs, keep within some 50 yards of our shell bursts so that when the barrage lifts the bayonets will be on the Germans before they can leave shelter and come into action.

'Carrying parties', orderlies with written messages, signallers laying telephone cables, and all others rehearse their parts exactly, except that officers may supervise for the first few days . . .

Since I think it imperative to prevent Germans who escape the artillery from coming into action at point-blank range, we are heavily manning our leading line with Lewis guns. Each gun is carried by two men, the first with arm looped round the muzzle to steady it, the second holding the butt to fire. We believe that an occasional spray of bullets, though not accurate, will keep the enemy under cover. I have further ordered that, should this fail, fire is to be opened instantly on any Germans appearing close at hand, but without checking the advance . . .

JULY 10TH

. . . The long exercises on the manoeuvre area continue to take place every second day . . . Our time is fully occupied indeed . . .

Nor is the office work light. In the Line and out of it, the volume of correspondence is astounding, between operations, training, administration and routine. Seldom are pen, paper and map laid down till bed-time. I have known battalion commanders pale with fatigue before a battle owing to the preparations for it. For myself, a very strong constitution enables me to carry out the great Duke of Wellington's sound principle of never carrying over arrears of work till the next day if it can be avoided.

Little as is the time for recreation, games have to be sandwiched

in somehow, since no British troops ever travel without foot-
balls or the energy to kick them . . .

. . . The day before yesterday a bloodthirsty fellow, Colonel
Campbell, the Army bayonet-fighting expert, gave a lurid
lecture to a large, thrilled audience on the most economical use
of the bayonet, and to arouse the pugnacity of the men. He
pointed out that to plunge the blade right through an opponent
is a waste of trouble, and that three inches in the heart are quite
sufficient. The cold-blooded science of the business seems to me
rather horrid, even if necessary.

'Instruction' after 'instruction', forecasting the Battle Orders,
keeps arriving. Intricate and lengthy as they cannot avoid
being, Lieut-Colonel H. Beddington, M.C. (16th Lancers),
G.S.O.1, 8th Division, has framed them simply and clearly,
besides issuing them in their proper sequence at a few days
interval to allow recipients to digest the contents. Each instruction deals with a separate phase of preparations and
operations . . .

The weather is sunny and warm, but sometimes broken by
thunderstorms. The men are fit as fiddles, comfortable and
happy. Football is an endless diversion in the evenings . . .

Today all the infantry of the 8th Division who are to be
launched into the first assault at Ypres go through the attack
together, everyone in his proper place . . . In the evening
General Jacob delivers an interesting lecture on the coming
battle to senior officers of the Division in the village hall . . .

. . . Yesterday the Commander-in-Chief comes to witness the
exercise. He arrives at the West Yorks with his aide-de-camp,
and an orderly carrying a Union Jack at the end of his lance,
all perfectly turned out and riding beautiful glossy-coated
horses. I am introduced to Sir Douglas who shakes my hand.
At this moment 'Zero hour' falls, and, seeing that the long,
kneeling lines of the companies, the officers watch in hand, are
uncertain whether to await inspection or to advance, I canter
forward on polished little Warts to set them in motion with my

horn. On my return, the Chief chats affably for a minute or two about the polo we played together in India; then, wishing my battalion 'good luck', he moves on to another unit.

Sir Douglas Haig paid two visits to the 8th Division in training. On July 13th he noted: 'The men looked in splendid condition and marched very well.' Seeing them again on the 18th, he commented: '. . . all ranks looked very fit and healthy.' Jack met him again at Cologne in 1919; when he was introduced, Haig looked at him for a moment, then said: 'Oh yes, I remember him. That was a nice little horse you were riding when we last met.' Jack remarks: 'Surely this must be a remarkable instance of memory, observation, and fondness for horses.' It was certainly quite a feat to remember one battalion commander, on the strength of two minutes' conversation, at an interval of a year and a half crowded with events, and from a time when he was daily visiting unit after unit.

The Battle preparations have become more intensive. Further 'instructions' arrive nearly daily, constituting a kind of 'paper barrage'.

On most evenings we attend conferences at Brigade Head-quarters, or lectures describing the plan of attack in the hall of this village, the largest room hereabouts. An exact clay model of the front at Ypres is at hand for study, and the lecturers are supplied with large-scale maps. Until yesterday most of those addressing us, with a comprehensive sweep of the pointer across the map, have declared that by 'Zero hour' all the German trenches will be 'obliterated' by our shells – a tale we have heard before. The last lecturer, however, on the artillery role, ominously omitted to provide this comforting assurance . . .

Our Air Offensive has already commenced. Now the Battle Bombardments have opened at Ypres; it is whispered that they have drawn a considerable reply from the enemy . . .

Three plump young subalterns from England have reported for duty. What a time for them to join! They should have been here weeks ago.

Yesterday being the last time on which we shall mess to-gether, all my officers dine with me.

Today we are packing up. Our quarters look empty . . . The final full guard mounting is over; the glass and china crockery are away; service tin mugs and plates are in use again. All ranks are in great spirits in anticipation of smashing the Germans this time.

JULY 20TH

. . . Our cavalry are assembled in the vicinity for the battle. High Command, with incurable faith in their luck, continue to expect that the infantry assaults will burst a gap in the German defences large enough for horsemen to ride through and create havoc in the enemy's rear. The 10th [Hussars], which lost some two-thirds of their men at the Battle of Arras last spring, do not appear to share this belief . . . But should the German defence be widely and completely broken, cavalry, supported by tanks and artillery, might get an opportunity of routing disorganised forces. The bare possibility of this justifies the readiness of the Cavalry Corps . . .

Cavalry were always held in readiness behind every large-scale attack, for the reason which Jack states. Since the attacks failed, time after time, to break through the German defences, the cavalry found little opportunity for mounted action, and their presence has been the subject of much derisive comment. The fact remains that, with all its evident weaknesses, cavalry was the only mobile Arm available during the First World War. What comment would be appropriate for a High Command which planned and launched great assaults, without making any provision for mobile exploitation, it is not difficult to see. In 1918, many eye-witnesses agree that the great German offensives were much handicapped by the absence of cavalry; and when open warfare was to some extent restored in the last weeks of the War, the need for cavalry (and any other mobile troops, e.g. cyclists) became acute.

JULY 21ST: RENNINGHELST

. . . The peaceful countryside . . . is far behind. The entire Ypres Salient, to a depth of some eight miles from the front line, is alive with infantry, artillery, repair workshops, hospitals and ambulances of Gough's Fifth Army, in billet, bivouac, mottle-painted tent and hut. The sheds and yards of buildings, copses and all other cover hide tanks, long-range guns, heavy howitzers and munitions. Renninghelst stands on the outer edge of the shelled areas. The military targets ahead are subject to periodical bombardments, the enemy paying special attention to main roads, railways, suspected shell stores and gun positions . . .

Tonight we must bivouac, and there seems to be scarcely a bit of vacant ground the size of a football pitch clear of troops, gear and stores.

The Battalion, having debussed, marched in at 10 o'c, very jolly and singing – or what passed for it in my wearied opinion. What with this noise, the all-night rumble of transport and the reverberations of our cannon in the vicinity, sleep is elusive; one's nerves are a little 'on edge'.

JULY 22ND: WINNIPEG CAMP, RENNINGHELST

. . . At 11 a.m. orders arrive for the 2/West Yorks to march to Ypres this afternoon.

At 2.30 the Battalion falls in in close column of companies to hear my final words on our last parade as a battalion.

Sitting on Warts I say that I am proud to lead soldiers with such a record, and have never seen men in better form before a battle. That every detail of plan and preparation has been arranged with the utmost care. That indifferent troops may win battles if there are enough of them and casualties do not matter; but I expect my men, as first-class soldiers, to defeat the enemy utterly without themselves suffering unduly. To this end they must use all their wits, and and engage every German in range without a second's hesitation. That I know they will fight with their usual tenacity and like gentlemen, respecting the lives of Germans whose surrender has been accepted. And God's blessing on them all.

On finishing this address I am on the point of ordering companies to come to attention and march off when, to my horror, a private whom I regarded unfavourably, in the front rank of the leading company, irregularly steps forward a few paces and takes off his helmet. I wonder 'What's up now? Is the fellow going to throw down his rifle, tell me to lead the charge without him, and cause a parting scene?'[1] Instead of this my

[1] *No doubt certain other variations on the well-known phrase 'I shall soldier no more' sprang into Jack's mind at this moment.*

230

friend, holding up his helmet, calls out 'Three cheers for the Colonel' – to which singular and warm-hearted compliment my feelings were, under the circumstances, too deep for reply . . .

IN THE LINE AND IN SUPPORT
(July 23rd–30th)

At 8.30 o'c this morning the Battalion, filing 3½ miles forward, relieves two companies of the 2/Wiltshire and two of the 9/Cheshire in the trenches about Bellewaarde Farm . . .

The relief is conducted in daylight – an unusual time for reliefs, especially with so much of the route in view from the enemy's higher ground. Sections of six men leave Ypres at five-minute intervals and move between the battery positions to Potijze; there the long string of groups enters a communication trench, pulverised in places, for the last mile and a half of the journey up the gentle, war-blighted open slope. This tedious relief is not finished till 7 p.m., with only two casualties, thanks to luck and to the good judgment of junior leaders . . .

Our trenches have been terribly knocked about by the hostile fire, but the Germans must be getting hell from our frequent intense bombardments. I have never seen such commodious dug-outs; those in the support trenches can hold hundreds of men; an immense amount of labour and material must have been required for their construction.

After a tour of the lines to see that the companies are settled, we are busy completing tomorrow's raid arrangements . . .

JULY 24TH

The weather is good. At daybreak, Fox and I proceed to the front trench and minutely examine the German parapet and wire through binoculars to make certain that the gaps cut in the wire by our shells and patrols have not been repaired during last night in spite of bursts of Lewis gun fire to prevent it . . . Our posts having previously been thinned and as many men as possible put in shelter to escape retaliatory shelling, the covering barrage opens at 1 p.m. Instantly the raiding party, under Lieut McConville and consisting of 2/Lieuts Spink and Exley, with 12 volunteers per company (51 in all), climbing out of their trench, coolly walks forward in a line of four groups in file a hundred yards apart, and enters the first German trench practically unopposed, Here two groups remain to guard against any undiscovered enemy, while the other two proceed to the second trench, 150 yards behind the first. Owing, however, to an error, about which I bitterly complain later, our barrage misses part of a flank holding a machine gun which kills Sergt McIntosh and Corporal Rumbold, besides wounding Spink and 10 other ranks.

The raiders take 5 prisoners of the 89th Grenadier Regiment, kill 15 others, and report that the Germans must have sustained a number of additional casualties when running back through our barrage to escape capture.

Raids by the battalions to right and left of us take place at the same time . . .

In the evening messages from Generals Heneker and Grogan arrive to compliment 'Mac' and his men on their excellent performance.

It may be noted here that the number of those volunteering for raids is smaller than formerly, although courage in action is as common as ever.

I am very sad about today's losses; they were most unlucky. I believe that our efforts to keep down casualties have generally resulted in my battalion suffering fewer than most others. For instance, a recent successful raid in the same strength as ours cost another battalion 36 men – half of whom had not been in action before.

JULY 25TH

The usual three-hour round of inspections soon after dawn; then a full day's office work.

The reports on small affairs such as yesterday's must minutely give High Command all information likely to be of use. For example, where the German counter-barrage fell during the raid and the number of minutes it took to fall will probably coincide with its place and time in the forthcoming assault.

At night the Battalion is relieved by the 2/Devonshire under pretty good conditions and with only three or four casualties . . .

We have not got far before a lump of shell striking my helmet knocks me down, unharmed . . .

JULY 27TH: YPRES

We have had 37 casualties since the 22nd . . . Many men are sick from German gas shells . . . Fortunately, there has never been any need for my wearing a respirator. They are too stuffy to work in, the eye-glasses become dim from moisture; one is often too busy and too weary to heed personal risks. Besides, I consider myself to be almost impervious to every enemy weapon after serving for thirty months at the Front with scarcely a scratch.

We are losing our long, good-natured and amusing McConville, who is going to the Royal Flying Corps after gaining a great reputation during his year with the 2/West Yorks . . .

Although incurring their displeasure thereby, I have ordered all company officers to wear tunics – with small rank badges – issued to the men, men's trousers and equipment, the subalterns to carry rifle instead of revolver. The junior leaders run sufficient danger from their positions in action without adding to it through the presence of trappings which the German marksmen can distinguish. The Quartermaster has therefore provided the necessary articles.

The German shell fire on Ypres is persistent and heavy in reply to terrific poundings by our artillery. Shell splinters and masonry are constantly flying about while the concussion seldom ceases altogether. All troops not on duty must remain under cover; but even so, the casualties in and around the town are severe, amounting, I hear, to 400 or 500 daily. Between dusk and dawn working and carrying parties, as well as transport bringing stores along the Poperinghe road into Ypres, have nerve-wracking experiences in this ghastly area . . .

Our office is in a tin hut a few yards from the ramparts into which we may adjourn when the fire becomes too hot. Concealed amid the ruins near us are some 8-inch howitzers, two of which lie overturned in their shattered emplacements.

The 'paper' strength of the Battalion is 41 officers and 917 other ranks, of whom 28 officers and 763 other ranks are present with it.

The assault, due today, has been postponed; it is, however, imminent. I wish the business were over.

JULY 28TH

. . . At 6.45 p.m. the Battalion commences its 22-mile march to the trenches. The companies, with platoons at 5-minute intervals, file through the Lille Gate . . . past several ruined farms, smashed limbers, dead horses and mules; then up treeless, war-stricken slopes north of Zillebeke Lake, now almost dry. We proceed through the entrenched Field Artillery positions, the pieces of the battery nearest us all out of action, lying with broken wheels and shields, or overturned by the successive bombardments that sweep the extensive lines of guns from end to end, and necessitate large replacements after dark.

Walking ahead of my leading platoon, I see on ascending a slight rise that the German observation balloons are still up. I therefore halt the long chain of groups and the men sit down for a smoke. Soon there are grumbles – 'What are we stopping for? Why don't we get on?' Palmes, a sound adviser, thinks it safe enough to go ahead, but I will not budge till the sun sinks deeper; the risk is too great of being discovered by the balloon observers with their telescopes, and of their turning artillery on to the Battalion while it is still in the open. Presently the balloons are hauled down for the night, and we file on again, later entering a communication trench. Our rear company, however, is caught by shell fire, and has ten casualties . . .

JULY 29TH: TRENCHES:
BELLEWAARDE FARM SUB-SECTOR

. . . The Battalion holds 500 yards of line with two companies in the front trench, and two in the support trench about 150 yards in rear. In many places the parapets and the sandbags revetting them lie scattered about from shells . . .

The sector is fairly quiet this morning, the atmosphere dull . . . Some 200 yards ahead of our wire entanglement with its shattered supporting posts, across the shell holes, rank grass, weeds and scarlet wild poppies in No Man's Land, we see the

German wire and the line of their riven parapet. A full half-mile beyond are the tree-stumps on low Bellewaarde Ridge, the West Yorks' sector on the First Objective of the Fifth Army. This objective is shown on our maps as the BLUE Line . . .

Westhoek Ridge, on the BLACK Line, 2,000 yards of which is the Second Objective of the 8th Division, is visible half-a-mile north-east of the First Objective. These are all that now concern the 23rd Brigade . . .

The aeroplanes of both armies are very active today, large formations of ours cruising over the German reserve and artillery positions, usually among the bursting shells from anti-aircraft guns.

A single hostile aeroplane passes over us only a few hundred feet up, its observer, clear to the naked eye, standing in the cockpit gazing down, doubtless to see if the British trenches appear to be unduly crowded preparatory to an attack. Any men who cannot hide in time remain motionless to escape detection. Some Lewis gun sections are slow in opening fire to drive this machine higher; the N.C.O.s in charge of them have to be roused. Courage in action is common to all ranks; but there is a shortage of properly trained junior leaders who will act at once on their own responsibility . . .

Major McLaren, Captains Clayton and Ingham, 7 subalterns and about 80 other ranks, the Battalion 'Minimum Reserve', were sent to the transport lines on our departure from Ypres yesterday. After deducting these, the personnel belonging to the Quartermaster, Transport, Band and other details, we have in the trenches for the assault 16 officers and 600 other ranks.

The blast of shells continues throughout each day and night with rare intervals.

JULY 30TH

Last night a 'D' Company patrol took a German prisoner, who was at once escorted back to the staff for interrogation.

At 5 a.m. Cropper, Fox and I proceed in drizzling rain[1]

---

[1] *The beginning of the break in the weather which, lasting all through August, did so much to frustrate British hopes, and give to 'Passchendaele' its eternal evil name.*

round the trenches. The morning shelling costs us a few casualties.

All ranks are confident. The men not on duty are crowded in smelly dug-outs whose accommodation is taxed to the utmost with additional troops -- a Trench Mortar battery, Machine Gun Company, message pigeons, etc.

A message arrives: 'Zero hour will be at 3.50 tomorrow morning, the 31st inst.' and is acknowledged. So we are for the 'high jump' once more.

I don't want to be mutilated, but death is a contemptible little enemy. Gone are the personal fears of the 1914 days. One has become accustomed to battles, besides being too strained, wearied and busy to care much about oneself. The certain loss of friends of all ranks will be the worst shock, a shock still keenly felt even after two and a half years of this bloody war. Tomorrow the French, British and German Press will all be hailing a victory, the first two for the capture of some ground, the last for losing so little. The National casualties will be described as 'slight', those of the enemy as 'heavy'. One must, however, keep these thoughts to oneself.

After a final look at the German positions to imprint the scarce landmarks (always being shot away) on the memory, there are many papers to tackle in the office. In the evening – for the second time today – a staff officer comes to synchronise all watches and to re-check compass bearings to our objective in case of misty weather.

At periods today – as on preceding days – large groups of our artillery open short bursts of hurricane fire on different German reserve and gun positions in turn. During these 'shoots' one sees the hostile area under 'treatment' in a whirlpool of exploding shells, clods of earth and débris. More slowly and methodically, by day and night, our heavy pieces search for the enemy's artillery, ammunition dumps, reserve billets, roads and railways still further away. There is a considerable reply to these and the concussion is often deafening . . .

At midnight, after a hot meal, the last before assaulting except for tea, bread and butter, the companies file silently to their battle positions in the trenches . . .

I have ordered the Provost-Sergeant with the Battalion Police to line up in the front trench as soon as the assault starts. They are to arrest any men who return improperly. Although I command a battalion whose courage and loyalty have never given me a trace of anxiety, one must guard against those inexplicable panics which may seize brave men on rare occasions and which are so infectious. Moreover, false orders to retire, emanating possibly from a concealed enemy or shouted in error, have to be taken into account . . .

On rounds alone tonight I come on a sentry fast asleep although trench routine allows of all getting sufficient rest before battle. If court-martialled he is liable to be shot. My fingers at once close on the fellow's neck and I give him a rough shake. He looks up indignantly and says in reply to me that he is not unwell. I tell him I shall forward to High Command any complaint he cares to make about me, and that, having taken the law into my own hands, I will not report him. I have not the heart to charge the man just before action in any case . . .

My final entry in the Battalion Diary reads: 'Battalion in front line awaiting attack which is to take place next morning at dawn.'

THE THIRD BATTLE OF YPRES: BATTLE OF PILCKEM RIDGE

At 2.30 a.m. on the 31st I personally reported to Brigade Headquarters . . . that the 2/West Yorks were ready to attack. The other three battalion commanders of the 23rd Brigade and Commanders of attached units made similar reports.

General Grogan asked me in my turn 'And you, Colonel Jack, do you understand your orders?' I replied 'Yes, sir.' He then read out the latest news from the Divisional front, saying in conclusion 'That's all, gentlemen; thank you, and good luck.' We reciprocated the good wishes, saluted and returned to our units . . .

At 3.40, after shaving, a last polish and brush-up by Holden, then a light breakfast, I proceeded with Palmes and our orderlies to a previously selected mound of sandbags outside Junction Trench, a couple of hundred yards from the front line. Although orders forbade battalion commanders to quit their headquarters during an assault lest the 'chain of command' were interrupted, I thought it right to see my companies start off correctly, and considered this post secure enough for a minute or two after 'Zero', due at 3.50 a.m.

Palmes, with Fox, some signallers and runners, was therefore to follow and command our assaulting 'waves', deal with local situations, and establish on Bellewaarde Ridge a new headquarters, in communication with those now occupied, to which Cropper and I would then repair.

In order to assist messengers in finding their way through the wilderness to the new headquarters, we had arranged for a white tape to be laid behind the battalion as far forward as tape would go; cleft sticks holding cards were to mark the rest of the route.

One minute before the time for the assault a drummer, his pre-War drum with pipeclayed cords and inscribed Battle Honours, was to beat a roll. I did not imagine that many would hear it, but anything to stir the blood on such occasions is valuable. Since we did not want to lose either drummer or drum the former had orders to be under cover by 'Zero' . . .

At 3.49, as we peered intently over our mound, the trench mortars suddenly opened, a minute too early. Although dawn was just breaking, there was not light enough to see more than a few yards; but we could tell by the muffled rattle of accoutrements and the blurred moving forms of the men nearby that the companies, in the tenseness of the moment, had mistaken the mortar barrage for that of the artillery and were mounting their parapets to advance.

'My God, Peter! What's up?' I asked.

'I don't know, sir,' came Palmes's strained reply.

Sick with anxiety lest our foremost lines would be 'blotted out' by our artillery through attacking too early, I immediately scrambled forward across the trenches, calling out repeatedly 'Steady West Yorks. Go steady.'

(I was told later that in the then comparative stillness the admonition was heard by parts of the companies, which I had almost reached.)

A few seconds later the ground just in front was all lit up by bursting shells. To make sure, however, that they were ours, not those of the enemy, I turned towards Ypres where I saw countless tiny gun flashes. Our barrage had opened; the inferno was deafening.

There was now nothing more to be done; so, cheering 'Forrard away, the West Yorks', I turned back for my head-quarters. Presently a small fragment of shell scratched my leg; then as if in answer to my contemptuous 'Pouf! They can't really damage me', a heavy shell, whose explosion I neither saw nor heard, buried me in the trench I was about to enter, wounded me severely and knocked me unconscious.

And so, on an unforgettable morning, cold grey dawn of the 31st of July, in battle dress, with bayonets fixed, buttons dulled and the polished helmets coated with a thin skin of mud to be less visible, 2nd Battalion The Prince of Wales' Own West Yorkshire Regiment, under Captain John Philip Palmes, M.C., with perfect discipline and undimmed courage, passed from me in a few minutes through the quaking shell holes into the hurricane of the battle.

*   *   *

THE 2/WEST YORKSHIRES AT 'PASSCHENDAELE' ('THIRD YPRES')

The Battle of Pilckem Ridge, marking the opening of the second phase of the Flanders Campaign, proved to be that most perplexing of circumstances in war: a partial success. Casualties were about 15,000 on July 31st – a striking contrast with the first day of the Somme in 1916, and a tribute to the British Army's much-improved battle techniques. Prisoners were taken; guns were captured; in places advances of as much as 3,000 yards were made and held. In other places, however, particularly on the right flank of the Fifth Army, in the sector adjacent to the 8th Division, gains were small if any. The Germans counter-attacked vigorously. The rain began to fall in torrents on British and Germans alike. The attack bogged down once more.

The 8th Division's casualties in the four days, July 31st to August 3rd, were 3,076 (5,121 on July 1st 1916). The 2/West Yorkshires were on their objectives by 5 a.m. On August 1st they drove off a German counter-attack, but lost heavily from enemy shelling. Their casualties in this tour of duty were 10 officers and 209 other ranks. Among those killed were Major Richard McLaren, Captains J. P. Palmes, M.C., and E. H. Bartley, Lieutenants G. May, M.C., A. Reese, M.C., and P. F. Drake.

After refitting, the Battalion returned to the line to take part in the Battle of Langemarck on August 16th, a failure in mud and rain which cost the 8th Division a further 2,111 casualties. Of these the West Yorkshires' share was 10 officers (not one who went 'over the top' returned; nine of the ten were killed) and 264 other ranks.

'So, to my infinite sorrow, nearly all my dear West Yorkshire friends were swept away. "How bright their Glorious Spirits shine." '

The return of two old comrades to the Battalion helped to alleviate some of the sorrow at these losses: 'Captain Charles Hinchcliffe, M.C., having recovered from his wounds of May, rejoined the Battalion after these engagements. And Captain Sidney Rogerson, with his invariable high sense of duty, at once applied to relinquish his staff appointment and return to help his battalion . . . Both of these came unscathed through the fierce fighting of 1918 . . .'

(The full fierceness of that fighting is well described in Sidney Rogerson's book, 'The Last of the Ebb', Arthur Barker, 1937.)

V

Sick Leave, Home Duty, Commanding 1/Cameronians in France

Jack's wounds on July 31st 1917 kept him in hospital until January 27th 1918; he then entered upon a prolonged period of sick leave during which he slowly regained his strength.

. . . On March 27th, April 12th and May 22nd I asked my doctors if they would pass me fit for active service. The first report was that my health at the Front would not last for six hours, the second that I must do nothing strenuous for six or eight months, and a third that my condition was good enough for, perhaps, a couple of months' work. Army Medical Boards took a less serious view, but not until May 28th was I pronounced recovered.

The War Office having good-humouredly agreed to accept my services for a month's light duty, to Whitehall I repaired on the day after my last Board. I selected the War Office in preference to Home regimental employment, because I knew the former would not seek to retain me, whereas a training centre might want an experienced Regular to instruct drafts, and so prevent my rejoining the B.E.F. . . .

Jack remained at the War Office until July 4th, and returned to France on July 11th.

The War which he now re-entered had changed greatly. Following the final collapse of Russia in October 1917, the Germans were able to bring almost a million troops from the Eastern Front to the West. With this accession of strength, Ludendorff gambled on a last throw against the British Army. The blow fell on March 31st; it was held only by prodigious efforts and with very heavy loss to the British forces. A second attack was launched against them in the Ypres area on April 9th; this, too, was held, partly with the help of French troops made available by the newly appointed Allied Generalissimo, Foch. It was on April 13th, when this battle was at its height, that Field-Marshal Haig issued his famous 'Backs to the Wall' Order.

Both sides were suffering from exhaustion, and a brief interval fol-

243

lowed the defeat of this attack. Then the Germans struck heavily at the French on the Aisne, on May 27th, and a series of battles followed which carried them once again across the Marne, threatening Paris. By July, however, when Jack returned to France, the impetus of the German assaults was perceptibly dying away. Their losses had been crippling: those of the Allies were increasingly offset by the arrival of American forces. The Germans still had one attack left in them, launched on July 15th, the day on which we resume Jack's diary narrative.

But first a word should be said about the Army which he was rejoining. His old division, the 8th, had had terrible losses both in March and again in April, being virtually 'wiped out' on each occasion. It then had the cruel luck to be sent to a 'quiet sector' to recuperate; this 'quiet sector' was the Chemin des Dames, beside the Aisne, where the Division found itself facing the brunt of the next German offensive. It emerged from that experience with a total ration strength of 1,500.

Divisions, it should be noted, had been reorganised before the German attacks began. Following the reduction of the B.E.F. by 141 battalions, in view of the alleged man-power shortage, British divisions were reduced to 9 battalions, 3 to a brigade. This reduction did not apply to the Dominion divisions, which partly accounts for the great part played by those formations in the subsequent fighting.

Jack's return coincided with a remarkable swing of fortune, which makes the next part of his diary read very differently from all the foregoing chapters.

JULY 15TH: 'M' SCOTTISH BASE DEPOT, BEAUMARAIS

... Two days ago a telegram from H.Q. Fifth Army[1] said that they have applied for me to command their Army School of Instruction, a flattering appointment. When at Home, however, I had asked to be sent to my own regiment, or to the 2/ West Yorkshire in the 8th Division, preferring to finish the War, or myself, at the Front ...

At the depot I am handed a telegram ordering me to go forthwith and take command of the 1/Cameronians, with which I have not served since February 1915.

JULY 16TH

1/Cameronians, still forming part of the 19th Infantry Brigade, were

[1] Now under General Sir William Birdwood.

244

now with the 33rd Division in Flanders, after many vicissitudes. Jack
set off by train on the 16th to join them.

. . . While awaiting [the train] a company of Americans
passes, big, loose-limbed fellows of a fine stamp . . .

The enemy must force a victory before the American strength
becomes too formidable; otherwise they are certain to lose the
War. (My original diary of 13th April notes: 'The race is a gift
for the Allies if all hold on. It is Waterloo over again, the
Americans taking the place of Blücher's Prussians.')

JULY 19TH: 'B' ECHELON CAMP, IN DIVISIONAL RESERVE

I take command of the 1/Cameronians from Lieut-Col W, a
keen Territorial officer from another regiment, whom I knew;
he then departs.

A ride to, and conference at, Headquarters 19th Infantry
Brigade in a house near Poperinghe occupies most of the morning. Brig.-Gen. Mayne, the commander, greets me pleasantly,
but to my sorrow says privately that my battalion is below form.
It is the only original battalion left in the 19th Brigade, the
others having been transferred elsewhere. We intend it to become again one of the best in the Army . . .

At lunch I meet my officers. The Second-in-Command,
Major the Hon. H. Ritchie, D.S.O., a New Army officer, has
been in France only a month following service in Salonika.
Dick Hunter (Major) and George Wood (Quartermaster)
are the only pre-War Regular officers now with the Battalion.
The former was wounded in 1914, and since his recovery has
served consistently and well with the Regiment, gaining the
D.S.O. The adjutant, Freddie Becher, a brother of my subaltern Harry, who was killed in 1915, has spent over two years
with the Battalion. The assistant-adjutant is a cheery young
fellow, Wigan. These are all first-class officers. I can only hope
that the remainder are better soldiers than they look.

There are, too, several old friends among the Warrant and
Non-Commissioned ranks, pipers, transport and cooks; the
chief of them being Tom Windram, M.C., Regimental-Sergeant-

Major, and Pipe-Major Alexander, both of whom I have known for nearly 15 years.

The other units in the Brigade are: 1/Queen's, 5/6/Scottish Rifles (Cameronians) and 19th Trench Mortar Battery.

The afternoon is taken up with detailed inspections of everything. The whole Battalion has been greatly upset by tactless handling, a minor example being the alteration of the tunics of this old Lowland Regiment to a Highland pattern. Unless efficiency demands it, one must never change the customs of a regiment to which one is temporarily attached for duty.'[1]

The first thing required is close-order drill, smartening up, and cleaning . . .

In the evening a staff car takes me to dine with the Divisional Commander, Sir Reginald Pinney . . . He gives me a good welcome, and an excellent dinner . . .

There is thrilling news from the Marne. The French (with American divisions attached) have opened a large-scale offensive between Château-Thierry and Soissons, with wonderful success.

JULY 20TH

A decent charger is my first personal requisite, and the sympathy of the divisional Veterinary Officer has been enlisted to this end.[2]

The Battalion is scattered among ruined farms and trenches . . . we can carry out little training and drill, that, too, only in small bodies at dawn and dusk, because the whole area is under German observation from Kemmel Hill.

At night about half the Battalion is at work repairing roads and improving trenches and wire . . .

JULY 23RD: IN BRIGADE SUPPORT

The next German offensive is expected to take place here any day . . .

A hostile attack will almost certainly sweep away all our

[1] *In 1916 the 6/Cameronians (T.A.) lodged a formal protest at being brigaded with Highlanders, on the grounds that their grandfathers had fought against the Highland men.*

[2] *Warts, also, was a casualty of 1917.*

246

thin advanced defences. In that case my battalion is to retake the crest-line south-east of St Eloi, and we are busy with plans for it . . .

There is a large amount of office work daily. We have been deeply engaged checking the organisation of the companies, which is fully explained in a General Order detailing the exact numbers of the different ranks, special units (Lewis gunners, bombers, runners, etc.) and stores to be maintained by each company. Casualties, besides other changes, necessitate constant revision, which has been neglected.

The thorough and prompt attention to orders, formerly the rule in the Regiment, is now notably absent. Pressure is required to get work properly performed. This is not due to unwillingness, but to the present officers (save those from the Royal Military College) not having been well grounded at Home in their duties.

Although my battalion is labelled 'Regular', it contains no greater number of trained personnel than Territorial or New Army battalions. Perhaps we have one or two more experienced warrant and non-commissioned officers than they.

Besides the daily round of inspections, we are making every effort to increase battle efficiency – slack soldiers are anathema. At dusk, therefore, as many officers and non-commissioned officers as feasible are collected for instruction which should have been given at Home. They are, however, bundled out here to face the most formidable army in Europe (at least, that was the state of the German Army till recently) and fail, or achieve success, at excessive cost of life and time . . .

JULY 25TH

. . . Last night 'H' Company, 2/119th American Regiment arrived for attachment to us, to become accustomed to routine at the Front. The men are of splendid physique. Unfortunately one of their officers was killed almost at once by a shell, said to be a British 'short'; it must, however, have been defective, as it fell over 1,000 yards behind our posts.

Considering the amount of their firing, our gunners are marvellously careful and accurate.

We are due for the trenches tomorrow . . .

In the evening Harold Ritchie comes up from the Transport lines for a talk. The permission of Brigade Headquarters is required for this meeting, because battalion commanders and their seconds-in-command are not allowed to be at the Front at the same time lest one shell should rob His Majesty of the services of both . . .

The French offensive, assisted by British, American and Italian divisions, has forced the Germans to abandon the line of the Ourcq.

JULY 27TH: VOORMEZEELE: FRONT TRENCHES

. . . The relief was expeditiously completed by midnight, but as the ground telephone cables had been broken the last reports that companies had taken over their posts did not arrive till 2 o'c this morning by runners . . .

The Battalion 'Trench Strength' is about 15 officers and 450 other ranks . . . The advanced posts of the enemy are 300–400 yards from ours . . .

The plan of defence has altered since I was last in Belgium. The continuous, wired, double trench lines have been replaced by these several lines of posts which, besides economising men, are harder for the enemy to locate and shell than trench lines. The new defence is not, however, initially as strong as the old, so supporting companies, besides other troops, are furnished with detailed plans for re-taking important positions gained by the enemy . . .

Jack is referring to the British adoption of 'defence in depth', first employed by the Germans in 1917. The advantages of the system are as he states, but it does depend for effectiveness on counter-attack, which presupposes adequate reserves. Also, of course, under certain circumstances (fog, darkness, or smoke screens) the mutual support of the posts is much reduced, making them vulnerable to penetration. When this occurs the successful offensive is described as 'infiltration' – a tactic used by both sides in 1918.

JULY 28TH

. . . Visiting the posts is an easy affair nowadays compared with former struggles along trenches knee-deep or more in mud;

the Germans, too, are rather farther away than they were in the old trench lines, and their snipers and machine gunners are unaccountably indolent – for the moment. Nevertheless, there being practically no cover, our inspections of the advanced posts must take place circumspectly, in the faint light of dawn or dusk . . .

Our artillery is very active in periods every night; the enemy's weak reply is chiefly on the support areas and roads in rear.

The French have captured Fère-en-Tardenois and the Americans have broken up fierce German counter-attacks.

JULY 29TH

At 6 a.m. today I accompany the Brigade Commander on his inspection of our lines. Orders seem to have lost their sacredness, and a few instances of gross neglect come to light. But on the whole things are improving; companies have made their trenches much more comfortable – an important contribution towards efficiency. The Battalion is excellent, as ever, at labour of all kinds.

Last night Corporal Bell, 'C' Company, captured a German, one of a patrol which ventured too far across No Man's Land. I have gladly sent Bell's mother – at his request – the £10 reward which I had offered for the first prisoner so taken . . .

For some days past plans have been in preparation for a local attack. These plans require minute arrangement. Success raises the valuable quality of self-confidence, whereas failure, especially if due to rashness and careless organisation, undermines it.

Tonight the bombardment is disturbing for a time, one shell nearly flattening our shelter. In circumstances of great discomfort I recall the flattering opinion of my old Colonel, 'Jerry' Macan, expressed on manoeuvres in India in bad weather: 'Jack, my boy, the best in this world is barely good enough for the likes of us.'

JULY 30TH

This morning our rounds are early – 2.30 o'c. I am happy to find matters in a much better state . . .

The Battalion had 14 casualties during the last tour in the Line, a tour of the now customary four days . . .

The Battalion spends its first day in Support or Reserve in resting, cleaning, and with inspections of accoutrements. On other days the platoons not detailed for work carry out drill and musketry exercise for a couple of hours in the mornings, Lewis gun and 'specialist' training for an hour in the afternoons. All available officers parade under Ritchie, Hunter or me for instruction, and the Regimental-Sergeant-Major coaches the Non-commissioned officers.

At sundown, when the pipes and drums play 'Retreat', the company guards mount with peace-time precision.

It has hitherto been the rule in the British Army for men, when passing officers, to salute with the hand farther away from them. But a new Army Order decrees that in future a salute is to be given with the right hand only. This seems a peculiar time to select for altering so small a matter.

Jack added later: 'It has been suggested that our altering the hand salute of the Army in the midst of critical operations did much to break the enemy's heart, the Germans considering, no doubt, that it was useless to continue the struggle against an opponent who had energy to spare for bothering with such a trifle at such a time.'

This would seem to be the perfect answer to those who scorn military minutiae.

This morning 'A' Company carries out a practice attack in the presence of the Brigadier . . . Battle training is circumscribed by the Battalion having to find every day 250 officers and men (nearly three-quarters of its available numbers) for work on roads, defences and dug-outs.

The close supervision of exercises, duties and organisation, besides dealing with office papers, leaves one absolutely no leisure time. Matters go so quickly wrong unless they are constantly attended to . . .

The Franco-American attacks make good progress . . .

AUGUST 4TH

. . . This morning I inspect 'A' Echelon of the Transport and find it in good condition. On the way back a mob of infantry straggling along the road towards Ypres forms a sorry spectacle for any soldier. It looks more like the remnant of a defeated army than fresh Corps reinforcements, as it is. With my advice the units get into better order.

In the afternoon unexpected orders arrive for the Battalion to return to the trenches tonight. There is at once a stir of packing up.

Poor Harold Ritchie is in a bad humour; we have had almost a quarrel. He considers it to be his turn to go into the Line, and mine to kick my heels with the 'minimum reserve'. Strictly speaking, that is the rule; but I will not surrender command of the Battalion until the Brigadier is satisfied with its state; General Mayne is persuaded to accept my view for this occasion. It would be manifestly unfair to hold an officer responsible for his command while depriving him of the course he thinks best for exercising that responsibility. I have, however, made it clear to Harold as well as to the Brigade Commander that my decision is not due to lack of faith in the former.

There is some grumbling because the canteens of the 33rd Division are forbidden to sell alcohol on account of the Americans – some of whose units are attached to ours – being 'dry' by order of their High Command. Luckily we and our overseas friends can purchase a reasonable amount of wine and spirits at the canteens of the unrestricted divisions.

AUGUST 5TH: VOORMEZEELE: FRONT LINE, CANAL SECTOR

. . . At dawn today the Brigadier visits our lines and has, with perfect justification, many faults to find. I therefore perform a second, and more leisurely, four-hour tour after breakfast to remedy defects . . .

AUGUST 7TH

A company of the 3/120th American Regiment is in the Line, attached to my battalion. Yesterday the commander of the regiment [*battalion*?], Major Phillips, accompanied me on my rounds. The Americans are big, manly fellows, free from brag and anxious to learn; but from our point of view they are a little careless about duties and lose too much of their gear. They are excellent friends with our men, and have expressed their gratitude, so I hear, for the return of a *portion* of their missing rations. The Americans are naturally strange to this life and, for practice, relieve their platoons, mixed up with ours, every night. The company commander does not impress me, but his senior subaltern is a splendid young fellow. I asked him what kind of shots his men are; he replied in a slow drawl, 'Well, sair, I guess they got lots of practice on Revenue officers in Arizona.'

Our sentries and other duties are improving slowly, at a depressing crawl, considering ceaseless coaching.

Today . . . a staff car whisks me away through Poperinghe to attend a lecture . . . The Inspector-General of Training, General Maxse,[1] delivers a very sound address and appears anxious to help us. It is, however, curious to hear him lay such stress on the need for carrying out orders, which we had imagined to be the foundation of military discipline, and the first thing to be impressed on all ranks when they join the Service.

Another point of the General's is: that every platoon commander should have his men at his disposal for a short period of training every day when out of the Line. This is entirely sensible in theory; but few of the present platoon commanders are professionally fit to instruct their men, and we prefer to educate them first, so that they shall teach correctly and not spread false doctrines among their subordinates.

Secondly, the greater part of platoons is not available for parade when companies are in reserve. Many men are on duties and working parties . . .

Thirdly, after a tour of four to eight days in the Line, almost the first essential is a day' rest, and not too much work in the little remaining time in reserve . . .

---

[1] *The post of Inspector-General of Training was not established until the second half of 1918, when it was ably filled by Lieutenant-General Sir Ivor Maxse, previously commanding the XVIII Corps.*

We have instituted two customs, practised when I commanded the 2/West Yorkshire. When possible, each front company sends before dawn a pair of sharpshooters into shell holes in No Man's Land to do what damage they can to the enemy before returning to our lines at dusk . . .

The second is the improvement of marksmanship through each man of the advanced companies firing at dawn and dusk daily two supervised shots at tins hung on our wire entanglement.

The hand-bomb was a necessity for trench warfare from the Spring of 1915 till that of the present year . . . The apparent return to open warfare makes the rifle once again of the greater importance . . .

An American officer has been accidentally shot dead by his men when he was examining the wire in front of their post in the dark. It seems that he failed to inform them of his intention to go in advance of the Line, and that he did not hear their challenge. The Americans are sometimes a little 'windy' – as we ourselves may have been when new to the game . . .

The British Fourth and the French First Armies have opened a large-scale offensive between Amiens and Rheims with striking success . . .

This was the Battle of Amiens, launched by Sir Douglas Haig on August 8th 1918, the date subsequently referred to by Ludendorff as 'the black day for the German Army'. It marks the beginning of the continuous series of Allied offensives which concluded the War.

AUGUST 13TH

Yesterday morning on inspecting the support companies, and at night those in front, we found the discipline and arrangements of both groups much improved . . .

Soon after lying down at 12.30 o'c this morning, a report arrives that a patrol of six men under 2/Lieut F has been ambushed by a party of Germans. Two of my men are killed, one is missing, and two are wounded. F's patrol seems to have regarded its mission too lightly, and to have taken insufficient precautions. A slovenly affair, just when the reverse is urgently desirable. I hate losing men needlessly, and patrolling has been a special subject of our lectures . . .

It appears that the Americans have their own way of conducting reliefs. On one occasion, at least, their front posts marched back as soon as they heard the incoming unit approaching. We regard this method as being too sketchy; all our duties must be actually relieved before quitting their stations . . .

The Battalion is being relieved tomorrow . . .

AUGUST 15TH: CATTERICK HUT CAMP

. . . The Battalion had 13 casualties during its last tour in the Line.

In the afternoon unexpected orders arrive for our relief by the 1/119th Infantry Regiment, United States Army. We forthwith set about preparing to receive it and to give what assistance we can; the camp is cleaned, guides are detailed to show each unit its quarters; tea and sandwiches are made ready.

The Americans march in before dusk, and I am soon informed that they have taken over their accommodation; but there is no sign of their Commanding Officer. After waiting some time for him in our hut above ground (so far from the Front we prefer huts to dug-outs), I learn that he and his staff have gone to the dug-outs. Thither I repair to offer any help, and am told that the commander has gone to bed; that they are satisfied with everything, and require no help. This being so, my battalion marches off . . .

LEAVING THE YPRES FRONT

AUGUST 18TH: IN CORPS RESERVE

We have spent three useful, undisturbed days . . .

On the 17th, following a day's rest, cleaning-up and inspections, we commenced training in earnest – the first opportunity the Battalion has had for such a thing since I took command a month ago.

The steel helmets, purposely covered with mud in the Line for camouflage, have been washed down to the regulation bottle-green paint and polished, exposing the small strip of regimental colours at the side . . .

Regarding the Battle Training parade, the Divisional and Brigade Commanders, not at first realising that my companies carried out their own exercises after the demonstration, thought that I interfered too much with details. But one had to begin by teaching these embryo soldiers the right lines on which to work. Without guidance it would have been a case of the blind leading the blind, and I consider my method the surest and quickest when time presses . . .

'*The results of the Battle of Amiens may be summarised as follows. Within the space of five days the town of Amiens and the railway centring upon it had been disengaged. Twenty German divisions had been heavily defeated by thirteen British infantry divisions and three cavalry divisions, assisted by a regiment of the 33rd American Division and supported by some four hundred tanks. Nearly 22,000 prisoners and over four hundred guns had been taken by us and our line had been pushed forward to a depth of some twelve miles in a vital sector.*' (*Haig's Despatch, December 21st, 1918.*)

AUGUST 25TH: LICQUES, 15 MILES EAST OF
BOULOGNE

. . . The Standing Scale of parades and tactical training is carried out daily . . .

The Army Training Staff have come to give us lectures. With them is a Demonstration Platoon of picked men, which accompanies them on their round of battalions, and we have been shown the approved handling of a platoon in action. So the soundness of teaching by demonstration, which I have applied for the past 18 months, is endorsed by the intellectual side of the British Army . . .

Generals Pinney and Mayne have inspected our battle training and told me of their satisfaction at last. The latter said how struck the French are with the soldierly mien and behaviour of the Battalion . . .

AUGUST 29TH: IVERGNY, 6 MILES N.E. OF DOULLENS

At 2 a.m. on the 26th we were awakened to receive orders warning the Battalion to prepare to march at once from

255

Licques. The camp was, therefore, immediately astir. The actual orders did not, in fact, arrive till 3 o'c in the afternoon.

At 5 p.m. we marched 12 miles to Bayinghem . . . reaching there at 10.30, and getting to bed after midnight . . . What an unnecessarily long, fatiguing day through some staff muddle! . . . I am not yet fully fit after my long time in hospital from wounds, and had a struggle [yesterday] to reach billets, on foot, according to our regimental habit of officers marching when the men march, except at 'attention', or when riding is otherwise necessary.

On this occasion the pipes struck up an infernally quick 'Rifle' step to play the Battalion into quarters, and forthwith transformed the companies into a mob. My order is that the pace on the line of march is to be 114 to the minute (which I have personally found to be the normal rate for loaded men), and 125 when marching into billets. The regulation pace is 120 per minute, but Rifle regiments – as we are – maintain on parade a step of about 145; we have therefore conceded a slight increase on the Line regiments' rate for sentimental reasons.

I spoke sharply to the Pipe-Major about the matter at the time it occurred, and today at Orderly Room, behold all the pipers formed up, with a request to be 'returned to duty' in the company ranks. This is the British soldier's manner of airing a grievance – at my remarks in this case. I tell the complainants that their duty is piping; that orders must be carried out; and that I am pleased with them otherwise. The interview terminates. Sergeant-Major Windram orders, 'Pipers, right turn. Quick march!' They are fine lads really, but have their stubborn moments, like the rest of us . . .

SEPTEMBER 1ST

. . . My officers are now properly turned out; they must be an example to their men in every respect. The excessively light-coloured ties, collars, shirts and breeches have been discarded at my request, and articles of the regulation colour have appeared. Harold tells me that his wife is highly indignant at my disapproval of his cream shade of breeches. These light colours are showy and attractive, but I do not desire to lose my officers in action owing to their being dressed so conspicuously that German marksmen cannot fail to single them out. Proper officers' canes, a present from me, have replaced on parade a miscellaneous collection of walking-sticks . . .

Yesterday afternoon Captain Rochfort-Boyd came to give us a clear and most interesting lecture on Tanks, which I have not yet seen in action. He said that the Germans are terrified of them, and that they completely demoralised their defences in recent operations . . .

Since Tanks on the move are so noisy, the difficulty is to assemble them in their positions, 300 to 500 yards in rear of the leading infantry, before an advance, without warning the enemy of their presence. This is done at night, of course, and when our bombardment will drown the sound of their approach . . .

Tanks must be withdrawn to refit after about eight hours in action. Their pace is from three to eight miles an hour, and the cramped interior becomes stiflingly hot. Their worst enemy is boggy ground . . .

The Germans are placing field guns in their front line to knock them out at point-blank range, and are arming some of their infantry with specially designed heavy rifles firing armour-piercing bullets. The enemy has practically no Tanks.

Our Fourth and Third Armies have taken Péronne, Mont St. Quentin and Bapaume. The capture of the second-named by the Australians was a brilliant affair. The First Army, east of Arras, has gained a portion of the formidable Hindenburg Line.

Apart from a slight exaggeration of German 'terror', the information about Tanks which Jack here conveys is very accurate. There is a perceptible elision in the reference to speeds: the first four Marks used (1916-17) had a maximum speed of 3.5 m.p.h.; the Mark V (1918) had a speed of 4.6. m.p.h.; the Medium Mark A ('Whippet'; 1918), 8.3 m.p.h. The peak moment of the War for Tanks was at Amiens on August 8th, when 534 took part in the battle, of which 415 were fighting Tanks; but only 145 were fit to continue the action on the following day.

SEPTEMBER 5TH

On the 2nd instant a message, terminating with the warm congratulations of the Divisional Commander and staff, said that I am being appointed to command a brigade, for which I was first recommended in the Spring of 1917, prior to being wounded. This promotion is a great slice of luck for a regimental captain . . .

We have been assiduously studying and practising the attack while not entirely neglecting the defence, which may be forced locally on troops during any operations. The whole of the mornings are devoted to battle training and I am satisfied with the result, tedious as the road has been to reach it. I do not pretend that we have nearly gained perfection; but the companies are smart, well-balanced, quick in moving and using their weapons. The officers and non-commissioned officers have made great progress in tactical leading. All ranks are in good form, doing their best for the reputation of the Regiment. The certainty of having to repeat exercises badly executed is an incentive to brain and physical effort . . .

Today at 8 a.m. a military motor bus takes a party of officers of the brigade . . . to witness demonstrations by the Tank Corps. We see the 'landships' negotiating very steep thirty-foot banks with ease; then they advance on trenches sheltering us, the spectators. One can well imagine the terror they must strike into an enemy . . .

Our First Army has carried a further portion of the Hindenburg Line. In consequence of the Allied progress, the Germans are evacuating positions on the Douai—Lille front, which is still outside the scope of operations.

What Haig called in his Despatch the 'Battle of Bapaume' was fought by the Third (Byng) and Fourth (Rawlinson) Armies between August 21st and September 1st. During that time, 23 British divisions 'by skilful leading, hard fighting and relentless and unremitting pursuit . . . had driven 35 German divisions from one side of the old Somme battlefield to the other, thereby turning the line of the River Somme' (Haig). In the course of doing this the British captured 34,000 prisoners and 270 guns. Then followed the Battle of the Scarpe (August 26th–September 3rd), in which General Horne's First Army prolonged the front of attack, against the Hindenburg Line. In this battle 10 British divisions defeated 13 German divisions, taking 16,000 prisoners and about 200 guns.

These were merely the first stages of the majestic British advance dur-

ing the remainder of the War. German divisions were, of course, very much reduced by now, and their quality much impaired. The British exploits in 1918, therefore, well illustrate the difference between fighting a 'worn-out' enemy, and the grim, bloody business of reducing him to that condition, which had been the duty of Haig's armies in earlier years.

SEPTEMBER 7TH

The last few days have entailed an incessant rush to finish work and hand over the Battalion to Harold Ritchie, in whose ability and thoroughness I have complete confidence . . .

As late as yesterday we were called upon to submit by 6 p.m. today names recommended for the New Year's Honours List. During my command nothing of importance has happened to the Battalion, so this duty – a happy one in any case – does not take long, although instances of merit displayed before my arrival have to be carefully investigated . . .

Today is occupied in the office, with calls on Generals Pinney and Mayne – under whom I have had pleasure in serving – and on their staffs. On the morning parade I said good-bye to the Battalion, wished all ranks good luck, and thanked them for their services. Visits to the sergeants' and corporals' messes followed to amplify my regards more specially to them . . .

One's feelings about leaving the Battalion are rather mixed. Against the great honour of such early promotion – albeit among strangers of, to me, unknown quality – must be set the disappointment to be quitting unfinished work. The Battalion is not quite first-class, as I had hoped to leave it. However, I have done my level best, and have tasted, if only for a short and uneventful time, a Regular's ambition, that of commanding a battalion of his Regiment in the field.

Although my criticism of shortcomings has often been sharp, appreciation has been equally freely expressed. As soon as my views on soldiering had become thoroughly understood, all ranks did their utmost to carry them out, without demur, and generally with success.

*　　*　　*

After Jack's departure, the 33rd Division took part in the main assault on the Hindenburg Line, and in other hard-fought actions. 1/Cameronians had 7 officers killed and 14 wounded. 'To my deep sorrow, Harold Ritchie, who had been wounded three times in three weeks, died on 28th October.'

VI

SEPTEMBER 1918 TO THE ARMISTICE

Commanding
28th Infantry Brigade

THE 28TH INFANTRY BRIGADE

Jack's new brigade belonged to the 9th (Scottish) Division, a most distinguished formation. Not only was it the 'senior' New Army Division, formed on August 21st 1914, but also the first to arrive in France (May 9th 1915). Its first major action was the Battle of Loos, where it performed magnificently, and sustained 5,868 casualties.

Its original brigades were the 26th, 27th and 28th, but the last of these was broken up in May 1916, when the South African Brigade arrived to take its place in the Division. The South Africans took a large part in the furious fighting at Delville Wood in July 1916, being reduced from 121 officers and 3,032 other ranks to 29 officers and 751 other ranks in the space of a week. In 1918 they again suffered terrible losses during the German April offensive on the Lys, and were withdrawn from the 9th Division to refit. The 28th Brigade was then re-formed under Jack. It was, in effect, a quite new unit.

SEPTEMBER 8TH: IVERGNY, ARRAS SECTOR,
XVII CORPS RESERVE

My seven weeks' service with my old battalion terminates this morning . . .

Lunching in Hazebrouck at the headquarters of my new division, the 9th, I meet its commander, Major-General H. Tudor, an active, quick-witted and agreeable little man who, when a Royal Artillery subaltern, was one of the best lightweight boxers and gentleman riders in our Army . . . He is a convinced believer (the originator, I am told) in 'smoke screens' discharged from shells to hide movements in action. These came into use last March and were most successful . . .

On leaving General Tudor, I call on 'Billy' Croft (Cameronians) commanding the 27th Infantry Brigade in our division, to glean more of the divisional commander's idiosyncrasies.

Then I motor to Lumbres, 6 miles south-west of St Omer, where my brigade is re-forming . . .

At Divisional Headquarters I heard of the magnificent performance of the 9th Division – especially, perhaps, the South Africans – at Moislains last April during the great German offensive.

Two battalions of the Brigade, 2/Royal Scots Fusiliers (Lieut-Col J. E. Utterson-Kelso, D.S.O., M.C.) and 9/Cameronians (Lieut-Col W. Lumsden, D.S.O., M.C.), besides a few other details have arrived. The 10/Argyll and Sutherland Highlanders, from another division, are due about the 15th to complete us.

As regards Brigade Headquarters, only one staff officer has reported, and since our single clerk has no typing machine the considerable daily correspondence must be hand-written . . . After a ride round on a borrowed horse with General Tudor, my staff-captain and I motor some 30 miles to Calais to buy mess crockery and stores, as well as to choose chargers from the Remount Depot.

When near the town my Don Juan of a companion suggests our offering a lift to a couple of smart-looking young damsels walking shopwards, but I inhospitably describe the car as being full enough . . .

My staff-captain, who joined yesterday, leaves tomorrow for another appointment – a queer arrangement. His place is taken by Captain L. J. Will, M.C., Worcestershire Regiment.

Bits of the Brigade keep arriving: a cook, a couple of orderlies, some harness, parts of our Trench Mortar Battery – minus mortars . . .

The Mess of the Scots Fusiliers is also in our château. In the evening, hearing a tumult there, I run upstairs to learn the reason for it. Round the walls of a large empty room stand the officers, and in the ring thus formed Kelso, their boy colonel, and a tall subaltern, both stripped to the waist, are pummelling each other with boxing gloves. Presently the watch-keeper calls 'time', and two fresh lads take their place for 'battle training'. Being satisfied with the righteousness of the row, I return to the office.

The 9th Division is transferred . . . to the II Corps (Lieut-Gen Sir Claud Jacob), Second Army (General Sir H. Plumer) . . .

Sir Herbert Plumer ('Plum') calls at my headquarters. I have not previously met him although his name is familiar as a column commander in the South African War, and as the commander of our Second Army in its entirely successful attack at Messines last June – a model of arrangement and execution. He is elderly, and has the appearance of the best type of country squire . . .

The General asks how the Brigade is getting on, and laughs – a little uncomprehendingly – when I put a typewriting machine as our first requirement. This is not so frivolous a request as it sounds. Our borrowed typewriter makes a noise like a travelling tank and mutilates the paper copies – and manuscript is too slow for the volume of office work. The Army Commander now laughs more genuinely and says he will do his best . . .

SEPTEMBER 12TH

Heavy showers. Our Trench Mortar Battery (28th) has been sent – rather late in the day – to a trench mortar school to complete its training . . .

Today the Fusiliers are keeping fit by route marching, and the Rifles (Cameronians) are practising an attack using live smoke grenades. Both battalions are commanded by distinguished young Regular officers of most attractive personality. We have received orders to move tomorrow . . .

SEPTEMBER 13TH

. . . General Tudor . . . tells me secretly that the 9th Division is to attack soon, which is, I confess, disagreeable although expected news.

SEPTEMBER 14TH

. . . At 3 p.m. the Brigade marches 4 miles south-east to billets in Wormhoudt. The Fusiliers and Rifles look very soldierly as they pass at 'attention' with pipes playing. Marching past Battalion or more senior commanders daily in this manner is good for discipline, and provides these officers with an opportunity of accurately gauging the general form of their troops ...

... The 1/Royal Newfoundland Regiment (Lieut-Col T. G. Mathias, D.S.O.) has joined the Brigade with an excellent record in the 29th Division. It is only lent to us, as the 10/Argyll and Sutherland Highlanders, engaged with another division in the south, are still expected here officially. I am warned to be 'careful' of the newcomers, but how this is to be managed when we go into action is not clear. 'B' Company, 9th Machine Gun Battalion, the 63rd Field Company, Royal Engineers, No. 4 Section, 9th Divisional Signal Company, the 107th Company, Army Service Corps, and the 76 Field Ambulance are in the Brigade Group ...

Yesterday, after calling on the Newfoundland, I inspected the Fusiliers, and am well pleased with them.

At 7 p.m. battalion and other unit commanders attended a conference at our château and then dined with me. During our cheery meal the remarkably good string quartette of the Fusiliers played popular selections; then three Cameronian pipers arrived and we danced reels, to the huge delight of M. de Charpentry[1] and his domestics ...

Today ... Sir Claud Jacob calls and stops to tea. I am so pleased to be back in his Corps again. His quiet, thoughtful manner always gives one great confidence. There is nothing 'slapdash' about any of his arrangements; all are most carefully prepared, and he never sacrifices his men needlessly ...

At 8.30 a.m. the Brigade, as a whole unit, carries out a three-hour practice attack. On its conclusion commanders of battalions, companies, and of other units in the Brigade Group, parade at the château to hear a short address by the Corps Commander on 'a possible future offensive' (not specified).

[1] *Owner of the château.*

266

Later Sir Claud outlines to me privately the plan, but not the date.

In the afternoon 'Move Orders' arrive. They include instructions for the usual Minimum Reserve (10% of the fighting strength of each unit) to remain behind at the Divisional Reception Camp, and for 'scrupulous care' to be taken henceforth to conceal troops from the enemy's aircraft. This first is a pointer to all ranks at operations ahead . . .

SEPTEMBER 19TH

We spend nearly all day dealing with large files of orders which have been drafted by Higher Command with infinite care and clarity. Many amendments crop up, but although annoying they are unavoidable in plans for operations on a wide scale.

General Tudor calls to ask if the orders are quite understood, and if there are any questions regarding them. He and his staff take no end of trouble; it is a pleasure to serve under him. On his departure I ride round the camps to ensure that our orders are clear to units, and to say a few words to their officers, who are by now aware of the coming attack.

At 7.30 p.m. (dusk) I go over to the Newfoundlanders to wish them 'Godspeed' as they start on their 6-mile march forward to shelters 2 miles north-west of Ypres. They are a splendid body, mostly fisher-folk; I have chaffed them on being 'land-sailors'.

The remainder of the Brigade stands fast . . .

SEPTEMBER 20TH

Fine weather. We are busy writing the Brigade orders for battle . . .

Failure may follow the best laid plans, carried out by the finest troops, because after all, one can only guess the enemy's strength and what he will do, the weather and other factors. But the risks of failure, or even of unduly long casualty lists, are tremendously increased by unsound or incomplete plans; by troops not thoroughly knowing their role, or being insufficiently rested before action; by slack discipline, shortage of training and poor leading. Having had ample time to prepare, time fully used, we must make no avoidable mistakes.

For the many instant decisions required in action one has to rely on the courage and training of junior leaders. The general plan can be little altered once battle is joined, except by the use of reserves. I have added my coaching to that of my experienced battalion commanders, and have no misgivings about the fighting qualities and efficiency of the Brigade Group . . .

A report is to hand that a number of Germans have surrendered to our posts, and that more would have done the same but for the interference of their Non-commissioned officers. The enemy's morale must have dipped; one has rarely heard of such a thing happening before an action . . .

IN THE FRONT LINE

SEPTEMBER 21ST

. . . In the afternoon I bicycle through Ypres, along the Menin road to a company headquarters near Hellfire Corner to inspect the line . . .

The desolation of the countryside is beyond belief. Shell holes and rank grass cover the whole area; the débris of battle is strewn all about; rusty wire entanglements, the rotting sandbags of disused dug-outs and trenches, a few helmets, portions of uniform, smashed rifles, quantities of empty ration tins and boxes, empty shell cases, and some field guns beyond repair . . . All troops are underground in cellars while daylight lasts . . .

SEPTEMBER 22ND

. . . In the afternoon I visit the Front . . .

Few landmarks are left anywhere; battles have blotted out all traces of villages, churches and farms, besides reducing the large woods in the vicinity to a tangle of short stumps. But maps show the shell-pitted ground to be covered with the network of British and German trenches, wire and 'pill-boxes' of the 1917 struggle for Passchendaele Ridge, as well as defences constructed by the enemy since we vacated the Ridge last April, the nearest being faintly visible some 400 yards away . . .

The weather keeps fine . . .

I have told the Newfoundland to put up some new (not rusty) wire, and a few trench shelter roofs visible to the enemy. We hope that the Germans, seeing this fresh *defensive* work, will think that an attack is not imminent.

Last night the enemy, covered by a heavy bombardment, raided the Belgian trenches just north of ours, and still hold some of them. This is most unfortunate as we cannot tell what maps and orders may have been captured, nor what information regarding the Allied plans may have been obtained from prisoners. The above constitutes one reason why troops are not told of prospective attacks till as late as possible . . .

This morning the Corps and Divisional commanders call. The assault has been postponed; this is a *nuisance* as I cannot leave the Newfoundland too long in trenches, neither can I well relieve them as I want the Fusiliers and Cameronians (leading assault battalions) to be perfectly fresh when the 'flag falls for the start'.

This is to be a big battle; the whole of our Second Army, the Belgian Army north of us, and possibly several French corps will be engaged on the 20-mile front from Ypres to Dixmude . . .

SEPTEMBER 25TH

. . . How familiar the place-names of today were 14 months ago: the Menin and Lille Gates, Bellewaarde and Westhoek Ridges, Zonnebeke Redoubt. We shall presently assault the identical positions then attacked by the 8th Division, containing the 2/West Yorks under my command. The bones of most of my officers and many of the other ranks lie between here and Zonnebeke. I hope the 28th Brigade will have better luck . . .

All is ready for the battle; we can think of nothing left to chance . . .

SEPTEMBER 26TH

. . . Near the barrier on the Menin Road, some 400 yards from our line, I am astonished to see several officers from administrative corps, with maps and binoculars, reconnoitring. In the group is a 'tubby' Royal Engineer major, sitting recklessly on horseback, looking for a suitable place for his advanced store 'dump'. Since orders are stringent against advertising the attack by reconnaissance or otherwise, I 'persuade' the delinquents to conceal their persons and paraphernalia from the enemy forthwith, and we post sentries to ensure that such enterprises are not repeated . . .

Our Brigade strength is about 80 officers and 1,700 other ranks. For heavy fighting I think that the present organisation of infantry brigades in three battalions, instead of the former four battalions, is unsound. In the event of severe casualties, or otherwise trying operations, the two leading assaulting battalions cannot both be relieved at the same time, as is desirable – perhaps vital. A further immediate attack must therefore be carried out with one relatively inefficient battalion and one fresh battalion, an ill-balanced arrangement . . .

SEPTEMBER 27TH

. . . all ranks are in high fettle at the prospect of licking the 'Huns'. High Command are confident of a great success here; they are always incurably optimistic. Last year it took four months of bitter fighting to gain Passchendaele Ridge, which we and the Belgians are expected to carry in one day – tomorrow.

At dusk the 9/Cameronians and the 2/Royal Scots Fusiliers . . . move four miles eastwards to their assembly positions, slightly ahead of the outpost line, from Hellfire Corner to Mill Cot, a frontage of 1,800 yards . . .

After nightfall advanced parties erect posts marking the assembly boundaries of platoons, and 'direction posts' to start companies correctly on their way in the half-light of dawn. At the same time the Newfoundland cut step-ways leading out of the trenches, and eight gaps in our wire, laying white tapes from steps to gaps . . .

While Grant Taylor (R. Scots Fusiliers, Brigade Intelligence Officer, a fine young soldier) and I, near the outpost line, are awaiting the arrival of the troops we are horrified at the loudness of their approaching tramp on an open piece of plank road, and go a short way into No Man's Land to judge how much the Germans can hear of it. The noise is still terrible and must be audible to the enemy; however, except for the usual few shells, rifle shots and Very rockets, all remains quiet, to our thankfulness as the routes to the forming-up positions are very exposed.

The assembly is complete by 2.30 a.m. (28th) with little interruption, and soon telephone messages containing the code words 'Rations arrived', signifying 'ready to attack', come from all battalions.

My Headquarters are officially at the Ramparts in Ypres, much too far back for keeping touch with one's command; so, having seen battalions arrive, and having earlier received permission from the Division, I proceed with a small staff to a company dug-out on the Menin Road near White Château, some 350 yards from the advance line, and there remain till 'Zero' hour.

By coincidence, Jack had selected for his command post the very locality – White Château – used by Haig when commanding I Corps during the First Battle of Ypres in 1914.

Jack calls the battle which now followed 'The Last Battle of Ypres', which is as good a name as any. For the occasion, the British Second Army was placed under the command of the King of the Belgians. Haig described the entire operation as 'a brilliant success. The enemy who was attempting to hold his positions with less than five divisions was driven rapidly from the whole of the high ground east of Ypres, so fiercely contested during the battles of 1917. By the end of the day the British divisions had passed far beyond the farthest limits of the 1917 battles . . . the British forces alone captured at light cost over 5,000 prisoners and 100 guns.'

Even better results would probably have been obtained, but for a break in the weather on the night of September 29/30th, which rapidly transformed the whole area once more into a morass. This in turn produced a further development in a relatively new technique of war, when 80 aircraft dropped 15,000 rations to the forward troops who could not otherwise be supplied.

THE LAST BATTLE OF YPRES
THE ASSAULT ON THE WESTHOEK –
FREZENBERG RIDGE

SEPTEMBER 28TH

... At 5.30 ('Zero' hour) on a dark wet morning, the crash of our field artillery barrage falling on the enemy's advanced trenches 300 yards ahead of our assembled infantry, and that of machine guns and heavier pieces firing beyond, suddenly breaks the silence on our front.

After five minutes the field guns 'lift', and the barrage creeps forward at the rate of 100 yards in three minutes, with a three-minute pause every 500 yards. Immediately the four widely extended lines of infantry groups advance in 'quick' time (walking) from trench and shell hole with bayonets fixed . . . keeping as close to our barrage as possible . . .

When dawn presently breaks, two-thirds of the field guns use smoke shells; these blind the enemy's view, and greatly assist the infantry in getting through wire entanglements and in surrounding trenches and 'pill-boxes'.

Soon walking wounded trickle back along the Menin Road; then prisoners, and wounded on stretchers . . . It always makes me sick to see so many fine fellows mangled and bloody from this God-forsaken war.

In action the first reports of progress – or failure – usually come from wounded; junior commanders are far too busy to write messages until there is a pause in the operations. I am informed that the attack started well; then that we have taken Railway Wood; so thither I proceed with a small headquarters marked by a red pennon on an Uhlan lance.

The Cameronians, passing round both sides of marshy Bellewaarde Lake, together with the Fusiliers on their left, gain Bellewaarde Ridge; then pressing on through more wire belts, across the sodden shell field, and rapidly overwhelming trenches and 'pill-boxes' on their way, these battalions capture, by 7.30 a.m., Westhoek Ridge, the First Objective, two miles ahead of their Zero positions, with little loss . . .

Brigade Headquarters, walking forward from point to point as planned, and delayed through having to stop to deal with wet and nearly indecipherable messages on the way, reach Westhoek about 8 o'c.

A telephone cable laid ahead enables us to maintain communication at each progressive point with Divisional Headquarters and, to some extent, with battalions. We have also a small wireless set, pigeons and dogs for this purpose . . .

Engineers and pioneers, who went forward soon after 'Zero', are hard at work repairing the plank road, all smashed and uneven. Up this difficult, winding way teams struggle to drag the close support field guns to Westhoek Ridge; they are under considerable shell fire; one team is 'blotted out' not far from me . . .

THE ATTACK ON THE BECELAERE – BROODSEINDE RIDGE

At 8 a.m. Cameronians and Fusiliers begin the Second Attack, supported by those field batteries which have been able to arrive, as well as by the Corps long-range guns and howitzers.

The 'creeping' barrage – searching all the ground – which assisted us till now is no longer practicable; artillery support for this stage is confined to 'shoots' at known and likely enemy positions with smoke and high-explosive shells.

Soon after the outset of this attack the boggy and heavily-wired Hannebeek brook is crossed, with the aid of portable bridges in places, and the Germans in trench or 'pill-box' are rushed or surrounded.

Then Anzac Ridge and Glasgow Spur (on both of which a 15-minute halt is allotted) with their scattered yet dense belts of wire, are taken in the same spirited manner against considerable opposition.

By about 11 o'c the 28th Bridge is established on its Final Objective, with patrols well forward . . . The 29th Division has taken Gheluvelt and villages southwards; the Belgians Passchendaele and places to the north. Our aeroplanes have given hostile aircraft no freedom during the day . . .

The day's success has been astonishing: an advance of over five miles (more than in four months' bloody fighting last year). No doubt the hostile shelling has been less severe than formerly, and his infantry, behind ample defences, have not put up their wonted resistance. Nevertheless, allowing for every mercy (including our smoke screens), the good leading and drive of all ranks from sunrise to sundown, through this bullet-swept wilderness, has been admirable, hustling the enemy off his feet.

The Brigade casualties are 306; the Fusiliers have lost 12 out of 22 officers. We have taken several hundred prisoners and some guns.

Following a scratch supper we lie down at 1 a.m. (29th), tired, wet, cold and blanketless, in a large German dug-out in Polygoneveld; the floor is inches deep in water. Presently orders arrive for the Brigade to attack again at 9 a.m., supported by the 26th and 27th Brigades. We therefore rise at once, telephone a 'warning order' to battalions and, getting out paper, dividers and compass, write in the light from two or three candle stumps the full orders, which are sent to units by one of their runners always at Brigade Headquarters.

THE ATTACK ON THE LINE OF THE MENIN–ROULERS ROAD

SEPTEMBER 29TH

At 8 o'c, after personally reporting on horseback to General Tudor on Anzac Spur that we are ready to attack, I ride forward to the highest point of the crest to see Battalions start.

The dismal belt of land devastated by four years of war lies behind. In front and slightly below us is spread a flat, unshelled plain, intersected by winding 'beeks' (brooks), and dotted with undamaged farms, hamlets, and a few trees. The ground, neglected agriculturally, is covered with long ripe grass . . .

9 a.m. The night's downpour of rain gives place to a bright autumn morning. There is no barrage today; our guns, however, lightly shell the southern portion of Kaiberg Spur and their smoke shells are bursting on the lower land in front of us.

The Cameronians, in open successive lines of sections, set

off down the gentle slope under negligible shell fire, but meet a considerable fusillade from distant machine guns. The Newfoundland are less prompt and I canter over to them to ascertain the reason. They are about to create a smoke screen from rifle grenades; it is unnecessary, and they quickly advance to catch up with the Belgians, visible half a mile on their way already.

On a mound nearby General Tudor – habitually well turned out and collected – stands telescope to eye.

About 10 o'c we watch the Belgians and Newfoundland clear Kaiberg Ridge, the Germans in parties of 20 to 30 retiring when our men reach the foot of it . . .

Towards noon the Newfoundland enter Waterdamhoek, but they and the Cameronians – who have been under severe enfilade machine gun fire all morning through their getting ahead of the 36th Division – are checked when crossing the marshy bottom south of that place.

On perceiving this I ride over to the Fusiliers to find out the exact situation and to ask them to help; Kelso, however, with his quick wits, has already sent two of his companies forward to strengthen our right. With this assistance Potterijebrug is taken, the brook crossed, and the advance continues, the enemy's flank having been turned . . .

A little after 4 o'c, from a roof-top in Strooiboomhoek, it is thrilling to see troops of all three brigades, now greatly intermingled, flooding across the Kanterhoek Brook to cut the Menin–Roulers Road south of St Pieter . . .

At nightfall, in the rain, the Brigade . . . is withdrawn to Potterijebrug in divisional reserve . . .

Today's advance is 4½ miles. The action cannot be described as more than a smart skirmish. Battalions were at times under extremely hot machine gun fire, but the shell fire over the area did little harm. The Brigade has only 57 casualties. It has captured about 100 prisoners and 6 guns, making the bag in the last two days approximately 400 prisoners, 12 field guns and 2 heavy guns . . .

This day, for the first (and last) time, scattered groups of cavalry followed the leading battalions. Although conditions here are all against mounted troops, I think that small resolute

bodies, able quickly to charge or disperse, presenting, too, a
fleeting, difficult mark, do not run undue risks and may get
occasional chances of rounding up parties of the enemy, or
at any rate hurrying his retirement with the gleam of their
lances . . .

*It should be noted that the absence of cavalry was due to the concentration
of the Cavalry Corps on the fronts of the Third and Fourth Armies,
where the main British attacks were being made. In 1918 the Cavalry
Corps consisted of only 3 divisions (some 15,000 sabres and lances in all),
an altogether insufficient number for open warfare, but it was impossible
to reinforce them effectively in the time available.*

THE ADVANCE FROM YPRES TO THE SCHELDT

SEPTEMBER 30TH: POTTERIJEBRUG

A horrid drizzly day . . .

At 7.30 a.m. I ride a mile north to Waterdamhoek to attend
General Tudor's conference there . . . The Division is standing
by, ready to attack if the 36th Division and the Belgians can
get on. Strong hostile wire is reported all along our front,
and the enemy is thought to have been reinforced considerably . . .

OCTOBER IST

. . . Towards noon, by Divisional instructions, the Fusiliers
move to Kanterhoek in close support to and under the orders
of the 27th Brigade. Billy Croft is a fine, determined and
capable commander, but it is a little tiresome to have my
battalions detailed so often to assist his brigade; they have
enough work of their own to perform. However, since I hate
bickering, and the additional work not being excessive, I have
made little complaint on the subject.

At night the 28th Brigade relieves the 27th Brigade in the
line from near Klephoek to the northern outskirts of Ledeghem,
a frontage of 2,000 yards . . .

The 26th and 27th Brigades lost heavily this morning; it

was an unfortunate setback, as we thought we had got the Germans 'on the run'.

The Brigade casualties today number 14.

OCTOBER 2ND: IN THE FRONT LINE

This sector is most disagreeable. Our two advanced battalions hold a thin line of posts in ditches, several 'pill-boxes' and a few hastily-dug trenches. At dawn the enemy puts down a barrage on them, perhaps with a view to counter-attacking; but the field guns reply at once, and we are obviously too ready . . .

In the afternoon Grant Taylor and I accompany General Tudor and Murray (his A.D.C.) to survey the Front. The Divisional Commander must have a view to gratify his Gunner instincts; he is always climbing on to the roofs of exposed buildings as near the line as he can find them.

While we are peacefully ensconced behind the banked-up, tree-lined main road a quarter of a mile from the advanced infantry north of Ledeghem, and are leisurely identifying landmarks through telescopes and binoculars, a tremendous hostile barrage suddenly claps down on the road. We crouch in the shelter of the bank with shells exploding all round.

Feeling sure that the barrage is the prelude to a hostile attack, I keep watch, and am presently horrified to see considerable numbers of men from another brigade drifting back from the Front over the open ground; we suppose the Germans will be on their heels at any moment.

Springing across the road and running forward pistol in hand, I threaten to shoot the first man who passes me. The rascals halt. One must make a joke. So although half expecting my cane, held up at arm's length, to be blown out of my hand, I swear that the shells are too high to reach. Thereupon a sergeant – no officers are visible among the retiring warriors – generously remarks 'You're a topper, sir.'

The General and our two companions are alongside in an instant; we push the men into the nearest ditch to defend it if necessary; Taylor and Murray hurry off to fetch up reserves and warn the artillery.

There is no excuse whatsoever for these fellows quitting their posts; the line is quite quiet. It is just a rare example of panic due to lack of discipline, a rough time in yesterday's action, the loss of many of their officers, the fear of being isolated by the barrage and overwhelmed by a German assault.

Tudor and I 'fall the men in' in the open – it is safe enough as the shells are bursting more than 100 yards behind. When we have sorted out the different posts, the General, monocle in eye and cool as a cucumber, orders 'Slope Arms', 'Quick March', and himself leads the parties back in extended formation to their posts, accompanied by a rally on my hunting-horn. During this half-hour there have been few casualties.[1]

I now hasten alone to my nearest battalion, the Newfoundland, in a salient at Ledeghem, to see if their nerves are all right, and to warn them to strengthen their flank in the direction of the foregoing débâcle . . .

The shelling has died down; Colonel Mathias and his adjutant, both the acme of composure, are leaning against a hut beside the advanced lines of their Newfoundlanders, who lie behind a shale bank in the goods yard, bayonets fixed, waiting for the Germans, and unconcerned as their officers. Indeed, part of their support companies have most improperly left their trenches in rear to join the forward companies in the threatened fight.

The enemy evidently intends attacking, because 100 to 200 yards away one can momentarily see many heads moving about behind the cover of buildings and hedges in an unmistakable manner.

While Mathias and I stand talking together, too exposed, there is a loud 'crack', and one of the men lying at our very feet is stone dead with a bullet from a house nearby in his brain. How the shot missed us and hit the poor fellow, apparently completely protected by the bank, is quite unaccountable. (I had omitted to replace the khaki cover, torn off my polished, red-banded helmet to give me more authority during the panic . . . One never, of course, walks up to forward posts conspicuously dressed, and I am very sorry if neglect on this occasion may have contributed to the fatality. – J.L.J.)

. . . The anticipated attack does not materialise, owing, I

[1] *See Appendix IV.*

suppose, to the prompt reply by our artillery, as well as to the steadiness of battalions like the Newfoundland.

We pass a normal night. Today's Brigade casualties are 29. Splendid news; Bulgaria has given up the struggle.

OCTOBER 3RD

Our patrols frequently approach the German lines after dusk to discover if there is any sign of a withdrawal, but their lines are still strongly occupied . . .

My right battalion, the Fusiliers, is continually subjected to fire from Hill 41, whose capture has defied repeated attempts by the division south of us. From this hill the enemy has good observation over much of our area.

Opposite us are units of the German 6th and 7th Cavalry Divisions – identified from dead and prisoners. They are a tough lot, nicknamed by other Germans for their stubborn quality 'the war-prolongers' . . .

The Brigade casualties today number 37.

OCTOBER 4TH

. . . battle patrols from both front battalions, covered by a light barrage, enter Ledeghem twice today and find the vicinity strongly held. They take a few prisoners, who have lost their wonted confidence in final victory; in fact, German morale has been sinking for some time . . .

We have 17 casualties today.

OCTOBER 5TH

Following a pretty strenuous eight days the Brigade is relieved at dusk . . . under considerable shell fire, the Fusiliers, the chief sufferers, losing amongst others Colonel Utterson-Kelso and his adjutant, both severely wounded . . .

Our casualties today are 20.

OCTOBER 8TH: IN DIVISIONAL RESERVE

. . . I am very sorry to lose Johnnie Kelso. He is so full of life, courage and quick, sound decision. I have yet to meet a better or more lovable leader. As a mere boy he has greatly distinguished himself in this War . . .

The Divisional Commander visits the Brigade on horseback nearly daily and is most generous in his praise of its work. Sir Claud Jacob has issued a Special Order of appreciation, in which he says that the recent achievements of the Division will be considered in history to have eclipsed its previous fine performances. Yesterday the Army Commander called to add his warm compliments . . .

Sir Herbert Plumer arrived in a large car with his chief staff officer . . . and asked heartily 'Well, Jack, how are your men?' He seemed astonished to be told that they are pretty tired, but will be fit to attack again with a few days' rest. After all, when he put the question, the Brigade had been out of the line for little over 24 hours, following eight days of more or less severe fighting, outposts, marching, hard work in bad weather, without shelter, without sufficient rest, and sometimes short of food. 'Plum' is most human, but it is the old story: those who live right away from the troops engaged cannot possibly understand the strain and weariness affecting fighting troops at the Front . . .

Besides visiting units and attending a divisional conference, I have held two conferences with battalion commanders – all other officers being present – to discuss our past errors as well as improvements that have been noticed . . .

The Brigade is returning to the Front tonight . . .

OCTOBER 9TH: FRONT LINE: LEDEGHEM

Following a bare snatch of sleep I am up at 4 a.m., and at dawn assume command of the Divisional front. This command is not changed during the hours of darkness in order to obviate confusion should the enemy attack then. After daybreak this risk is reduced . . .

The German machine guns and snipers are less active than they were a few days ago; their barrages at dawn, however, and 'area shoots' at other times of the day and night are still severe . . .

Twice daily at irregular hours our barrage lightly rolls through Ledeghem to cover the investigations of patrols, which usually take one or two prisoners. These are always wanted by the staff to help in identifying the divisions opposite, and so to deduce from this, in addition to other information, the enemy's wastage, morale, and possibly some of his plans . . .

The Brigade has four casualties today.

General Tudor informed Jack that another attack was imminent.

. . . Battalions are busy overhauling their organisation, promoting junior leaders to fill vacancies, inspecting weapons, kits and battle stores. These duties are ever-present, particularly before action.

Today, when again reconnoitring the Front, Taylor and I get an unpleasant share of an 'area shoot' and are sniped at near the posts. Two orderlies always follow us at an interval as we do not fancy being left undiscovered for hours punctured by bullets.

At 4 p.m. a car calls to take me to a conference at Divisional Headquarters in a farm near Broodseinde. The seven miles of road from Ypres over Passchendaele Ridge have been pretty well repaired with prodigious labour; many long-range guns, heavy howitzers and stores have therefore arrived in the forward area to enable the suspended advance to continue.

The enemy's night-bombing aeroplanes and his shell fire are most disagreeable . . .

The Brigade has had no casualties yesterday or today.

. . . 'Zero' is fixed for 5.30 a.m. . . .

Throughout the afternoon staff and administrative officers keep calling at our headquarters; one to synchronise watches, others on the business of their departments. Their visits are rather a bother at the moment since we are busy; but all come to assist; there is no friction in the 9th Division. I am happy to assure them that we believe there is not a button out of place in the 28th Brigade . . .

At dusk the Brigade (less the Minimum Reserve) files with intervals to the Front by tracks marked across the plain. On the way severe shell and gas-shell fire causes the Newfoundland 15, the Fusiliers 50 casualties.

We relieve the 26th Brigade as silently as possible . . .

The 29th Division is on our right, the 3rd Belgian Division on the left.

The heavy 6-inch trench mortars are just behind us, and the divisional artillery brigades have closed to within 1,500 yards of the Front.

Single 18-pounder guns, trench mortars and machine guns, placed a few yards in rear of the leading infantry and aligned on all near German strong points, are ready to fire at 'Zero' over open sights . . .

The Brigade Final Objective tomorrow is the road running north and south through Steenen-Stampkot, 2½ miles ahead of our 'Zero' line . . .

The night passes fairly quietly, but sleeplessly.

At 3 a.m. (14th) battalion commanders report to me personally that all is ready, and having finished my work I lie down for a short rest.

The Brigade has about 70 casualties today (13th).

THE ATTACK ON THE
STEENEN–STAMPKOT RIDGE

Haig's Despatch summarises the second phase of the Flanders advance as follows: 'The Allied attack was again attended by complete success . . . Before nightfall on the 15th October Thourout was surrounded, and next day the enemy retired rapidly. Ostend fell on the 17th October, and three days later the northern flank of the Allied line rested on the Dutch frontier. In these operations and others of a lesser nature . . . the British forces operating on this battle front captured over 6,000 prisoners and 210 guns.'

OCTOBER 14TH: FRONT LINE: LEDEGHEM

I rise at 5 a.m., swallow some tea, bread and butter, two boiled eggs, and look at the weather. The morning is misty, with a very faint south-easterly air – not very suitable for our smoke.

At 5.30 our guns, trench mortars and machine guns open with a crash; the front is speckled with shell flashes; the foremost German defences are under a hail of fire.

Three minutes later . . . the Newfoundland and the Scots Fusiliers, in normal battle formations, advance forthwith, bayonets fixed. The Fusiliers have early difficulty with 'pill-boxes', and Black Watch companies from the 26th Brigade at once press in on their northern flank.

Ledeghem is rushed by the 29th Division; the hamlets of Boonhoek and Hennekot fall to my brigade with little trouble . . .

Many German 'pill-boxes' in this neighbourhood have no loop-holes, and their garrisons, sheltering in them too long, are trapped when the exits are under fire . . .

About 11.30 a.m. the Newfoundland and the Fusiliers gain the gentle, wired crest just west of the Drie-Masten – Smisse-Knok Road after sharp fighting . . .

Beyond this crest the field artillery barrage, now at the limit of its range, can support us no further; and although an advanced battery or two can gallop up almost immediately, a long pause in the operations is necessary to prepare the next attack . . .

From the Steenen-Stampkot Ridge several large parties of the enemy are visible in the valley retiring towards Drie-Masten and Laaga-Kapel; and a mounted German leisurely towing a light cart follows a track of his own. Since it appears to me that some of the forward companies are showing too little vigour in chasing and firing on these fellows, I canter forward to the Newfoundland to ask them to 'turn on more steam', and even seize a Lewis gun myself to shoot, although the range is rather long.

I am, however, too hasty in questioning the enterprise of my men, because about this time Private Ricketts of the New-foundland is personally responsible for the capture of four field guns, four machine guns and eight prisoners, whilst other patrols of both battalions, pushing far ahead of their com-panies, are fired on by friends – fortunately without loss.[1]

The Brigade has now reached all its objectives.

On returning to the crest after this errand I find McLean (Lieut-Col commanding the 50th Field Artillery Brigade) waiting for me. His batteries and those of the 51st Brigade stand under cover, sweating from galloping forward. McLean

[1] *Pte. Ricketts was awarded the V.C.*

always happens to be just where he is wanted, and after a brief talk together he disappears to complete arrangements for a second attack which we are to execute.

At this stage of the War, Divisional Artillery consisted of two brigades, each containing three 18-pdr. and one 4.5-inch howitzer batteries.

THE ATTACK ON THE STEENBEEK RIDGE

About 1 o'c the Newfoundland with two Cameronian companies thrown in on their right, and the Fusiliers with the 26th Brigade on their left, descend into the shallow valley and advance on the more formidable Steenbeek–Laaga-Kapel Ridge some 2,000 yards ahead . . .

By 2.30 . . . despite the gallantry of the gunners, quite exposed and firing over open sights, particularly those under Captain Hoggart, recklessly serving a piece within a few hundred yards of the enemy, our infantry, although supported by the 12/Royal Scots, can make little progress.

Part of their extended lines, 'glued' to the slopes three-quarters of a mile eastwards – though we can hear little firing there – are plainly visible to McLean and me.

Nettled – as a Foot soldier myself – at his remark 'I don't see what is to stop your infantry getting on', I reply that I will trot forward to find out the cause of the delay. Riding quietly up to one of the advanced groups – there is no fire to speak of – I lean over my horse's neck and address the men lying at my feet: 'My good fellows, there's nothing to stop you. Do get on.' Instantly several German machine guns open on me at under 500 yards range and I am forced to beat a retreat under a shower of bullets. McLean is content with my certificate that my battalions are not halted unreasonably.

Since it is evident that the enemy have been reinforced and intend holding their strong position, further attacks are cancelled . . .

The Brigade has again done splendidly, perhaps especially Mathias's Newfoundlanders . . . Today we have 244 casualties, and have captured about 300 prisoners, besides 8 guns, during an advance of nearly 4 miles.

Some bodies of the enemy fought very well; others did not. They belong to a beaten army and, worse, they know it.

OCTOBER 15TH

On this day the advance of the 9th Division was taken up successfully by the 27th Brigade and supporting units, 28th Brigade being in reserve.

My brigade spends a quiet, comfortable night in houses and barns little damaged by the fighting. We have 5 casualties today.

OCTOBER 16TH

The 27th Brigade forced the crossing of the River Lys.

A soaking day; we are lucky to be housed. The streets [of Cappelle-Ste-Catherine] are decked with Belgian and Allied flags, looking rather sad in the rain.

The inhabitants complain that the Germans have, ever since 1915, confiscated without payment all their goods and stock, leaving them with only the barest necessities; and that all men able to work have been conscripted to make munitions or to construct defences.

It is reported that the enemy's soldiery are highly indignant at the continuance of the Allied advance; they understand that, Germany having agreed to President Wilson's terms, the War is finished . . .

Today my brigade has 7 casualties . . .

OCTOBER 18TH

We are still standing fast in peace and comfort, and had 4 casualties yesterday from stray shells.

The 27th Brigade, however, have had a most anxious time . . .

The shallow 27th Brigade bridgehead over the Lys was vigorously counter-attacked, and held only with difficulty. Rations were again dropped by parachute to the defenders.

Had the Germans been in their old fighting form scarcely a man who got over the Lys would have come back.

The enemy has abandoned the Flanders coast and retired to Ghent. They have also given up Lille, Tourcoing and Roubaix.

Lille was retaken on October 17th by the British Fifth Army, under Sir William Birdwood.

Today has again been quiet for us with only 2 casualties. My battalions have had a glorious rest since the 14th.

But at 9.30 p.m. orders arrive for the Brigade to force the passage of the Lys tomorrow as part of a general attack. There is therefore an immediate stir in all our offices . . . and we are up till late . . .

THE 28TH BRIGADE CROSSES THE LYS

OCTOBER 19TH

. . . This is a very busy day. In the morning battalion, company, machine gun, trench mortar commanders and I independently reconnoitre as thoroughly as possible the approaches to the Lys and the sites selected for the footbridges being constructed by the Engineers, the Germans having destroyed all permanent bridges. Since the banks are within close range of their marksmen, reconnaissance is not easy.

At the same time companies usefully practise, as a drill, crossing an imaginary river, marked by tapes on the ground, and then forming up to attack . . .

The whole afternoon is spent in writing orders, and with a conference of commanding officers at my headquarters . . .

At 11 o'c our barrage falls on a line 200 yards beyond the enemy's bank, and the covering parties move silently along the tapes to the water's edge. They are followed by Sappers and pioneers carrying the bridges, pontoons and rafts, which were collected at hand after dark. Then the leading companies steal forward to commence their passage.

Half an hour after midnight, when very worried at getting no news of progress . . . we are horrified to receive a message, timed 11.30, from the Fusiliers, saying that their bridge has been smashed by shell fire and the pontoon sunk; that the raft has fouled the bank and no men are across. There is no report from the Cameronians. I at once send orders to these battalions to try using the bridges and ferries of units on their flanks, if necessary.

Our forming-up line on the German side is the Harlebeke–Beveren road, 400 yards from the river; we are due to attack from that line in the direction of Deerlyck at 6 a.m. (20th). In view of the recent experience of the 27th Brigade I am terribly anxious lest we be late in reaching the starting positions and miss the support of the artillery; or even that we may fail to get to them at all. We can, however, do nothing in time to be of any use; the troops have all the means available at their disposal, and we know they will do their best.

About 2 a.m. the intense strain is relieved by glad tidings that the Engineers and pioneers have managed to patch up one bridge and several of the ferries; that both battalions crossed the Lys half an hour after midnight, and hope to gain the forming-up line in time for the attack . . . So ends an exciting night.

THE ATTACK ON THE
ST LOUIS–BELGIEK LINE

OCTOBER 20TH

At 5.30 a.m. our smoke barrage opens. Both leading battalions, after a series of sharp minor encounters, are now practically ready to advance on a 1,200-yard front in conjunction with the brigades on either flank.

At 6 o'c on a fine morning, the H.E. shell barrage commences 250 yards in front of the line of assembly, its density being one gun per 50 yards. It then creeps forward at the rate of 100 yards in two minutes, with the heavier artillery engaged on more distant targets.

The extended lines of groups of Cameronians and Fusiliers forthwith move on their First Objective, a line a good half mile ahead. They are followed at an interval of thirty minutes by the Newfoundland in support.

The Fusiliers are immediately under severe flank fire from Beveren, and are forced to deviate slightly to assist the 36th Division in capturing that village.

About 'Zero' hour (6 a.m.) my small staff of officers, signallers and orderlies . . . cross the Lys by a single-file barrel bridge so rickety that we marvel how the companies got over it in the dark and in the face of the enemy.

Following the signallers' cable laid along the centre of the Brigade advance, we arrive at Donkere Farm, near our First Objective, which has everywhere been gained with moderate losses . . .

At 8 a.m. the fair-sized town of Deerlyck is in the hands of the Cameronians after sharp fighting . . .

The 26th Brigade is now some way behind, as they have had difficulty in clearing the Germans out of the very confined Harlebeke area. The progress of the 36th Division on our left has also been retarded.

As soon as the environs of Deerlyck have been made good, the Yorkshire Dragoons (on pedal bicycles, apart from punctures!) and No. 7 Motor Machine Gun Company, acting as 'Independent Cavalry', pass through our lines to seize the village of Vichte, and to do what damage they can to the enemy.

Dashingly handled and followed by the Cameronians together with the Fusiliers, they reach Belgiek, capturing a battery on the way; some of them get as far as the St Louis–Vichte road, 'mopping up' another battery, 40 prisoners, and some stores.

By 9.15 the Brigade Group has almost gained its objectives, after severe fighting, particularly in and around Belgiek, where the 'cavalry' and the Fusiliers have many casualties . . .

Reports from our right being favourable, the Newfoundland, assembled on the 12-foot-wide Gaverbeek brook, renews the attack at 1.45 p.m., covered by a short bombardment of selected areas . . .

On rising a crest south of Belgiek, however, they come under hot shell and enfilade machine gun fire . . . Although they persist with their task they can do no more than gain a line north and south through Vichte station, after sharp fighting. One of their patrols, however, succeeds in reaching the outskirts of Vichte itself, into which village one and a half companies of the Fusiliers have disappeared . . .

The attack 'fizzles out' in the afternoon; there is a limit to the

288

physical efforts troops can make, and in action there is mental strain as well. This is often not well realised by High Command and the Staff . . .

The casualties of the Brigade since yesterday evening are some 200. The length of our advance from the Lys is rather over four miles, during which [the 'cavalry'] and my battalions have captured about 120 prisoners and 15 guns . . .

OCTOBER 21ST: OUTPOSTS BEFORE VICHTE

. . . The 9th and 29th Divisions are remaining stationary today in order that those to the north may advance into line. The situation of the Brigade left flank near Belgiek has been rather disquieting as our posts are weak in numbers, very extended, and the enemy seems inclined to attack . . .

In the afternoon, when sitting alone in the office and desiring to give some instructions without disturbing the well merited sleep of the Brigade Signalling Officer (Lieut Duff), I send for Signal-Sergeant Sim and his corporal. While they stand in the doorway of the room receiving my orders, there is a terrific explosion from a heavy shell; the room is filled with dust, smoke and falling plaster. On the view clearing, the bodies of Sim and his comrade are disclosed lying dead before my eyes, and there is a gaping hole further along the wall. Luckily the remainder of the headquarters are safely in the cellar and hurry up the stairs to help. Apart from the loss of two fine Non-commissioned officers, the incident gives me a severe momentary shock, and being rather stunned, kind little Duff leads me outside . . .

The Brigade has 19 casualties today.

OCTOBER 23RD: IN DIVISIONAL RESERVE

The 27th Brigade captures Vichte and other localities.

. . . The capture of Vichte released those of the Scots Fusiliers who had been hiding in the cellars there since our attack on the 20th. They hastily came to the surface on the arrival of their friends, so as to avoid the risk of hand-bombs, intended for the Germans, rolling down the steps into their lairs . . .

This morning the Brigade presents a very good appearance

when marching past in column of route to the pipes and drums. The Newfoundland, alone of the battalions in this division, has bugles, fifes and drums for music – their only mistake from a Scotsman's point of view.

After this ceremony I visit battalions and, as is my custom on coming out of action, have a short chat with their assembled officers and platoon commanders on the 'error of the day'. This phrase, however, embraces the generally very good leadership of those who must be regarded as amateur soldiers, although extremely gallant gentlemen . . .

We had two casualties from shells yesterday, today none.

THE ATTACK ON THE
OOTEGHEM–INGOYGHEM RIDGE

OCTOBER 25TH: OUTPOST LINE SOUTH-EAST
OF VICHTE

At 8 a.m., on going outside the farm to see how the wind will suit our smoke shells, the first sight to greet my eyes is the body of Woods, my Intelligence Officer, lying dead under a sack.

A few Germans, captured by our patrols, are standing nearby. I speak to one of them; he answers pipe in mouth. He would not thus address his own officers, so, with the shock of poor Woods's death fresh in my mind, I flick the pipe to the ground; and then, annoyed at my temper, give the man some money, saying I am sorry.

The country in front is open, grassy, undulating, sprinkled with a few farms, their trees and enclosures . . .

At 9 a.m. our smoke, shell and machine gun barrage opens on the line of hostile posts some 300 yards from ours . . . The Fusiliers on the right and the Cameronians on the left, covering 1,200 yards of front, advance forthwith from their shelter trenches in the usual successive lines of small groups . . . The leading battalions immediately come under heavy shell and machine gun fire, suffering considerable casualties; but they press on . . .

By about 11.15 nearly all the Ooteghem–Ingoyghem Ridge has fallen to the 26th and 28th Brigades. But hostile fire has prevented battalions from completely gaining the new starting-line.

The 41st and 36th Divisions are reported to be also behind time.

McLean's batteries, trotting coolly and promptly along the very exposed Vichte road, are now in position in rear of the crest and only 500 yards from the infantry . . .

THE ATTACK ON THE SECOND OBJECTIVE

At 12.30 p.m. the barrage reopens; the Fusiliers and Cameronians thereupon advance on the Second Objective, two miles ahead. Some of their companies, however, have been unable to reach the starting-line, and consequently lose the close support of our artillery. Apart from this, the German enfilade machine gun fire from Klein-Ronsse (in the sector of the 26th Brigade) and from Kleineberg (opposite the 36th Division), as well as the fusillade on their own front, stops them almost at once . . .

The Newfoundland are now close to Ingoyghem with previous orders to press into the attack; but General Tudor, from his highly dangerous post near the top of the church spire of the village, some 400 yards from the infantry lines, at once realises that the enemy's positions are too strongly defended for the operation to succeed without entirely fresh plans. He therefore orders the troops to stand fast and entrench their ground.

Very frightened, I accompany the Divisional Commander up the interior of the spire. Although not under fire at the moment it has been holed by several shells. On arriving at each successive floor I suggest that the view could not be better, but the General keeps mounting—he has a new telescope to try. After an interminable climb with our staff officers, we halt on the top platform. The outlook is certainly extensive, but is rather spoilt, to my mind, by the imminent risk of a shell crashing the spire—which is a notable mark for the enemy—along with us to the ground . . .

I am most relieved when the General's eyes are satiated with the panorama and we descend to earth.

At 5 p.m. the 36th Division again fails to carry the stoutly-held Kleineberg, but gains a footing on its western fringe, thereby easing the situation of the Cameronians . . .

The situation is pretty quiet except for severe shell fire. The men are fairly comfortable, although tired after their arduous day.

I reach my headquarters at 8 o'c exhausted. When supper is over, my staff and I settle down to several hours' office work . . . The Brigade casualties today number 204. We have taken about 40 prisoners and advanced one-and-a-third miles. The enemy, in exceedingly strong positions, fought with determination . . .

OCTOBER 26TH

Soon after daylight I visit the headquarters of my battalions on foot; the shell fire on and near the Ridge is most unpleasant.

Last night and at dawn today, patrols of the Fusiliers and the Cameronians, covered by machine and Lewis guns, succeed after several attempts in slightly improving some of our positions by the capture of minor features, in the face of severe fire from commanding crests . . .

At nightfall the 9th Division is relieved by the 31st Division . . . After a period of roughing it, how much one enjoys the simple comforts of a hot supper, a fire in the room, wash, change of clothing, warm blankets, and a good sleep away from the blast of those damned shells!

The Brigade has 63 casualties today . . .

IN II CORPS RESERVE

OCTOBER 28TH: HARLEBEKE

Yesterday all ranks had a good rest. We expect to return to action very soon and must be fresh. Half-stale soldiers have not nearly the attacking value of those who are fresh. In the afternoon I held my customary conference with commanding officers to discuss our last operations as well as improvements for the future. All the same, I am delighted with the performances of the Brigade since its initial assault at Ypres just a month ago—and said so.

Two relatively minor shortcomings concern Guard Duties and Dress.

Guards are to troops in quarters what Outposts are to troops in action: in each case meticulous vigilance is imperative. If sentries are too unobservant to notice the Corps Commander's car bearing a large distinguishing flag, they are unlikely to notice individual movements of the enemy. Training in Guard Duties, intelligently and throughly carried out, provides excellent practice for battle by quickening eyesight and wits.

Regarding Dress: I have already remarked that junior leaders in action run their full share of risks without wearing conspicuous trappings. The proportion of officer casualties to those of 'other ranks' is high . . .

The men are comfortable; they have all had a good wash at the well-arranged military baths in this town.

Today I inspected all three battalions on the march. They looked soldierly, especially considering that they are just back from a month in action. One can quickly and easily get a fair idea as to the condition of troops by seeing them in column of route.

Jack informs us here that the 9th Division, during its month of offensive action, mounted nine prepared attacks, drove the Germans back 25 miles, captured 2,600 prisoners and 64 guns. 'Its casualties in this period amounted to 188 officers and 3,604 other ranks, and nearly all battalions had been reduced to about 200 bayonets.'

He gives 'corrected figures' for the performance of the 28th Brigade. Thus, in his diary (p. 270) he gave the ration strength of the Brigade as 'about 80 officers and 1,700 other ranks'; the actual figure was 80 officers and 1,620 other ranks. Of these, by October 27th, 54 officers (12 killed) and 1,124 other ranks had become casualties. It is interesting to note that his daily casualty returns during the period add up to 1,345; the discrepancy between this and the corrected figure is due partly to the stress under which the first reports were made, and partly to 'missing' men returning to duty. The fact remains that one month's fighting, against a beaten enemy, cost the Brigade two-thirds of its numbers.

OCTOBER 30TH

In the morning I pay my customary visit on horseback to battalions and our Trench Mortar Battery; then lunch at

Divisional Headquarters to meet the Army Commander, who wishes to see all brigadiers.

Sir Herbert Plumer, dear old gentleman, holds the confidence of his troops whether times be good or bad. The operations of his Second Army have been notably soundly planned and successful.

He says that the Enemy Powers are all very shaky – thank Heaven – but that we are not to relax in the least degree our battle preparations on account of rumours that the Germans intend to cave in.

Battalion commanders come to Brigade Headquarters for tea and to be told about General Plumer's views, besides discussing other matters . . .

OCTOBER 31ST

. . . In Italy, the Italians, French and Lord Cavan's Army have defeated the Austrians, 30,000 of whom are prisoners.

In Mesopotamia our army has routed the Turks.

In Palestine, Aleppo has fallen, and the sweeping victories of Allenby's Army have forced Turkey to capitulate . . .

NOVEMBER 3RD

We have daily been assiduously carrying out battle-training, route marching, refitting, and short close-order drills . . .

In the afternoon the chatter of the signallers in the telephone room next to my office is interrupted as a message arrives. A moment later I hear the matter-of-fact announcement, 'Listen to this, Bill. Austria's chucked in her mitt.' Thus Thomas Atkins describes the collapse of the proud Habsburg Empire.

NOVEMBER 4TH

Reinforcements of quite good quality have just arrived for the Brigade: 304 Scots Fusiliers, 126 Cameronians and 206 Newfoundland Regiment. They will be much needed if we are to fight again . . .

NOVEMBER 5TH

At 7.45 a.m. the Brigade marches 7 miles to Bavichove. There the whole of the 9th Division forms up for inspection by

King Albert, who is accompanied by his Queen and by his heir, the Duke of Brabant . . .

In a sea of mud and torrents of rain, the Divisional Mounted Troops march past, the Royal Artillery in lines of batteries, Trench Mortar units, Royal Engineers and Signal units. Then come the Infantry brigades, each battalion, in column of double companies, being played past the saluting base to its own regimental air by the massed pipe bands of the brigade to which it belongs. The Machine Gun and Pioneer battalions, Army Service Corps and Army Medical Corps complete the parade . . . In spite of the mud, the vile weather, and with only one rehearsal, the ceremony is performed most creditably, and the King, a gallant and soldierly figure, expresses his great appreciation of the services of the Division.

Still in the rain, we have dinners from the field kitchens which accompanied us, and then march back to Gulleghem, arriving there at 2.30 p.m., soaked, the men rather tired, too, from their 14-mile 'trek'.

The day's proceedings have not improved a bad chill which I caught last week . . .

NOVEMBER 7TH

. . . The British Armies are across the Sambre; the Americans, too, have won a great battle in the south.

General Ludendorff, Commander of the German Armies, has resigned.

In the afternoon Sir Claud Jacob calls and says he thinks that the War is virtually over. German delegates have left Berlin for Marshal Foch's Headquarters at Compiègne to sue for an Armistice.

This news is almost too good to be true; we still hear the distant boom of guns.

NOVEMBER 9TH

. . . I ride round my brigade area daily from 10 a.m. till 1 p.m. and we are occupied in the office all afternoon and evening. When battles are to the fore, the General Staff branch keeps us busy with papers; the moment operations finish, the Quarter-master-General's branch takes up the running. So, between

'G' and 'Q', less exalted headquarters get no peace at all . . .

At night I dine with the Corps Commander at his Head-quarters in Courtrai . . . Sir Claud, a first-class commander, is also a charming host. His personal kindness to me never shrinks.

The Brigade is at one hour's notice to advance if the Germans will not accept the Allied terms.

NOVEMBER 10TH

The weather is perishing cold.

In the morning I am president of a Court Martial in a neigh-bouring village. The accused is a cavalry officer, and the charge is 'drunkenness on active service'. My duty is the more distasteful since I knew Captain 'X' in India . . . We reluc-tantly decide to convict, and, after weighing Captain 'X's' good service record, sentence him to be reduced in rank . . . When the trial is over I am impelled to tell 'X' how sorry I am for his misfortune . . .

The Kaiser has abdicated and fled to Holland; Bavaria has declared herself a Republic. Nevertheless, we are under orders to be ready to march forward forthwith, if necessary.

THE ARMISTICE

NOVEMBER 11TH: CUERNE

A 'priority' message states that an Armistice has been concluded with Germany, to take effect from 11 o'c this morning. What a relief!

On a short parade of battalions in fatigue dress at their billets I congratulate them on their services, shake hands with all recipients of decorations during my period of command, and express the hope that the behaviour of the Brigade under Peace conditions will remain unsullied as it has been in the field.

In the evening I and many officers are most hospitably enter-tained to dinner by the Burgomaster of Cuerne and his Council. The town band, having hurriedly disinterred and cleaned their blue, silver-laced uniforms and instruments after four years' burial, is in grand form. Champagne and other wines flow generously but not in excess. The healths of King George and King Albert are drunk. A few speeches are made in spite of linguistic difficulties – what does that matter on an occasion like this? The Allies toast one another cordially; the enthusiasm passes description.

Throughout the night the noise of singing, the shrill hooting of railway whistles, and the blast of factory sirens might awaken the dead. Rockets hiss skywards as long as the supply lasts. Officers' pickets in the town ensure that there is no other kind of disturbance, and when the celebrations are concluded we have only one or two cases of simple drunkenness to report.

At last I lie down tired and very happy, but sleep is elusive. How far away is that 22nd August 1914, when I heard with a shudder, as a platoon commander at Valenciennes, that real live German troops, armed to the teeth, were close at hand – one has been hardened since then. Incidents flash through the memory: the battles of the first four months: the awful winters in waterlogged trenches, cold and miserable: the terrible trench-war assaults and shell fire of the next three years: loss of friends, exhaustion and wounds: the stupendous victories of the last few months: our enemies all beaten to their knees.

Thank God! the end of a frightful four years, thirty-four months of them at the front with the infantry, whose company officers, rank and file, together with other front-line units, have suffered bravely, patiently and unselfishly, hardships and perils beyond even the imagination of those, including soldiers, who have not shared them.

*   *   *

So ended the First World War, in which Jack served from first to last, as a Regular officer, chiefly in Regimental employ, on the Western Front.

The 'stupendous victories' of the British armies during the last months of the War, which did so much to hasten the Armistice, form, oddly enough, a little-known chapter of British military history. Marshal Foch has listed nine major battles during that period:

The Battle of Amiens, August 8th – 13th (Fourth Army).

The Battle of Bapaume, August 21st – September 1st (Third and Fourth Armies).

The Battle of the Scarpe, August 26th – September 3rd (First Army).

The Battle of Havrincourt and Epéhy, September 12th – 18th (Third and Fourth Armies).

The Battle of Cambrai and the Hindenburg Line, September 27th – October 5th (First, Third and Fourth Armies).

The Battle of Flanders, September 28th – October 14th (Second Army).

The Battle of Le Cateau, October 6th – 12th (First, Third and Fourth Armies).

The Battle of the Selle, October 17th – 25th (Third and Fourth Armies).

The Battle of the Sambre, November 1st – 11th (First, Third and Fourth Armies).

The cost of this immense effort was very great: in the three months August, September and October, the British armies lost 17,426 officers and 340,723 other ranks. To this figure something has to be added for the November fighting; the grand total is probably about 375,000.

The reward, however, was commensurate. Above all, this sustained offensive brought Peace. The British contribution to that result may be judged from the following figures: from July 18th, when the Allies passed to the counter-attack, the

				Prisoners	Guns
British Armies took	..	..	..	*188,700*	*2,840*
French Armies ..	..	..	..	*139,000*	*1,880*
American Armies	..	..	..	*43,3000*	*1,421*
Belgian Armies ..	..	..	..	*14,500*	*474*

Lord Haig wrote: 'In three months of epic fighting the British Armies in France have brought to a sudden and dramatic end the great wearing-out battle of the past four years ... The work begun and persevered in so steadfastly by those brave men has been completed during the present year with a thoroughness to which the event bears witness, and with a gallantry which will live for all time in the history of our country.'

These truths, long obscured, should be remembered.

*   *   *

Appendices

APPENDIX I

EVENTS AFTER THE ARMISTICE

The 9th Division was among those selected to form the British Army of Occupation in Germany, under the command of Sir Herbert Plumer. Jack adds brief notes on that period of service, only a few points from which need concern us.

On November 17th, during the march through Belgium, he relates:
. . . a charming English-speaking Belgian curé dined with us. The German resistance had crumbled so quickly and so utterly that I asked him when the enemy had begun to 'crack up'! He paused a moment, and replied that our terrible shell fire on the Somme (1916) had shaken them deeply; some, brave lads as they were, even wept when ordered to the trenches from his village behind that Front. Terrible as was the strain on our men, I never saw any so overcome as that.

On December 16th Lord Haig said 'Farewell' to the senior officers of the Army. Before departing Sir Douglas said 'Thank you, gentlemen.' Then passed from us a redoubtable, well-liked Chief, who for nearly four years had calmly borne a crushing load of responsibility.

In early 1919 there were serious troubles in Germany, partly political, partly the result of dire food shortages. Apart from these troubles, great dissatisfaction has been caused among our troops, and even serious insubordination *in the back areas* – none at the front – by the unfair way in which demobilization is being conducted. The carefully planned War office scheme for discharging soldiers in their proper turn has been upset by the Home Government. Men happening to be on leave have been liberated from the Army, and large numbers serving here have been ordered Home on the grounds that they are required in industries, in both cases irrespective of length of service. More equitable arrangements have had to be made by the civil authorities.

Sir Winston Churchill, then Secretary of State for War, has supplied his own interesting gloss on these events.

On March 15th 1919 the 9th Division ceased to exist. Jack reverted to battalion commander (9/Cameronians), but never served with his designated unit. On April 28th he sustained severe injuries in a steeple-chase, which led to his retirement from the Regular Army in 1921.

APPENDIX II

DAILY ROUTINE OUT OF TRENCHES
2/WEST YORKS, NOV. 1916

(See p. 162)

7 a.m.	First sick parade, for those unfit for duty.
7.15–7.30	Running, saluting, physical exercise, under one officer per company.
8 a.m.	Breakfast.
9–9.45	Close-order drill under the Regimental-Sergeant-Major. Officers of less than one year's service in the ranks. The drums on parade.
10–11.45	Battalion or company parades for tactical training, or musketry, bayonet exercise, etc. 45-minute periods for the former and 20-minute periods for the latter.
12 noon	Companies and headquarters units march past the Battalion Commander in column of route to the drums and fifes.
12.15–12.45	Officers' and N.C.O.s' classes under the second-in-command. 'Specialist' classes, for Lewis gunners. scouts, pioneers, bombers, signallers, cooks and transport, under the instructors concerned.
12.15	Commanding Officer's Orderly Room, to deal with 'accused', and with company as well as Quarter-master's papers.
1 p.m.	Dinners (meals are visited by one officer per company).
2–3	'Specialist' instruction, as above. All men are trained in one or other of these, in addition to carrying out their ordinary duties.
3.15	Second sick parade, for trivial cases.

4 p.m.	Tea.
4.30	Guard mounting under the adjutant. Attended by officers of less than one year's service, field punishment men, defaulters and 'marked' men.
5 p.m.	'Retreat', played by the drums and fifes.
9 p.m.	Supper.
10 p.m.	Lights Out.

APPENDIX III

JACK'S ATTEMPT TO PREVENT THE VAIN ATTACK BY THE 2/DEVONSHIRES ON VILLERS-GUISLAIN (APRIL 13TH 1917)

(*See p. 212*)

23rd Inf. Bde. J. 14. 13th

1. I have just returned from my Advanced companies, where I had a long talk with Coy. Comdrs. & think it right to inform you that I consider the projected assault by 2/Devons quite impracticable *without* further preparations for the following reasons:

a. Strong wire exists approximately N-West & S-East of the South edge of VILLERS-GUISLAIN.

b. The wire is continuous & can be seen extending from the South end of the village over the crest about X.21.b.

c. The wire is thick (reported very thick) in places.

d. Behind the wire are series of Posts – in some places trenches.

e. Many enemy were seen there today. At a rough estimate the village and vicinity are held by about ½ a battalion.

2. It does not therefore at all appear to be a question of an occupation, such as of the villages heretofore, but of an assault under disadvantageous conditions.

In spite of the foregoing, I, at 8.30 p.m. repeated my orders:-

a. For the most careful reconnaissance of the enemy's line N-West & S-East of the South end of the village.

b. Reconnaissance of the village by strong Patrols.

c. The occupation of the village if Patrols report it vacated or held by Posts only.

303

3. I may further add that a great many of our shells today are reported to be 'BLINDS',[1] & that our guns did not deal with the 2 Southernmost houses, previously reported, which contained most active snipers, who have been dealt with by my Lewis guns, which houses, I hope, will soon be occupied by my men.

J. Jack, Lt.-Col. VAST, 11.35 p.m.

By Telephone
J. 15. 14th
In continuation of my J.14 sent by orderly at 11.30 p.m. A Strong Patrol attempted to enter the village, was heavily fired on & bombed, and had several casualties. aaa Village line reported held in considerable strength. aaa Shall send reports as they come.

VAST. J.L.J. 12.15 a.m.

*   *   *

APPENDIX IV

CITATIONS

On May 21st 1917 Jack received the Distinguished Service Order from Major-General Heneker, commanding the 8th Division. The recommendation read as follows:

'*This Officer has shown conspicuous ability and leadership since our advance began on March 14th.*

'*He has been quick to seize the initiative throughout and has availed himself of every opportunity of following up the enemy after a success. In particular he conducted the attack of his Battalion on Villers-Guislain, after previous failure by other troops, with very marked skill and foresight and attained all his objectives in the minimum time with very small loss to his troops.*

'*His gallantry and soldierly example to all around him is most inspiring.*

'*He is worthy of special reward.*

(sd) G. Grogan, Br-General.
Commanding 23rd Infantry Brigade.'

[1] *Did not explode.*

Jack comments: It was not the fault of the "other troops" that they failed. (*See pp. 212-15.*)
The 'London Gazette' citation for the Bar to his D.S.O. (*December 10th, 1919*) *reads:*

'*Major and Brevet Lieut-Colonel* (*Temp./Brig.-Gen.*) *James Lochhead Jack,* D.S.O., *Scottish Rifles* (*Cameronians*) (*G.O.C. 28th Infantry Brigade*).

"*He commanded his brigade with great dash and gallantry throughout the operations east of Ypres from 28th September to 28th October 1918. On 2nd October the enemy opened a heavy barrage and counter-attacked at Ledeghem. Troops on the immediate left of his brigade gave way. He formed them up in the barrage and personally led them forward again and re-established the front line. He then went across to his own front line under heavy machine gun fire and, by his energy and example, inspired his men to save an awkward situation.*" '

Jack adds: N.B.—Gen. Tudor led the retiring troops back to their posts while I saw to my own brigade who were as steady as rocks. (*See p. 278.*)

Jack had been admitted to the Legion of Honour in October 1914 (see p. 24), and in February 1920 was also awarded the Belgian Croix de Guerre, the citation reading: '. . . s'est particulièrement distingué par son courage et dévouement au cours de l'offensive de Flandres'.

APPENDIX V

SOME GENERAL OBSERVATIONS BY J. L. JACK

At the end of each of the four volumes of his diary, Jack wrote a few pages of general notes. Some points from the last of these sections, embodying recurring themes, are worth quoting.

[The author] reluctantly considers that after 1914 the German Army, as a whole, was the best in the Field until its débâcle in July 1918. It had been prepared exclusively for a European War, a war likely to demand the maximum effort. Its leaders and highly qualified staff were accustomed to handle large bodies of troops; some of the former had experienced a European war – against France in 1870. It was trained to close with an enemy and its driving force was tremendous; in defence it was no less formidable. Behind the Fighting Forces stood, schooled to weapons, the entire manhood of Germany and all her resources . . . .

Our seven Home Regular Divisions (one of cavalry), their commanders and staffs, were practically untrained *as divisions on a war footing on adequate manoeuvre areas.* Besides forming the first Expeditionary Force, these troops were bled of men in peacetime to furnish drafts for foreign garrisons. The only other soldiers in the United Kingdom were Militia and Territorial units of little value for immediate action, the latter not even obliged to serve abroad.

Handicapped as they thus were, besides carrying at the commencement of the War over 50 per cent of half-fit reservists, the British Regular divisions were fully a match for the Germans, especially in defence . . .

The Territorial and New Army divisions, their men all Volunteers of splendid quality, were for a long time short of qualified instructors, as practically all the Regulars were in France when the second-named were first raised . . .

While eagerness hastened the learning of these civilians, it takes over a year to make efficient soldiers – soldiers, for instance who will instinctively act correctly when surprised under adverse conditions – and far longer to turn out officers. Thanks, therefore, to our pre-War objection to National Military Service, large numbers of these fine fellows, slung into battle against a fully-trained enemy before they were ready, fell, partly at least through ignorance of their job . . .

In June 1918, Brig.-General Grogan, v.c., told the author that, when disciplined, the Colonial[1] troops were probably the finest in our armies, being more self-reliant and of better physique than the Europeans . . .

Frequently . . . our infantry were overworked by High Com-

---

[1] *'Colonial', of course, in this context, means 'Dominion'.*

mand till shortly before assaulting. Exhausted troops can *hold* a position, but men must be fresh to produce the energy *needed to attack* . . .

Our plans were usually too stereotyped . . . It is probable that properly trained troops would not have required such set plans for operations, nor so many men to hold the front as was the case with us after 1914; that they would generally have made more headway in attacks; have withdrawn in less disorder during the German offensives at Cambrai in 1917 and the Somme in 1918; and would have suffered fewer casualties than the New Army battalions for the same reason that an expert boxer delivers to a less capable opponent more punishment than he receives.

Public esteem is apt to be bestowed on the basis of the casualties suffered by a corps. Those corps defeating the enemy at least cost to themselves, and so remaining fit for the next effort are the more worthy . . .

The errors of politician and commander were finally liquidated by the exceptional tenacity of the regimental soldiers, the creation of a great National Army amply equipped, a Tank arm of which the enemy had practically none, and a superlative Air Force. Whatever the Germans may say now, the result was a complete military defeat for them . . .

Criticism of military leaders is, of course, made easier after a war, when documents have laid bare the state and plans of both sides. Confronted, however, with the danger of war, no Government can be absolved from blame which hazards National Safety by neglecting its armaments and the training of the personnel wanted to handle them . . .

When determined and equally matched opponents meet there is no short cut to victory; the struggle must be long; the way hard . . .

To any fire-eaters who say they were sorry when the War was over, the reply is that none who was 'through the mill' with the infantry or others as exposed was known to utter this view during hostilities.

The author held himself responsible, as far as possible, for the lives of all his men, and worked nearly every day of his service at the Front until he could work no longer. The loss of so many friends, coupled with almost continual personal strain of one kind or another, made the War a 'living hell', solely redeemed by the unflagging, nearly Divine, courage, patience and unselfishness of his comrades, their tenacity probably never before surpassed by mortal man.

APPENDIX VI

GENERAL JACK'S VALEDICTION TO THE CAMERONIANS

. . . For nearly eighteen years I lived with officers and other ranks who faithfully and unostentatiously performed all their duties, whose instincts were those of gentlemen, whose interests off duty lay with manly sports, whose grumbles were superficial, who met setbacks with a smile, danger and death without flinching – death in this war having claimed over seven thousand of the Regiment.

It is a great privilege to have served in a company of such high quality, a privilege realised perhaps more fully as time rolls on, and one meets at gatherings of old comrades so many who express the ardent wish that they were back with the Regiment.

Sept. 30th 1938.

APPENDIX VII

CORRESPONDENCE BETWEEN THE EDITOR AND GENERAL JACK

The editor corresponded spasmodically with General Jack between 1960 and his death in 1962. Since this correspondence played a considerable

*part in causing this book to be compiled, some extracts from the General's
letters to me are appropriate.*

If you mention my name pray do so *with reserve*. I do not wish
it brought into greater prominence than it is worth.

(April 6th 1960; *referring to a request for permission to quote him in
my book* 'Douglas Haig: The Educated Soldier'.)

We may have cursed the Germans, the mud, our loads, but
NOT our senior commanders who, experienced officers, did their
level best, often with amateur staffs.

Let us remember that the result of a hard-fought action is
nearly always a GUESS.

(April 12th 1960)

One must carefully consider the REASONS for mistakes and
failures.

(April 19th 1960)

I hate harsh, exaggerated or ill-formed criticism. Criticism
can be pointed and firm without being rude and aggressive . . .
One may legitimately consider that 'the other fellow' is wrong,
without insinuating that he is a damned fool – unless it is
crystal clear that he is one.

(April 28th 1960)

Please mark that my diaries are those of a mere regimental
officer only faintly aware *at the time* of the problems facing
High Command and the reasons for the plans to meet them.

(July 1960)

I served in almost every battle on the Western Front in 1914–
1918, and resent unjust, malicious slurs on my old commanders,
despite any mistakes they may have made.

(April 5th 1961)

I can scarcely believe that I took part, with the infantry, in those *quite frightful* 4½ years. Even after almost 50 years I can scarcely speak of parts of them without emotion.

(April 19th 1962; *his last letter to me.*)

APPENDIX VIII

NOTE ON INFANTRY FORMATIONS, 1914

Unlike Continental and U.S. practice, the British Regular Infantry fought by battalions, not by regiments. It was not until Territorial and New Army formations entered the field that battalions of the same regiment were frequently to be found brigaded together. This makes the British Order of Battle somewhat confusing: not a bad thing in war.

British

1 Battalion = 4 Companies = 16 Platoons = 30 officers, 992 other ranks.

1 Brigade = 4 Battalions.

1 Division = 3 Brigades = 18,073 all ranks +76 guns (54 18-pdrs., 18 4.5-in. field howitzers, 4 60-pdrs.) +24 machine guns. (*Marching depth, about 15 miles.*)

French

1 Battalion = 4 Companies = 8 Pelotons = 16 Sections = 22 officers, 1,030 other ranks.

1 Regiment = 3 Battalions + H.Q. Company.

1 Brigade = 2 Regiments,

1 Division = 2 Brigades = 15,000 all ranks +36 guns +24 machine guns.

German

1 Battalion = 4 Companies = 12 Platoons = 26 officers, 1,050 other ranks.

1 Regiment = 3 Battalions + machine gun company of 6 guns.

1 Brigade = 2 Regiments.

1 Division = 2 Brigades = 17,500 all ranks + 72 guns + 24 machine guns.

It will be seen that the division was an approximately equal formation for all armies, the main difference being that the French preferred to group more of their artillery under Corps command.

Conclusion

30 Septr, 1938.

THE OLD HOUSE,
KIBWORTH HARCOURT,
LEICESTERSHIRE.

TELEPHONE 33.

After commanding our Regimental Depot at Hamilton as a major during 1919-21 I resigned my commission; and since my career as a Regular soldier practically concluded with the last date in the diary I should like to add a few lines.

For nearly eighteen years I lived with officers and other ranks who faithfully and unostentaciously performed all their duties, whose instincts were those of gentlemen, whose interests off duty lay with manly sports, whose grumbles were superficial, who met setbacks with a smile, danger and death without flinching — death in this war having claimed over seven thousand of the Regiment.

It is a great privilege to have served in a company of such high quality, a privilege realised perhaps more fully as time rolls on, and one meets at gatherings of old comrades so many who express the ardent wish that they were back with the Regiment.

James Jack

Index

Infantry, 181; 89th Grenadier, 232

Richardson, Lieut. R. C. (W. Yorks Regt.): 213

Ricketts, Pte. (Newfoundland Regt.): 283

Riddell-Webster, Lieut.-Col. T. (Cameronians): 77

Ritchie, Capt. A. G. (Cameronians) 69; views on German Army, 72, 73, 76, 84

Ritchie, Major the Hon. H. (Cameronians): 245, 248, 250; argument with Jack, 251, 256, 259, 260

Robertson, Maj.-Gen. Sir P. R. (Cameronians): 26, 41, 43; opposes foolish attack, 90, 91, 93, 100, 101, 184

Robertson, Field-Marshal Sir W.: 137

Robinson, Cpl. (W. Yorks Regt.): 216

Rogerson, Sidney: 5, 6, 184–6, 199, 240

Rooke, 2/Lieut. C.W.D. (Cameronians); 87, 92, 101

Rose, Rifleman (Cameronians): 96

Roumania: 162

Royal United Service Institution: 17

Rumbold, Cpl. (W. Yorks Regt.): 232

Russia: 22, 23, 112, 190; revolution, 199, 243

Salonika: 245

Sandilands, Lieut.-Col. V.C. (Cameronians): 108, 111, 115, 117, 118, 125, 127, 129, 132, 133, 136, 141, 150, 151, 157

Sankey, Lieut. R. (W. Yorks Regt.): 179, 203

Sassoon, Siegfried: 6, 131

Savile, Major (Middlesex Regt.): 148

Schlieffen Plan: 27

Seely, Brig.-Gen Hon. J.: 205

Selle, River: 32, 35

Sim, Sgt.: 289

Smailes, 2/Lieut. G. (W. Yorks Regt.): 167, 168, 177

Smith, Lieut.-Col. H. C. (Cameronians): 108, 115

Smith-Dorrien, Gen. Sir H.: at Mons, 27–31; at Le Cateau, 33–40

Snow, Lieut.-Gen. Sir T. d'O.: 40

Snowdon, Sgt. (Cameronians): 114

Soissons: 52, 54–7, 61, 246

Somme, River: 42, 153, 220, 258

South African War: 5, 17, 22, 265

Spink, 2/Lieut. G. A. (W. Yorks Regt.): 231

Staines, Sgt. (Cameronians): 69

Standish, Pte. (W. Yorks Regt.): 168

Steenwerck: 62–4

Stewart, Sgt. T. (Cameronians): 139

Stirling, Lieut.-Col. C. R. (Cameronians): 108, 115, 117, 118

Stirling, Capt. J. (Cameronians): 84, rash adventure, 86, 92 and fn.

Tailby, Lieut. (11th Hussars): 46

Tanks: 176, 229, 255, 257, 258, 307

Territorial Army: 5, 306

Thiepval: 132, 141, 142.

Thompson, Rifleman (Cameronians): 154

Transloy, Le: 177–81

Trenches (trench warfare): Flanders 1914, 70, 73; development, 81–2; routine in, 82–3; flooding, 83; conditions, 84–5; winter flooding 1914, 88; conditions Jan. 1915, 93; breastworks, 95; conditions Sept. 1915, 108–9; mining, 110; raids, 123; Somme trenches, 134; raids; 135; German on Somme, 142; Loos 1916, 153–4; Hohenzollern sector, 156; sniping, 165; raids 1916, 166–8; trench feet, 196–6; 198

Tudor, Maj.-Gen. H.: 263–5; 267; 269, 274, 276–8, 280, 281, 291, 305

Turkey: 294

Turner, Capt. R. V. (D.L.I.): 35, 36

Tuson, Brig.-Gen. H. D.: 114, 134, 162

U-boats: 222

Uhlans: 28, 33, 44

Utterson-Kelso, Maj.-Gen. J. E.: 264, 275, 279

Valenciennes: 27, 28, 30, 58, 297

Verdun: 44

Vichte: 288–91

Villers-Guislain: 211–16, 303, 304

Vimy Ridge: 112, 210, 217

Wales, Prince of: 175

Wallis, Capt. Braithwaite (Cameronians): 120, 121, 124

Ward, Lieut.-Col. E. E. (Middlesex Regt.): 43, 45, 68

Wellington, Duke of: 16, 155, 226

Westhoek: 235, 269, 272, 273

Wigan, Lieut. C. R. (Cameronians): 245

Wilson, Field-Marshal Sir Henry: 40

Will, Capt. L. J. (Worcestershire Regt.): 264